ART AS A WAY OF TALKING FOR EMERGENT BILINGUAL YOUTH

This book features effective artistic practices to improve literacy and language skills for emergent bilinguals in PreK-12 schools. Including insights from key voices from the field, this book highlights how artistic practices can increase proficiency in emergent language learners and students with limited access to academic English. Challenging current prescriptions for teaching English to language learners, the arts-integrated framework in this book is grounded in a sense of student and teacher agency and offers key pedagogical tools to build upon students' sociocultural knowledge and improve language competence and confidence. Offering rich and diverse examples of using the arts as a way of talking, this volume invites teacher educators, teachers, artists, and researchers to reconsider how to fully engage students in their own learning and best use the resources within their own multilingual educational settings and communities.

Berta Rosa Berriz is an Instructor of Creative Arts and Learning at the Graduate School of Education at Lesley University, USA.

Amanda Claudia Wager is an Assistant Professor of Bilingual/TESOL Education at the Graduate School of Education at Lesley University, USA.

Vivian Maria Poey is an Associate Professor and Director of the M.Ed. in Art, Community and Education program at the Graduate School of Education at Lesley University, USA.

ART AS A WAY OF TALKING FOR EMERGENT BILINGUAL YOUTH

A Foundation for Literacy in PreK–12 Schools

Edited by Berta Rosa Berriz,
Amanda Claudia Wager, and
Vivian Maria Poey

Routledge
Taylor & Francis Group

NEW YORK AND LONDON

First published 2019
by Routledge
711 Third Avenue, New York, NY 10017

and by Routledge
2 Park Square, Milton Park, Abingdon, Oxon, OX14 4RN

Routledge is an imprint of the Taylor & Francis Group, an informa business

Library of Congress Cataloging-in-Publication Data
Names: Berriz, Berta Rosa, editor.
Title: Art as a way of talking for emergent bilingual youth : a foundation
    for literacy in Prek-12 schools / edited by Berta Rosa Berriz, Amanda
    Claudia Wager, and Vivian Maria Poey.
Description: New York : Routledge, 2019. | Includes bibliographical
    references and index.
Identifiers: LCCN 2018009368 | ISBN 9780815384519 (hbk) |
    ISBN 9780815384526 (pbk) | ISBN 9781351204231 (ebk)
Subjects: LCSH: Language arts. | Literacy—Study and teaching. |
    Art—Study and teaching. | Education, Bilingual. | English
    language—Study and teaching—Foreign speakers.
Classification: LCC LB1575.8 .A74 2019 | DDC 370.117/5—dc23
LC record available at https://lccn.loc.gov/2018009368

ISBN: 978-0-8153-8451-9 (hbk)
ISBN: 978-0-8153-8452-6 (pbk)
ISBN: 978-1-351-20423-1 (ebk)

Typeset in Bembo
by Apex CoVantage, LLC

We dedicate this magical volume to Sonia Nieto for her guidance, tireless support and mentorship through this first editorial journey. And to all of the emergent bilingual children for their inspiration, courage, and creativity.

CONTENTS

SECTION III
Lift Every Voice: Democratic Practice Before, During, and After School

FOREWORD

As the editors of *Art as a Way of Talking for Emergent Bilingual Youth* make clear in their introduction, combining language, culture, and the arts in education is not only timely but also a needed innovation in educating children for whom English is an additional language. No longer the exception, English learners—who the editors and authors refer to more appropriately as *emergent bilingual students*—are now the fastest growing and largest population in many school systems around the nation. Yet in many classrooms they are still left to metaphorically "sink or swim," often isolated from their peers with teachers who know little about them and their communities. Despite what may be their best intentions, too many teachers have limited preparation in second language and immigration issues. Consequently, both novice and veteran teachers are often left to puzzle things out on their own. Add to this the current context of education characterized by negative discourses about immigration, and it is no mystery that in too many cases both emergent bilingual children and their teachers are isolated and marginalized.

In addition to language and immigration issues, the authors also take up the matter of the arts in education. As contributors demonstrate throughout the chapters, the arts have long been recognized as aiding not only artistic growth and expression, but also academic achievement. Nevertheless, in the high-pressure, high-stakes testing era, the arts have been systematically decimated and, in the case of some of the most impoverished schools serving the most vulnerable populations, the arts have been eliminated altogether in the name of "the basics" and "rigor." Although reduced in more highly resourced schools as well, the arts have maintained some level of visibility in schools populated by middle-class and wealthy students. The result: once again, the most privileged students retain their advantage while the most marginalized are further overlooked. This situation is the backdrop for *Art as a Way of Talking for Emergent Bilingual Youth*.

Enter editors Berta Rosa Berriz, Amanda Claudia Wager, and Vivian Maria Poey, and their talented contributors. The editors begin the book by introducing themselves, their immigration stories, and the rationale for the book. Extraordinary and yet familiar stories of migration and "fitting in," their stories are poignant and heartfelt, demonstrating a deep and personal understanding of what their emergent bilingual students go through in schools that have little knowledge of their realities. Berta, an immigrant from Cuba at the age of 8, Vivian, who came to the United States at 14, and Amanda, raised in Los Angeles and later Amsterdam, and exposed to English, Yiddish, Dutch, and Spanish: all three write powerfully about what it meant to be a stranger in a new country, having to learn a new language and different customs while having their home languages and customs disregarded and dismissed.

Joining the editors in this imaginative odyssey is a diverse group of teachers and artists who make the pages of the volume come alive. The arts take a front seat in all the chapters, though in different and inventive ways. The contributors—practitioners from classroom teachers to administrators of language programs to university researchers—each bring a nuanced eye to the discussion of the arts in the education of emergent bilinguals. From theoretical discussions of translanguaging to impressive examples of classroom-based arts including drama, counterstories, graphic novels, hip hop, spoken word poetry, drawing, collage, videography, art backpacks as family outreach, and more, the authors offer inspiring stories of using the arts for communication, authentic skill development, and empowerment. Even the title says so much about what the authors try to convey in this lovely book: "Art as a way of talking" could just as easily have been "Art as a way of seeing," "Art as a way of thinking," or "Art as a way of teaching." Here, the arts are understood as tools connecting language to other kinds of expression. In the process, multiliteracies and multimodal learning help to make the book not only relevant but also current. These chapters shine with creativity and energy, defying the business-as-usual way in which so many emergent bilinguals are educated today.

Emergent bilinguals are too often left with the "scraps" of pedagogy in the quest to provide them with a rigorous education. As a result, educators have often bemoaned the lack of creativity in teaching emergent bilinguals. I am glad to say that they will find inspiration here. They will see that rigor need not be dreary, that it need not rely on fill-in-the-blank sheets, or on memorizing dull lists of lackluster grammatical rules. Readers will be inspired with the Freirean perspectives included in the chapters, as well as with the stories of activism and social action. They will understand that coming to voice is not only about learning a new language but, more importantly, about learning how to use it to make themselves heard in the world.

Every reader will find something to cherish in this book. Whether it's being introduced to an exciting idea for the first time, or learning how to incorporate particular art expressions into daily lessons, the book has something for everyone.

In fact, while reading *Art as a Way of Talking for Emergent Bilingual Youth*, I couldn't help but think back to my own experience as a 6-year-old starting school so many years ago. Speaking no English, with parents who had little knowledge of how to navigate their way around US schools, I had to rely on my sister Lydia, a year older than me, and my teachers to help me not only learn English but also learn how to "do school." The arts were a luxury reserved for special occasions, not for English lessons. I remember feeling alone and isolated in school, as if I didn't belong. It makes me wonder how much better it would have been for me, and for countless others in my situation then as well as now, had there been teachers like Berta, Amanda, Vivian, and the other authors who've contributed to this valuable book. It is my hope that many teachers, families, researchers, and others will take up the challenge set down by the editors and authors of this pioneering book to give these children the education they deserve. They are, after all, our children and our future.

Dr. Sonia Nieto,
Professor Emerita of Language, Literacy, and Culture
College of Education
University of Massachusetts, Amherst

PREFACE

The Art of Creating Literacy with Emergent Bilingual Children: Book Organization

"History is what you do to change the future."
Clara, emergent bilingual student, fifth grade

Art as a Way of Talking with Emergent Bilingual Youth offers no magic formula for effective teaching and learning or in responding to the wide range of linguistic histories of students within our schools. Instead, its authors link language acquisition theory with artful practices, such as through the imaginaries of role-playing, in schools that honor students' cultural ways of knowing. Indeed, writers and editors are guided by the belief that students are engaged in making academic literacy their own, as critical readers, writers and artists.

How the book is organized

The first section of the book, *Walk the Talk: Breathing Life into Theories with Families, Schools and Communities*, begins our volume with an emphasis on the knowledge, language and creativity that each member of the learning community brings to the learning project. Artist-educator, Shabaash Kemeh chronicles his family success story using the arts to increase proficiency of both heritage language and English, as well as highlighting sociocultural benefits for his own children. Cristina Alfaro and Lilia Bartolomé then focus on the importance of valuing and utilizing emergent bilinguals' creative use of language as a bridge to academic literacy. Mariana Souto-Manning and Jessica Martell expand the ways in which young children engage, represent, act, and express their knowledge of science and identities as scientists. In their chapter, collage is the medium for academic communication across languages. Closing this first section Dorea Kleker and Mika K. Phinney offer a transportable curriculum, The Family Art Backpacks, to build family-school relationships and elicit students' contributions to school learning on their own terms.

The second section, *In the Heights: Lifting Potential, Expanding Possibilities*, builds on the cultural resources of families and communities to deepen learning and academic success through artful practices. Mary Beth Meehan and Julie Nora use photography to engage students in developing multiple literacies in the social studies curriculum, while providing a vehicle for the rich lives of students to be shared from within. With a focus on assessment, Whitney J. Lawrence and Janelle B. Mathis explain how the arts and multimodalities further educators to gain a more accurate picture of what students know and are able to do. Katherine Egan Cunningham and Grace Enriquez offer evidence that picturebook illustrations provide rich resources for powerful transactions between child and text to construct response poems that deepen both their written and oral language.

The final section, *Lift Every Voice: Democratic Practice Before, During and After School*, offers several inspiring stories of political agency through the arts. Beth Murray and Gustave Weltsek work with drama to challenge their students to see themselves as active participants in the creation of a democratic society as they play with English language invention within arts-infused learning. Debi Khasnabis, Catherine H. Reischl, along with other artists and educators, describe a state-funded program involving a partnership across a public-school district, a university, and a community-based organization to engage students in multimodal affirmation of their culture and agency to define success on their own terms. Laura Cranmer, Jocelyn Difiore, and Jeffrey Paul Ansloos illuminate ways that individuals and communities use community languages, second languages, and an intermixing of languages to explore their collective identities. Native Hip Hop artists, in this chapter, demonstrate how Indigenous youth are (re)visiting, (re)claiming and (re)birthing Indigenous languages across Canada. Jie Park and Lori Simpson collaborate, in school and in afterschool settings, to document and describe how graphic novels support emergent bilingual learners in critically representing and expressing their analysis. Each of the three sections is followed with questions for reflection and further applications for practice.

ACKNOWLEDGMENTS

We could not have navigated this journey without the fine editors at Routledge, particularly Naomi Silverman for reaching out to us after reading our calling, as well as Karen Adler and Emmalee Ortega for carrying on Naomi's torch and supporting us through the rest of the process. Our Lesley University community of exceptional colleagues: Grace Enriquez and Arlene Dallalfar who served as our guides through the process of finding publications and answered our ongoing questions and Prilly Sanville who listened and held our heads up high. We are also grateful to the time and funding provided by the Russell Fellowship and Margery Miller Grant. And most importantly, special thanks to our families who generously gave up time with us as we worked through endless evenings and served as encouragers, listeners, readers, and editors with embracing enthusiasm:

Berta's husband, Ty dePass, for his wordsmithing and critical eye;

Amanda's partner, Drew Smith, and her wee ones, Sylvain and Eric, who made her stop and just play with cars;

Vivian's husband, Guy Michel Telemaque and daughter Camila, who not just encouraged her, but also kept her sane.

GLOSSARY

Activism: Direct vigorous undertaking in support of or opposition to one side of a controversial issue.

Basic Interpersonal Communication Skills (BICS):   Termed coined by Jim Cummins to differentiate between social and academic language acquisition. Basic Interpersonal Communication Skills (BICS) are language skills needed in social situations.

Bilingual: The ability to speak in two languages fluently.

Biliterate/Biliteracy: The ability to read and write in two languages fluently.

Codeswitching: The practice of alternating between two or more languages or varieties of language in conversation.

Cognitive Academic Language Learning Approach (CALLA):   An approach that was created specifically for emergent bilingual students. There are three modules of CALLA, which include learning strategies, development of academic language, and a related curriculum. Many public schools incorporate this into their ESL programs.

Cognitive Academic Language Proficiency (CALP):   Termed coined by Jim Cummins to differentiate between social and academic language acquisition. Cognitive Academic Language Proficiency (CALP) are language skills needed in formal academic learning, as opposed to BICS above for social learning.

Critical Framing: From the New London Groups concept of Multiliteracies, in critical framing students are guided to analyze designs critically in relation to whose interests are served by the meanings (ideology), and by considering the audience to whom the meanings are directed. Learners consider how these meanings relate to the cultural and social context of designs.

Collaboration: Interpersonal collaboration is a style of direct interaction between at least two coequal parties voluntarily engaged in shared or joint decision making as they work toward a common goal. (Adapted from a definition by Joanna D. Bertsekas, Lesley University)

Community-Based Language Learning (CLL): A language-teaching method in which students work together to develop what aspects of a language they would like to learn. It is based on the counseling-approach in which the teacher acts as a counselor and a paraphraser, while the learner is seen as a client and collaborator.

Comprehensible Input: A hypothesis first proposed by Stephen Krashen (1981) who purports that EBs acquire language by hearing and understanding messages that are slightly above their current English language level.

Critical Literacy: An instructional approach, stemming from Marxist critical pedagogy and Paulo Freire (1970), which advocates the adoption of "critical" perspectives toward text. Critical literacy encourages readers to actively analyze texts and offers strategies for what proponents describe as uncovering underlying messages.

Critical Pedagogy: A teaching approach inspired by critical theory and other radical philosophies, especially that of Paolo Freire's (1970) *Pedagogy of the Oppressed*, which is a teaching method that aims to help in challenging and actively struggling against any form of social oppression and the related customs and beliefs.

Cultural Capital: Acquired tastes, values, languages, and dialects, or the educational qualifications, that mark a person as belonging to a privileged social and cultural class . . . it is unconsciously learned. . . . "It is the best hidden form of hereditary transmission of capital" (Bourdieu, 1986, p. 246).

Cultural Competence: A set of congruent behaviors, attitudes, and policies that come together in a system, agency or among professionals and enable that system, agency or those professions to work effectively in cross-cultural situations.

Culturally Relevant/Responsive Teaching: A pedagogy grounded in teachers' displaying cultural competence: a skill at teaching in a cross-cultural or multicultural setting. They enable each student to relate course content to his or her cultural context.

Culture: The values, traditions, social and political relationships, and worldview created, shared, and transformed by a group of people bound together by a common history, geographic location, language, social class, or religion (definition by Sonia Nieto).

Discrimination: The differential allocation of goods, resources, and services, and the limitations of access to full participation in society based on individual membership in a particular social group.

Dual language Program: A form of education in which students are taught literacy and content in two languages. Dual language programs generally start in kindergarten or first grade and extend for at least five years, although many continue into middle school and high school.

Dynamic Bilingualism: The intermingling of past and present language practices, or the multi-competence of holding two languages at the same time, pushes us to understand the complexity of languaging in an increasingly multilingual global village. Dynamic bilingualism results when engaging our varying languages, past and present, in order to communicate across social contexts.

Emergent Bilinguals: Refers to culturally and linguistically diverse individuals who are utilizing their native language in the process of becoming dynamic bilinguals. The linguistic repertoire of these students taps into both languages as resources and students can be in developing stages of the native language and/or the second language. This term is used as a way to reject the deficit-oriented terminology of LEP (Limited English Proficiency), ELLs (English Language Learners), or ESL (English as a Second Language) students (García & Kleifgen, 2010). "One of today's most misunderstood issues in education throughout the world, and particularly in the United States, is how to educate students who speak languages other than English. In the United States, these students are most often referred to as English language learners (ELLs) by educators or as Limited English proficient students (LEPs) by legislators and the federal government. I argue here that *emergent bilinguals* might be a more appropriate term for these children. Labeling students as either LEPs or ELLs omits an idea that is critical to the discussion of equity in the teaching of these children. When officials and educators ignore the bilingualism that these students can—and must—develop through schooling in the United States, they perpetuate inequities in the education of these children" (García, 2009, p. 322)

English as a Second Language (ESL): Refers to the teaching of English to students with different native or home languages using specially designed programs and techniques. English as a Second Language is an English-only instructional model, and most programs attempt to develop English skills and academic knowledge simultaneously. It is also known as **English for Speakers of Other Languages (ESOL), English as an Additional Language (EAL), and English as a Foreign Language (EFL)**.

English Language Learner (ELL): A deficit-based term, used by most state departments of education and school districts, to mean emergent bilingual learner.

ESL Pull-Out: The pull-out method consists of the ESL teacher pulling students out of their general education classes to work with the teacher either one-on-one or in a small-group setting.

ESL Push-In: Some schools prefer for ESL teachers to work directly in students' classrooms, providing instruction in a push-in setting.

Empowerment: When members of oppressed groups refuse to accept the dominant ideology and their subordinate status and take action to redistribute social power more equitably.

Ethnicity: Social construct, which divides people into smaller social groups, based on characteristics such as nationality, ancestral geographical base, language, religions, socioeconomic status, and shared values.

Funds of Knowledge: Defined by researchers Luis Moll, Cathy Amanti, Deborah Neff, and Norma González (2001) "to refer to the historically accumulated and culturally developed bodies of knowledge and skills essential for household or individual functioning and well-being" (p. 133). When teachers shed their role of teacher and expert and, instead, take on a new role as learner, they can come to know their students and the families of their students in new and distinct ways. With this new knowledge, they can begin to see that the households of their students contain rich cultural and cognitive resources and that these resources can and should be used in their classroom in order to provide culturally responsive and meaningful lessons that tap students' prior knowledge. Information that teachers learn about their students in this process is considered the student's funds of knowledge.

Heritage Language: In foreign language education, heritage language is defined in terms of a student's upbringing and functional proficiency in the language: a student raised in a home where a non-majority language is spoken is a heritage speaker of that language if she/he possesses some proficiency in it.

L1: A first language, native language, or mother tongue (also known as father tongue, arterial language) is a language that a person has been exposed to from birth or within the critical period.

L2: The second language learned by an individual.

Latinx: We use the term Latinx when referring to communities and people in order to signal inclusivity instead of more 'genderized' terms such as Latin@, Latina/o.

Language Immersion Programs: An approach to foreign language instruction in which the usual curricular activities are conducted in a foreign language. This means that the new language is the medium of instruction.

Limited English Proficient (LEP): A deficit-based term used by the federal government to mean emergent bilingual learner.

Limit Situations: In Pedagogy of the Oppressed (1992, p. 89) Paolo Freire characterizes limit situations as barriers imposed on the oppressed that prevent them from being humanized. They can be effectively eliminated by educating those who are oppressed by these limit situations using the problem posing method of education.

Linguicism: Linguicism can be open (the agent does not try to hide it), conscious (the agent is aware of it), visible (it is easy for non-agents to detect), and actively action oriented (as opposed to 'merely' attitudinal). Or it can be hidden, unconscious, invisible, and passive (lack of support rather than active opposition), typical of later phases in the development of minority education (Tove Skutnabb-Kangas, Linguistic Genocide in Education, or Worldwide Diversity and Human Rights? Lawrence Erlbaum, 2000).

Microaggressions: Everyday verbal, nonverbal, and environmental slights, snubs, or insults, whether intentional or unintentional, which communicate hostile, derogatory, or negative messages to target persons based solely upon their marginalized group membership.

Multilingual: The ability to speak in more than two languages fluently.

Multiliterate/Multiliteracy: The ability to read and write in more than two languages fluently.

Multiliteracies: Refers to a variability of meaning making in different cultural, social, or domain specific contexts, which are becoming ever more significant to our communications environment. Literacy teaching no longer focuses solely on the traditional rules of reading and writing in the national language. Communication and representation of meaning today increasingly requires learners to navigate differences in patterns of meaning from one context to another. These differences are impacted by such variables as culture, gender, and life experience. Meaning is made in ways that are increasingly multimodal—in which written-linguistic modes of meaning interface with oral, visual, audio, gestural, tactile, and spatial patterns of meaning. Literacy pedagogy has also expanded to the new, digital media, providing a powerful foundation for a pedagogy of synesthesia, or mode-switching (Cope & Kalantzis, 2015). The multiliteracies pedagogical approach involves four key aspects: **Situated Practice, Critical Framing, Overt Instruction, and Transformed Practice**.

Multimodal Literacies: First proposed by Professors Gunter Kress and Carey Jewitt, is about understanding the different ways of knowledge representations and meaning-making. Multimodal literacy focuses on the design of discourse by investigating the contributions of specific semiotic resources, (e.g., language, gesture, images) co-deployed across various modalities (e.g., visual, aural, somatic), as well as their interaction and integration in constructing a coherent multimodal text (such as advertisements, posters, news report, websites, films).

Native Language Literacy Program: Programs that emphasize the importance of meaning and place learners' native language, cultural background and experiences at the center of the educational program, using them for instruction. The use and development of the learners L1 and L2 literacy skills are used throughout.

New Literacies Studies: "New literacies" that arise from new technologies include things like text-messaging, blogging, social networking, podcasting, and videomaking. These digital technologies alter and extend our communication abilities, often blending text, sound, and imagery.

No Child Left Behind (NCLB): The No Child Left Behind Act, created during the Bush administration in 2002, authorized several federal education programs that are administered by the states. The law was a reauthorization of the Elementary and Secondary Education Act. Under the 2002 law, states are required to test students in reading and math in grades 3–8 and once in high school.

Oppression: A systemic social phenomenon based on the perceived or real differences among social groups that involve ideological domination, institutional control, and the promulgation of the oppressors' ideology, logic system, and culture to the oppressed group. The result is the exploitation of one social group by another for the benefit of the oppressor group.

Sheltered English Immersion (SEI): Sheltered instruction is an approach to teaching emergent bilingual learners, which integrates language and content instruction. The dual goals of sheltered instruction are: to provide access to mainstream, grade-level content, and to promote the development of English language proficiency.

Sheltered Instruction (SDAIE): Sheltered Instruction, also referred to as SDAIE in California, is a teaching style founded on the concept of providing meaningful instruction in the content areas (social studies, math, science) for transitioning EB students towards higher academic achievement while they reach English language proficiency.

Sheltered Instruction Observation Protocol (SIOP): The SIOP model is a research-based and validated instructional model that has proven effective in addressing the academic needs of emergent bilinguals throughout the United States. The SIOP Model consists of eight interrelated components: Lesson Preparation. Building Background, Comprehensible Input, Strategies, Interaction, Practice and Application, Lesson Delivery, Review and Assessment

Situated Practice: Originally formulated by the New London Group (1996) as one of the related components of Multiliteracies Pedagogy, it is constituted by immersion in meaningful practices within a community of learners who are culturally and linguistically diversified.

Transformed Practice: When students recreate and recontextualize meaning (Cope & Kalantzi, 2000; New London Group, 1996).

Transformative Intercultural Pedagogy: This stance, which Cummins (2000) calls Transformative Intercultural Pedagogy, requires educators' appreciation of family involvement as a mutual border crossing and a shared responsibility (Bartolomé, 2006; Nieto, 1992, 2000).

Transitional Bilingual Program (TBE): A program that facilitates the transition of emergent bilingual learners into the all-English curriculum. Instruction in the students' native language ensures that students learn subject matter in the language they understand best. Classes in the native language continue as students acquire English language skills sufficient to function successfully in English-only mainstream classrooms. Transition to the English-only classroom is expected to occur within three years.

Translanguaging: Includes codeswitching but goes beyond this concept. For example, reading in one language and using another language to take notes, discuss, or write (García & Kleifgen, 2010).

Two-way Bilingual program (TB): A program that develops full bilingualism for all participants, regardless of their linguistic background. These programs serve emergent bilingual learners, both English language learners and native English speakers, who are seeking to learn a language other than their first language. All students receive instruction in English and a second language from the outset. Typically, native English-speaking students come from middle-class homes where parents understand the long-term value of investments rendering their children bilingual.

Unz Initiative: "End bilingual education in California by June 1998." That's the slogan of the Unz ballot initiative that was entitled English for the Children. In November 1997, California's Secretary of State certified that anti-bilingual activists had collected at least 510,796 petitions from registered voters—more than enough to qualify the measure for the primary ballot. The campaign was led by Ron Unz, a Republican candidate for governor in 1994 and a multimillionaire software developer, who funded the bill to get passed. Due to the results of the Unz Initiative in the early 2000s, California, Arizona, and Massachusetts restricted the implementation of bilingual education. As a result of this policy, in 2011 the US Department of Education and the US Justice Department found that Massachusetts had failed to adequately prepare teachers and school departments to implement English-only instruction (Berriz, 2006; Vaznis, 2011). Fortunately, California recently voted for the return of bilingual education in November 2016 and in Massachusetts, the bilingual education LOOK Bill passed in November 2017. It also passed a bill that puts the Seal of Biliteracy (https://languageopportunity.org/seal-of-biliteracy/) on graduation diplomas of high school students, in recognition of those who speak, read, and write proficiently in a language other than English. Progress on recognizing multilingualism as an asset is slowing emerging in the United States.

Zone of Proximal Development (ZPD): Psychologist Lev Vygotsky coined the term "zone of proximal development" (ZPD) in the 1930s to describe where instruction is most beneficial for each student—just beyond his or her current level of independent capability.

1

INTRODUCTION—BIENVENIDOS

*Berta Rosa Berriz, Amanda Claudia Wager
and Vivian Maria Poey*

FIGURE 1.1 Playing with Friends

"My friends here and at home are good. Some of them speak English, some Spanish and some both. Some of us like to play the same things. Some of us are all Puerto Rican and Americans."

—*Third grader in Berta's doctoral dissertation: The Emergent Cultural Identity of Puerto Rican and Dominican Third-grade Students and Its Relation to Academic Performance*
—*(Berriz, 2005)*

The picture in Figure 1.1 is but one example of how we, the three editors, and the many inspirational contributors to this volume have connected to students' *funds of knowledge* while utilizing the arts for language learning with *emergent bilingual* (EB) students, families, and communities (González, Moll, & Amanti, 2006). *Knowing who our emergent bilingual students are and honoring their voices is essential to the development of their academic identities.* In this introductory chapter, we begin by introducing ourselves, so that you immediately know our positionalities—who we are and the lens we see the world through—to make visible why this work is so close to our hearts. We proceed by contextualizing the work with demographic information regarding emergent bilingual learners, followed by the theoretical foundations and connections among the three disciplines represented: the arts, literacies, and language acquisition. Along the way, we provide rich examples from within this volume, using the arts as a way of talking, and conclude with an invitation to read onwards as we briefly describe the heart of each chapter within *Art as a Way of Talking.*

Our Journeys: Multilingual Students, Artists, Activists, Teachers, Researchers, and Scholars

The three of us—Berta, Vivian, and Amanda—come from distinct walks of life, with overlaps and similarities. We have been teachers, specializing in one of the three areas of arts, literacies, and language acquisition; however, we view these distinct areas as interwoven within the education of emergent bilingual learners. We continually seek to further educate ourselves, each other, and reach out to a broader community in these realms. This drive led us to form our collaborative and to seek out other voices in the field. In order to understand the lens that we bring to this text, we provide our histories and lived experiences as an entry point.

Berta's Story

Recently, as I searched for documents of our move to the United States, I came across this poem stitching my identity in my passion for dance, the land I left behind, as well as the constant presence of mi Abuelita, America. Abuelita is my spirit guide as I move through new contexts, challenges, and landscapes. I wrote this poem as a dancer taking a leap into the world of public education. In my view, artists were the original teachers. We are the ones who observed nature (scientists) and created ritual celebrations (philosophers). Artists documented everyday life experiences in drawings, stories, song, and costumes (historians). Storytellers captured traditions, values, advice, and humor and passed them on to communities (healers).

a dancer
all that she could
bring to the night
dance
was a dress
she stitched
for time
in preparation
carefully
in again out
with her
Grandmother's own needle
she stitched
appliqués
of people
rich red
brown earth
under their feet
their skin
next to sun blue air
working
tending to one another
familia
hermana
compadre
on silk she painted
creatures weaving
days and nights
spiders
humming birds
star fish
alacrán
the earth life weave
bonded with the heavens
rivers flowing
marshes sucking moisture

fish flipping
in the nets
gathering
flechas
lanzas
machetes
maracas
marimba
tambor
renewing in the weapons
her own firmness
reliving the soft song
reworking the tools
massing seeds
pounding the dough
casabe
enmeshed
in a thick
knotted border
a tight thread
encircled
still spinning
flaring
to meet the night dance
I still have my Abuelita's needles.

I moved to this country from Cuba at the age of eight. As a third grader, I was compelled to give up my country, my language, and my name. In many ways, I am my students; I have felt their confusion, embarrassment, and anger firsthand. I understand how the imposition of a new language and culture can profoundly affect the process of identity-formation, self-esteem, and the capacity for learning of a young child. My immigration story motivates my activism as an artist and educator. My journey as a bilingual teacher has included dual language and native language literacy settings, including African American students as well as Latinx students in transitional bilingual and special education programs in severely seg-regated public school contexts. Critical awareness of socio-structural impositions and limitations placed on my students required that I discard standardized cur-riculum in favor of engaging my learning community in a critical analysis of their own potential to excel and make their mark in a changing world. My teaching experience necessitated a deeper look at the relationship between my students' identities and their academic progress.

Stepping out of my classroom into the world of research at Harvard's Gradu-ate School of Education, I searched for answers regarding the persistent racial and ethnic disparities among third-grade students' academic achievement (BPS Office of Assessment and Evaluation, 2003). I was both lifted and led by pioneers in the anthropology of education, George Spindler and Carola Suárez-Orozco, who focus on the psycho-social impact of immigration on those called "other" in school (Suárez-Orozco, 2004). Children's drawings centered interviews exploring the relationship between the cultural identity and academic performance of these emergent bilingual youth. Voices from my doctoral studies at Harvard stay with me. Families are the foundation of a sense of belonging for my students that define their engagement with mainstream society. As Pedro, a third grader in my study put it, "family is part of the heart." Language is an important part of staying close to family. Toña, another student, visited her grandmother in the Dominican Republic and spoke to her in Spanish, "I love it there." Pedro describes how he thinks about language, "Yo le hablo en inglés a mis amigos y a los que no saben inglés, yo le hablo en español." (*I speak English with my friends and I speak Spanish with those who do not speak English*). Pedro also gives us insight to the importance of Spanish in his life. "We speak Spanish because in my family, my parents do not speak English. My mom wants me to speak Spanish and it feels good to speak Spanish" (Berriz, 2005).

Keeping this history close to heart, my hope for *Art as a Way of Talking* is to empower teachers, families, and communities with a guide for subverting the *limit situations*, which are barriers imposed on the oppressed that prevent them from being humanized and that can be effectively eliminated by using an arts-based problem posing method of education (Freire, 1970). The arts encourage our emergent bilingual scholars to use their imaginations as a way of linking their lived experiences to solve academic problems (Brice-Heath & Roach, 1999). It is our intention that *Art as a Way of Talking* broadens possibilities for young scholars of diverse cultural and linguistic backgrounds.

Vivian: an Artist's Journey Through her Family History

As Berta describes earlier, history shapes who we are. Nearly every generation, as far as I can trace in my father's family, has spent time in exile. This image (Figure 1.2) represents my grandfather's trajectory. He was born in Tampa in 1900 as my great-grandfather was in exile during the Cuban War of Independence (known in the US as the Spanish American War). The faint pencil lines show his trajectory from his birth in Tampa to Havana followed by his exile in Mexico City and finally Miami, Florida, where he settled until his death. I have included this as part of my own history by layering an image of my feet in the ocean at Varadero, Cuba—a place described in family stories as a paradise where "la arena es como el azúcar y el agua tan transparente que puedes ver hasta la mugre de las uñas" (*the sand is like sugar and the water so clear that you can see the dirt under your nails*).

I was 14 and in ninth grade when I moved to the United States. Before moving to Miami, I had lived in three different countries, sang three national anthems,

FIGURE 1.2 Aguirre exile 1898

and learned three different versions of history with varying historical figures and geographic regions. Everything I knew seemed irrelevant to my education in this country. It was not until I took a photography class in community college that I began to understand that my own experience was relevant, and that I could explore and share it though my artwork. While looking at contemporary photographers I began to feel connected. I was inspired by the work of Latin American artists, such as Graciela Iturbide and Manuel Alvarez Bravo, to look deeper into my own experiences and further my learning—not just about photography but about everything. Photography provided both a thirst for knowledge and a language to make meaning of the world. Later, I began to connect with the work of other artists, such as Fred Wilson, who created an alternate historical narrative by reorganizing and re-presenting the collection of the Maryland Historical Museum; Mary Beth Meehan, who photographed the bedrooms of immigrants, bringing an intimate view of a silent community; and Gustavo Perez Firmat, whose bilingual poetry says more than even two languages can speak.

Through my work I have been investigating my family history and its place in the larger history of Cuba, tracking my father's family history and creating a visual biography of past generations, leading up to my daughter who is a trace, a document, of Cuban, Haitian, and American history (www.lesley.edu/stories/vivian-poey). This work led me to do historical research, to read news archives, and to unearth family stories. Trying to connect to and represent places that are far away and stories that happened long ago, I researched maps during the time of my ancestors. I went back as far as the 1700s when my great-great-great-grandfather moved from France to Cuba. Creating these photographs forced me to connect to the details of my ancestor's lives. The times and places became real and alive, and the stories I learned made visible how those who came before me shaped my present context. These stories, both extraordinary and in some ways shameful, create personal connections across time and space that resonate in ways that are still relevant today.

I have been working in this historical research vein since my graduate thesis *On Fictional Ground and Culinary Maps* (https://digitalcommons.lesley.edu/jppp/vol2/iss3/5/), where I investigated the intertwined ideas of authenticity and assimilation. Working through the arts with these ideas about investigating and communicating our worlds translated into invaluable learning about my own students. As a photography mentor with teens from every public high school in Pittsburgh and later as an artist teacher in Washington DC with a young student body representing multiple countries from Africa and Latin America, I listened to my students' voices as they developed eloquent multimodal artwork that spoke to the personal and academic alike.

Amanda: Playing with Languages and Places

Connecting to Vivian's use of maps to tell her history, my "Life Map" collage (Figure 1.3) is the accumulation of the many different places I have lived; reflecting the space of displacement—of neither being here nor there, from this place or that place—that I often feel. My family history, through various moves and displaced moments in time, has made me adapt to new locations and languages quickly. Being a White, cisgender able-bodied English-speaking woman from the middle class, I come to this space of displacement with a great deal of privilege.

My name is Amanda Claudia Wager. My late father is Peter Polland Wager of Chicago and my mother is Marilyn Dee Pincus of Los Angeles. Both sides of my biological family stem from Jewish Ashkenazi ancestry. In the beginning of the 20th century, my great-grandparents came to the United States from Poland/Russia—the borders were constantly shifting—fleeing the Jewish genocide of the Russian Red Army. My grandparents spoke English and Yiddish, and we spoke English and eventually Dutch in our house. My stepfather Paul Logchies, from Amsterdam in the Netherlands, raised me from age 12 onwards. Growing up in Amsterdam, a small global city surrounded by countries that speak many other languages, we learned and heard languages everywhere. We played with languages by moving in and out of one on to another. Language learning and

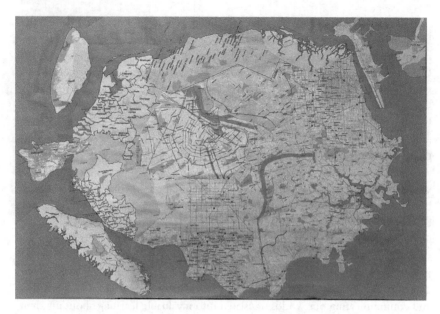

FIGURE 1.3 Amanda Life Map

teaching was an art form in itself and has led me to where I am now, with a passion for teaching languages and literacies via the arts.

Growing up in Los Angeles, I learned Spanish in school and I was often surrounded by it in friend's homes and on the streets. When I was 5 years old my family moved to London for a year, where I was told my first day of school to "Queue up for the loo!" and was the only child who stayed sitting on the rug while others laughed because I had no idea that I was supposed to line up for the bathroom. This is only a tiny taste of how emergent bilingual learners feel much of the time. Then in seventh grade, I watched a drama performance about two people stranded on a desert island. They spoke different languages and at first were petrified of each other. Eventually they were able to communicate without words and survive together. This was the beginning of my interest in using drama in education in order to communicate across differences. During these formative years growing up in Amsterdam, I gained the values of humility and a deep respect for humanity, nature, and myself, which guided me through my life as an educator, student, researcher, director, friend, sister, partner, and now, a mother.

From my experiences as a student and educator, drama can be used across cultures, languages, and perspectives (Schroeter & Wager, 2016; Wager, Belliveau, Beck, & Lea, 2009). In high school, I continued studying Dutch and Spanish, and spent much time with a Pakistani family tutoring their children, while also working as the theatre stage manager. I often used role-play with the family to communicate. My desire to study drama in education and language acquisition as an adult evolved and I eventually taught in a school in Chachapoyas, Peru, and in Chicago Public Schools as a bilingual elementary school teacher.

As an educator, I draw from critical and feminist pedagogies (Ellsworth, 1989, 1997; hooks, 1994, 2010) where collectivity, reciprocity, and reflexivity guide my teaching; that I may learn as much from others as they might learn from me through revealing who we are in relation to our histories and the contexts within which we work. Working through the arts, valuing and building off of the languages and literacies of those we work with, are key to the success of bi/ multilingual individuals. This is my hope for *Art as a Way of Talking*, that readers will recognize the importance of supporting bi/multilingual learning through the arts and become activists in promoting these efforts in their own community and collegial spaces.

Multilingualism: Recent Context and Unfolding Pedagogy

Throughout this book we refer to English language learners (ELLs) as "emergent bilingual learners" to honor the assets that multilingual students bring to our schools and communities (García, 2009). Since those who speak English as their first language began and still are English language learners, this work benefits all students. Being able to speak, read, and write in more than one language is significantly advantageous in our increasingly global society. As well, the United States and Canada have always been multicultural and multilingual countries. Bilingualism has existed in North America since the 17th-century European invasion (Wright, 2015). Seizing the land and displacing its indigenous populations, facilitated by the imposition of European cultural domination, resulted in the silencing of native voices. The enduring legacy of these policies is most evident in the longstanding resistance to language and cultural diversity, particularly in education (Motha, 2014). And yet, young people need to thrive regardless of whether English is their first, second, or fifth language. Creative, culturally responsive, and community-based ways of knowing within formal and informal education are essential for this to happen (Crawford, 1995).

Demographic trends of emergent bilinguals further the call for authentic ways of meaning-making to be shared, collaborated, and communicated by educators today.

- Over 350 languages besides English are spoken in US homes today. The United States lags behind most nations of the world, including European nations and China, in the percentage of its citizens who have some knowledge of a second language (Commission on Language Learning, 2017, p. viii).
- Emergent bilinguals have increased in all but 11 states in the US between the years of 2003 and 2013 (US Department of Education, 2015)

- The percentage of school-age children ages 5 to 17 in the US who were White decreased from 62 percent in 2000 to 53 percent in 2013, and the percentage of children who were Black decreased from 15 to 14 percent during this time. In contrast, the percentage of school-age children who were from other racial/ethnic groups increased during this period: those who were Hispanic increased from 16 to 24 percent; those who were Asian, from 3 to 5 percent; and those who were of Two or more races, from 2 to 4 percent (Musu-Gillette, Robinson, McFarland, KewalRamani, Zhang, & Wilkinson-Flicker, 2016)
- In US schools today, one in five children speaks a language other than English at home and more than 4.4 million students are classified at school as having limited proficiency in English (Imigration Policy Institute Fact Sheet, June 2015)
- Segregation by socioeconomic status, residential location, and language has increased since the 1970s. The Civil Rights Project notes that on average, Latinx emergent bilinguals attend schools where 60% of students are of Latinx descent (www.gse.harvard.edu/news-tags/civil-rights-project).
- The number of refugee children, as a percentage of all refugees resettling to the US, has increased over the past decade. For example, in 1998, only 13% of all refugees resettled by the US were children, but in 2008, 37% were children (www.brycs.org/publications/schools-toolkit.cfm).
- In California, Latinx students constitute more than half of all K-12 students (California Department of Education; www.cde.ca.gov/ds/sd/cb/ceffinger-tipfacts.asp).
- In the US 77% of the emergent bilinguals in grades K-5 and 56% in grades 6–12 were born in the United States and are simultaneous bilinguals, who learn two languages at once between the ages of 0 to 5 (Escamilla et al., 2014, p. 5).
- In Boston, Massachusetts, 35% of students are African American, 42% are Latinx, 30% speak a first language which is not English, while 62% of their teachers are White (2016–2017 demographic student data; www.bostonpub-licschools.org/domain/238).
- As a result of language subordination and marginalization of indigenous communities in Canada, speakers of indigenous languages are in alarming decline (Moseley, 2010).
- Native American languages are distinct in political status and history and are the object of school- and community-based reclamation and retention efforts aligned with the Native American Languages Act of 1990 (NALA) (Commission on Language Learning, 2017, p. ix; Crawford, J., 1995)
- Immigrant languages such as Tagalog, Mandarin, Arabic, Hindi, Creole, Bengali, and Spanish are reported as languages spoken at home in the 2011 Linguistic characteristics of Canadians (http://www12.statcan.gc.ca/census-recensement/2011/as-sa/98-314-x/98-314-x2011001-eng.cfm).

- One of the biggest obstacles to improved language learning is a national shortage of qualified teachers. Forty-four states and Washington, DC, report that they cannot find enough qualified teachers to meet current needs (Commission on Language Learning, 2017, p. ix). (www.census.gov/newsroom/press-releases/2015/cb15-185.html).

In the current political context, the topic of displaced populations, immigration policies (such as The Deferred Action for Childhood Arrivals [DACA]), refugees, as well as those who are undocumented is very alive in classrooms and relevant to our students' lives. This dramatic change in the faces and cultures of our students suggest that teachers, teacher educators, and community workers must develop new epistemological frameworks broadening the scope and depth of research supporting innovative literacy practices (Valdés & Figueroa, 1994). Particularly relevant are the stories, within this volume, of effective practitioners using the arts to create new linguistic pathways to learning for all students, families, and communities, especially the most marginalized.

Interdisciplinary Critical Pedagogy and Integrated Arts

So, how does art serve as a way of talking for these populations of emergent bilingual learners? Borrowing a metaphor from Seeking Educational Equity and Diversity (SEED) director Emily Style (1996), art is an expressive form that is simultaneously a "window and mirror." It is through art that we are able to access and honor authentic stories, lived experiences, and knowledge of diverse peoples. For students who are in process of learning a new language in a new land, while still holding on to their native language, the ability to investigate, reflect, and share this knowledge through rich multimodal literacies (i.e., through textual, gestural, visual, spatial, audio, and digital ways) that are not oral-language-dependent, is crucial (Franks, 2008). Applying a critical lens through the arts engages students through a wide range of literacies as they make meaning dependent on social, cultural, and historical contexts (Ajayi, 2015; Schroeter & Wager, 2016).

The arts, therefore, not only provide multiple entry points demanding complex problem-solving skills, but also provide tangible scaffolding for language learning and academic success. No test-driven, scripted curricula, pacing guide, or English-only-inspired set of standards can provide the rich relationships necessary for the learning process (Valdés & Figueroa, 1994). The arts create fertile ground for inspiring a sense of belonging in school, cognitive growth, and communication. The arts also call on students to draw from and contribute their cultural knowledge and linguistic background as they enhance their communication skills. *Art as a Way of Talking* is a call from fellow artists, educators, community organizers, and practitioners to co-construct learning using critical multimodal literacy tools through the arts.

Untangling the Disciplines: The Arts, Literacies, and Language Acquisition

In this next section we explore the foundations of the arts, literacies, and language acquisition by untangling the disciplines and providing a theoretical background to support this call. We elaborate on each of these foundations by providing examples from the artists, researchers, and educators featured within this book.

Why the Arts?

The arts are an integral part of our lives that represent our values, connect us with one another, provide avenues for research and learning, stimulate our imagination, and provide us with a sense of agency to create positive impact in our communities and the larger world. In addition to the richness of the process, a final product/performance also plays an important role in community building. Communities, families, staff, and teachers gather for exhibitions and performances, providing an opportunity not only to celebrate the community members' artful accomplishments, but also to engage all participants in teaching and sharing their knowledge and culture in both schools and the larger community.

The arts are more than an added benefit in any educational context; they are foundational literacies that engage participants in the process of observing, connecting, finding solutions, making meaning, and communicating/expressing (Kennedy Arts Center, 2014). For individuals who rarely see themselves or their experiences represented in schools or the media, the arts provide a way to make these hidden narratives and perspectives visible. When we are invited to "play" in art, we build on the complex and important work of translation through codeswitching, which in the arts can be represented not only through oral and written language (as in poetry and music), but also in images, gesture, tone, etc (Hetland, 2013). In a world fraught with challenges, it is helpful to have art to help us understand, translate, and transform both our place in the world and our vision of a better future (Greene, 1995).

In spite of the obvious benefits that the arts bring to schools and communities, arts funding is always at risk (www.nytimes.com/2017/03/15/arts/nea-neh-endowments-trump.html). Fewer students get access to arts education now than before *No Child Left Behind (NCLB)*. The disappearance of arts from public school curricula is listed first among the four areas of concern reported by the National Latinx Education Research and Policy Project Council (http://opencuny.org/nlerap4ne/casa/) (Valenzuela, 2016). With ever-increasing budget cuts nationwide, access to the arts has declined the most for students in the least privileged schools. Ironically, randomized and longitudinal research points to the greatest benefits from arts for these very communities (Bowen, Green, & Kisida, 2014; Caterall, Dumais, & Hampden-Thompson, 2012). Strengthening access to the arts is particularly crucial in this context. Whether as its own subject, integrated into the general curriculum, in afterschool programs or integrated into community practices, the arts are a powerful pathway for creative educators committed to tapping into their students' *funds of knowledge* (González et al., 2006), while opening doors to a sense of agency in their communities and their own lives, imagining new possibilities and developing academic excellence.

Within the pages of this volume, authors share inviting examples of where art is a foundational literacy for emergent bilingual students. For example, by constructing story through digital artwork, Sally Brown (Chapter 8), uses images as a tool for student talk that is essential to the success of emergent bilingual students as designers and writers. Through graphic novels, Jie Park and Lori Simpsons (Chapter 12) engage students' critical and analytic ways of "reading" their world. By embracing the arts within their teaching practice, these educators subvert this resource gap, while creating access for their emergent bilingual students.

Eclectic Approaches to Literacies: Multiliteracies, New Literacies, and Multimodality

> Multiple literacies projects build stories based on and arising from young people's lives and experiences and cultural forms of representation to engage with and gain access to student agency, cultural memory, and home and school learning within local contexts. . . . This makes it increasingly important for schools to attend to the literacy practices of students and diverse ways of making meaning, in particular, the multilingual, the multimodal, and the digital. In short, there is a need for further investigation of literacy practices as an intertextual web of contexts and media rather than isolated sets of skills and competences.
>
> (Jewitt, 2008, p. 255)

Literacy as a sociocultural practice encompasses the myriad of different spaces of students' lives: homes, schools, playgrounds, and similar public and private spaces. As well, literacies include the diverse representations that students use to interpret and represent their daily lives, such as through the modes of visual arts, song, dance, and drama. Informed by social semiotic theories that emphasize how the relationship between form and meaning is socially constructed with texts (Halliday, 1978; Hodge & Kress, 1988; Kress & Van Leeuwen, 1996), these concepts have recently been explained through the pedagogical theories of *multiliteracies* (New London Group, 1996, 2000), *new literacies studies* (Lankshear & Knobel, 2003; Street, 2003), *and multimodality* (Jewitt & Kress, 2008; Kalantzis & Cope, 2012; Kress, & Jewitt, 2008; Rowsell, 2013), which are a direct response to our growing multilingual and multimodal world with respect to technology, globalization, and the many English language variations spoken today (Cope & Kalantzis, 2013; Luke & Carrington, 2002).

The pedagogy of multiliteracies recognizes that students are "designers" in their meaning-making processes. This begins and continues with their immersion into rich learning environments that may include a diverse multilingual and multicultural classroom library, multilingual word walls, student multilingual and multimodal artwork posted, interactive teacher-student responses posted and digital representations within blogs and wikis. Within this volume educators Kleker and Phiney (Chapter 4) design "school-community art backpacks" that create bridges between family and school settings while creatively affirming home languages. Through art and story, they captivate us with a scene at the Family Art Night where a fifth grader and her mother are the teachers. Shabaash Kemeh (Chapter 1) documents how the educator and family collaboration can enrich academic performance while enhancing family language and cultural identity. Through his own family narrative Kemeh explains how he brings Ghanaian stories to educational spaces through interactive Reader's Theatre with young children. Laura Cranmer, Jocelyn Difiore, and Jeffrey Paul Ansloos (Chapter 11) demonstrate how Indigenous youth within Canada, via the art of Hip Hop culture, act as language brokers who contribute to Indigenous language revitalization and survivance.

These exemplary pedagogies focus on a student *situated practice* based on the learners' experiences which include their "funds of knowledge" (González et al., 2006). Jie Park and Lori Simpson (Chapter 12) engage critical multiliteracies with young emergent bilingual scholars who proceed to turn the League of Extraordinary Gentlemen *on its head* by using their voices to object to sexism. The culminating assessment of a dramatic jury trial provides a *critical framing* to connect the meaning of what students are learning, and a *transformed practice* where students recreate and recontextualize meaning (Cope & Kalantzi, 2000; New London Group, 1996). Our contributors recognize that these four factors expose students to rich learning environments by bringing with them the importance of the students' families, communities, and cultural backgrounds. They also expand on the functions of language and other nonverbal literacy representations in order to create critical learning spaces for learners to interpret new meanings from their lives in and out-of-school. Meehan and Nora (Chapter 5) bring voices of students documenting their cultural communities via photography and bilingual writing. Brown (Chapter 8) centers the sound of the classroom community at work constructing stories based on their own experiences and expressing them through digital art.

And finally, multimodality brings these ideas together to consider how each element, or mode that we use to "read the world" (Freire & Macedo, 1987) is situated historically, culturally, and socially, and contributes to the entire meaning of the text; the text now being a body, a book, a visual piece of art, a comic, a song. These meanings are made and mixed through various modes of meaning-making, such as gesture, gaze, image, sound, speech, writing, body posture, music, and so on. Multimodality places emphasis on how the many different modes within any given text intersect, interrelate, are interpreted, and remade, to make up new meanings (Kress, 2000, 2003). Debi Khasnabis and colleagues (Chapter 10) use music, spoken poetry, and video to tell stories of success by emergent bilingual students, which are multimodal ways of meaning-making demonstrated through gesture, gaze, image, sound, speech, writing, and body posture.

Each of these conceptions of literacies acknowledges that students, especially emergent bilinguals, bring a range of resources to meaning-making in and outside of the classroom. These multiple forms of literacies challenge traditional forms of schooling that merely spotlight restrictive print and language-based notions of literacy (Gee, 2004; Lam, 2006; Sefton-Green, 2006). A multimodal approach to literacy, as described via the arts and articulated within this volume and others (Chappell & Faltis, 2013; Donovan & Pascale, 2012; Flood, Heath, & Lapp, 2015; Latta & Chan, 2010; Wager, Poey, & Berriz, 2017), advances the call to deconstruct these restrictive forms of literacy assuring that educational settings connect to, and bring in our students' *funds of knowledge*—their homes, communities, and languages—to enrich schools and communities.

Navigating the Institutional Borders to Language Acquisition

This next section explains the foundations of language acquisition, and the importance of promoting bilingualism and family/community involvement throughout this process. We have all noted that many young students arrive and seem to be able to learn a new language in just a few months. We marvel at their ability to "soak it all in." But language acquisition is hardly that simple, and theories for how language is acquired have developed over time from B. F. Skinner's purely cognitive understanding that sees the brain as a blank slate needing to be filled to Noam Chomsky's more transactional perspective that sees language as developing through a social context. Additionally, there is the notion that there are two systems through which we acquire language: the subconscious process of learning language when we are babies, and language "learned" through more formal instruction, such as grammar, syntax, and vocabulary building. Furthermore, Cummins (2008) introduced the idea that there are great differences between language that we use socially (*BICS: Basic Interpersonal Communicative Skills*) and a more challenging academic language that is vital for academic success (*CALP: Cognitive Academic Language Proficiency*). While the former can take as little as six months to develop, explaining our perception that kids learn quickly, the latter can take between five and seven years to master.

Language is at the heart of teaching and learning because all classrooms and community settings are language-learning environments for both primary English speakers and emergent bilingual learners. Educators use knowledge of language as communicators, evaluators, educated human beings, and as agents of socialization. Drawing from Krashen's (1981) theory of *comprehensible input*, we see language acquisition being built and expanded upon input that is already understood at a certain proficiency level—much like Vygotsky's *Zone of Proximal Development* (1962, 1978, 1987)—and that students acquire language best through interaction in a non-threatening and low anxiety environment. Engaging pre-existing knowledge encoded in family languages encourages a deep understanding of concepts and factual knowledge for emergent bilinguals. The arts promote this kind of cross-language transfer and give students agency over their learning process while supporting *biliteracy* (Cummins, Baker, & Hornberger, 2001). Since there are a wide range of language variations represented in North America, teachers can benefit from pedagogically sound and culturally sensitive methods for helping students learn academic English in schools and other community settings while honoring home languages and cultures.

Second Language Teaching Methods and Approaches Today

There are various methods and approaches to second language acquisition in schools today. There is a content-based instruction, which is a type of communicative language teaching where a selected content area becomes a meaningful context for authentic communication as learners collaborate to complete carefully designed academic tasks. For instance, teachers use math, social studies, or science as vehicles for language instruction, which Souto-Manning and Martell (Chapter 3) demonstrate through the use of collage in the learning of ornithology.

English as a second language instruction (ESL), both pull-out and push-in, is utilized in schools as a means of specifically teaching the English language to support students to understand the content-area instruction in the mainstream classroom. *Sheltered Instruction*, which is also called *specially designed academic instruction in English (SDAIE)*, involves content-area teachers to custom-design their instruction to make it comprehensible for emergent bilinguals, while supporting students' English language development. Some popular ESL models known today are the *Cognitive Academic Language Learning Approach (CALLA)* (Chamot & O'Malley, 1994) and *Sheltered Instruction Observation Protocol Model (SIOP)* (Echevarría, Vogt, & Short, 2004).

There are also numerous models of bilingual education, such as transitional bilingual education, dual language programs, native language literacy programs, and language-immersion programs. A *Transitional Bilingual Education* (TBE) program facilitates the transition of emergent bilingual learners into the all-English curriculum. Instruction in the students' native language ensures that students learn subject matter in the language they understand best. Classes in the native language continue as students acquire English language skills sufficient to function successfully in English-only mainstream classrooms. Transition to the English-only classroom is expected to occur within three years. A *Native Language Literacy (NLL)* program constitutes a safe space for literacy development of emergent bilinguals who have had limited or no schooling in their home countries. The program is for students between the ages of 9 and 21 and is designed to help students eventually enter and succeed in the *TBE* program. The focus of the program is on developing native language literacy and *ESL* skills as well as subject matter knowledge. A *Two-way Bilingual* (TB) program develops full bilingualism for all participants, regardless of their linguistic background. These programs serve emergent bilingual learners, both English language learners and native English speakers, who are seeking to learn a language other than their first language. All students receive instruction in English and a second language from the outset. In *language immersion* programs learners are immersed into another language 100% of the time. Students in these programs often come from homes where parents understand the long-term value of the investment of rendering their children bilingual.

Due to the results of the *Unz Initiative* in the early 2000s, voters in California, Arizona, and Massachusetts restricted the implementation of bilingual education. As a result of this short-sighted and misguided policy, in 2011 the US Department of Education and the US Justice Department found that Massachusetts had failed to adequately prepare teachers and school departments to implement English-only instruction (Berriz, 2006; Vaznis, 2011). California recently voted for the return of bilingual education in November 2016. And Massachusetts passed the bilingual education LOOK bill in November 2017 as well as a bill that puts the Seal of Biliteracy (https://languageopportunity.org/seal-of-biliteracy/) on graduation diplomas in recognition of high school students who speak, read, and write proficiently in a language other than English. Progress on recognizing multilingualism as an asset is slowly emerging in the United States.

As educators, we all have a responsibility to work with students as human beings regardless of the systems we find ourselves in. The arts humanize these spaces and the work of teachers, administrators, community educators, and university professors can support this framework. In this book we bring together educators who work primarily in pre-k12 school settings. And because we find that work in schools is inextricably linked to what happens beyond school walls, we have included some voices that illuminate family and community contexts, making visible the important contributions of artful teaching across each of these realities.

Fostering Bilingualism: the hArt of Literacy Development with Emergent Bilingual Learners

Imagine, when you speak Spanish and English, and then add Mandarin, you will be able to converse with most of the people on this planet! Engaging the home language in school as a learning and teaching tool gives emergent bilingual students an academic advantage. This, in turn, creates access and accelerates both content area and basic literacy skills (Cummins, 2000). Teaching materials inclusive of home language and culture enhance proficiency in both the language of home and that of academic English (Kioko, 2015). This invitation to engage in the learning process with all that each student has to offer inspires a sense of belonging in school, to the extent that researchers have found a direct correlation between bilingual education and staying in school (Feinberg, 2002). Home language, then, is an asset, a valuable treasure worth preserving and enhancing, not only for families and cultural communities, but also to support cognitive development and academic achievement. As artists and educators, we are critically positioned as agents of multiliteracies to support students in communicating in rich ways across a wide range of contexts. The Commission on Language Learning (2017) cites various studies that support these findings:

- bilingual children have stronger working memory—the ability to retain and manipulate distinct pieces of information over short periods of time—than do monolingual children (Morales, Calvo, & Bialystok, 2013).
- the Utah Dual Language Immersion program showed that children in the program gained improved memory and attention, problem-solving capabilities, primary-language comprehension, and ability to empathize with other cultures and people (Utah State Office of Education, 2013).
- bilingual children have greater executive functioning—focus, planning, prioritization, multitasking—than monolingual children (Bialystok, 2011).
- "multilingual exposure may promote effective communication by enhancing perspective taking," a fundamental component of empathy (Fan, Liberman, Keysar, & Kinzler, 2015).
- bilingual patients at a memory clinic presented dementia symptoms four years later, on average, than their monolingual counterparts and that bilingualism delayed the onset of Alzheimer's disease (Bialystok, Craik, & Freedman, 2007).

The notion of *dynamic bilingualism*, intermingling of past and present language practice, or the multi-competence of holding two languages at the same time, pushes us to understand the complexity of languaging in an increasingly multilingual global village. *Translanguaging* includes codeswitching but goes beyond, for example, reading in one language and using another language to take notes, discuss, or write (García & Kleifgen, 2010). Translanguaging practices open up the pedagogical space to the imagination, knowledge, and linguistic gifts of emergent bilingual students. Since there are a wide range of language variations represented in North America, educators can benefit from pedagogically sound and culturally sensitive methods for helping students learn academic English while honoring home languages and cultures. For example, Cristina Alfaro and Lilia Bartolomé (Chapter 2) consider multilingual students linguistic geniuses as they engage in codeswitching, creatively bridging their linguistic resources within the context of schooling.

Researcher Jie Park and public school teacher Lori Simpson (Chapter 12) demonstrate how youth use different languages to express themselves during role-play in a jury trial. Debi Khasnabis and others (Chapter 10) shine the spotlight on center stage as emergent bilingual learners lay claim to the curriculum through multilingual spoken-word poetry, Hip Hop, and film. And Laura Cranmer, Jocelyn Difiore, and Jeffrey Ansloos (Chapter 11) share examples of how Indigenous youth masterfully translanguage Hip Hop music, while revitalizing their indigenous language and healing their histories.

Summoning Family and Community Voices

Tapping families and community as valued sources of cultural knowledge, and rooting learning in the histories and traditions of students' home communities embeds new knowledge in the fiber of everyday life while supporting rigorous academic standards. Students are engaged in constructing new knowledge from a position of strength—as one of Berta's third graders described it: "I am a student teaching and a teacher learning" (Giroux, 2011; Valenzuela, 2016).

Teaching and learning in this manner also enhances cross-cultural understanding, particularly since the diversity in most educational contexts includes a variety of languages, nationalities, and family immigration histories. Most certainly, this affirmation of cultural groups and their languages strengthens the transition between home and school (García & Kleifgen, 2010). The arts invite students to bring their histories and culture to express their ideas. Moreover, the arts support agency (Hanley & Noblit, 2009). Taking a social justice stance beside families turns the cultural deficit model, which blames students for their own deficits and lack of cultural capital, on its head, establishing a mutual base of support for students, families, and teachers (Berriz, 2002; Bourdieu, 1986). This stance, which Cummins (2000) calls *Transformative Intercultural Pedagogy*, requires educators' appreciation of family involvement as a mutual border crossing and a shared responsibility (Bartolomé, 2006; Nieto, 2000; Nieto & Bode, 2012). When an educator utilizes and invites home languages and cultural resources, students are not compelled to choose one over the other, rather they experience how education enables them to learn from and contribute to their communities (Moll & González, 2004). We are proposing that the arts engage students in exploration of ideas, making meaning of challenging concepts and weaving invisible cultural knowledge, and making it a visible part of our curriculum and pedagogy.

From preschool to high school, educators use critical democratic practices within their classrooms to create spaces for students to imagine themselves in multiple roles as users of language. In assessing language use, Murray and Weltsek (Chapter 9), emphasize how prekindergarten-aged students use their home language to show their understanding of a political situation and the dramatic power to influence the story.

In Conclusion: an Invitation

In this introduction we have described the context, setting the stage and making the case for much needed *activism* to engage resources within our multilingual educational settings and communities. The chapters included in this volume accentuate the power of artful teachers and researchers as agents of multiliteracies. You will discover innovative ways to invite students, and all that they represent, to fully engage with their own learning. We hope that you will find inspiration in the democratic spaces presented here where everyone is able to speak and be heard in the process of understanding how what is taught is connected to their communities and everyday lives. Read on!

References

Ajayi, L. (2015). Critical multimodal literacy: How Nigerian female students critique texts and reconstruct unequal social structures. *Journal of Literacy Research, 42*(2), 216–244.

Bartolomé, L. (2006). The struggle for language rights: Naming and interrogating the colonial legacy of "English Only". *Human Architecture, 4*, 25–32.

Berriz, B. (2002). Connecting the classroom and the community: Making the bridge with arts and oral history. In Z. F. Beykont (Ed.), *The power of culture: Teaching across language difference*. Cambridge, MA: Harvard Education Publishing Group.

Berriz, B. (2005). *The emergent cultural identity of Puerto Rican and Dominican third-grade students and its relation to academic performance* (Doctoral thesis), Harvard Graduate School of Education.

Berriz, B. (2006). Unz got your tongue: What have we lost with the English-only mandates. *Radical Teacher,* (75), 10–21.

Bialystok, E., Craik, F.I., & Freedman, M. (2007). Bilingualism as a protection against the onset symptoms of dementia. *Neuropsychologia, 45*(2), 459–464.

Bialystok, Ellen (2011). Coordination of executive functions in monolingual and bilingual children. *Journal of Experimental Child Psychology,* 110 (3): 461–468.

Bourdieu, P. (1986). The forms of capital. In J. G. Richardson (Ed.), *Handbook of theory and research for the sociology of education* (pp. 241–258). New York, NY: Greenwood Press.

Bowen, D. H., Greene, J. P., & Kisida, B. (2014). Learning to think critically: A visual art experiment. *Educational Researcher, 43*(1), 37–44.

Boston Public Schools. (2003). *Class of 2003: In-depth analyses-MCAS performance: Update with December 2002 re-test*. Boston Public Schools Office of Research, Assessment and Evaluation. Boston, MA.

Brice-Heath, S., & Roach, E. (1999). Imaginative actuality: Learning in the arts during the non school hours. In E. Fiske (Ed.), *Champions of change: The impact of the arts on learning* (pp. 19–34). Washington, DC: President's Committee on the Arts and the Humanities, Arts Education Partnership.

Caterall, J., Dumais, S., & Hampden-Thompson, G. (2012). *The arts and achievement in at-risk youth: Findings from four longitudinal studies.* Wahsington, D.C.: National Endowment for the Arts.

Chamot, A. U., & O'Malley, J. M. (1994). *The CALLA handbook: Implementing the cognitive academic language learning approach*. Reading, MA: Addison-Wesley Pub. Co.

Chappell, S. V., & Faltis, C. J. (2013). The arts and emergent bilingual youth: Building culturally responsive, critical and creative education in school and community contexts. Routledge.

Commission on Language Learning, American Academy of Arts & Sciences. (2017). *America's languages: Investing in language education for the 21st century*. Retrieved from www.amacad.org/multimedia/pdfs/publications/researchpapersmonographs/language/Commission-on-Language-Learning_Americas-Languages.pdf.

Cope, B., & Kalantzis, M. (2000). Introduction: Multiliteracies: The beginnings of an idea. In B. Cope & M. Kalantzis (Eds.), *Multiliteracies: Literacy learning and the design of social futures* (pp. 3–8). London, England: Routledge.

Cope, B., & Kalantzis, M. (2013). Towards a new learning: The scholar social knowledge workspace, in theory and practice. *E-learning and Digital Media, 10*(4), 332–356.

Crawford, J. (1995). Endangered native American languages: What is to be done and why? *The Bilingual Research Journal, 19* (1), 17–38.

Cummins, J. (2000). *Language, power and pedagogy: Bilingual children in the crossfire.* Clevedon, UK: Multilingual Matters.

Cummins, J. (2008). BICS and CALP: Empirical and theoretical status of the distinction. In B. Street & N. Hornberger (Eds.), *Encyclopedia of language and education* (2nd ed.). Vol. 2: Literacy, pp. 71–83. New York, NY: Springer.

Cummins, J., Baker, C., & Hornberger, N. H. (Eds.). (2001). *An introductory reader to the writings of Jim Cummins* (Vol. 29). Clevedon, UK: Multilingual Matters.

Donovan, L & Pascale, L. (2012). *Integrating the arts across the content areas.* Huntington Beach, CA: Shell Education.

Echevarría, J., Vogt, M. E., & Short, D. J. (2004). *Making content comprehensible for English language learners: The SIOP model.* New York, NY: Allyn Bacon.

Ellsworth, E. (1989). "Why doesn't it feel empowering? Working through repressive myths of critical pedagogy." Harvard Educational Review, 59(3), 297–324.

Ellsworth, E. (1997). *Teaching Positions: Difference, Pedagogy, and the Power of Address.* New York: Teachers College Press.

Escamilla, K., Hopewell, S., Butvilofsky, S., Sparrow, W., Soltero-Gonzalez, L., Ruiz-Figueroa, O., & Escamilla, M. (2014). *Biliteracy from the Start: Literacy squared in action.* Philadelphia, PA: Caslon, Inc.

Fan, S. P., Liberman, Z., Keysar, B., & Kinzler, K. D. (2015). The exposure advantage: Early exposure to a multilingual environment promotes effective communication. *Psychological Science, 26*(7), 1090–1097.

Feinberg, R. C. (2002). *Bilingual education: A reference handbook.* Santa Barbara: ABC Clio.

Flood, J., Heath, S. B., & Lapp, D. (2015). Handbook of Research on Teaching Literacy Through the Communicative and Visual Arts, Volume II: A Project of the International Reading Association. New York, NY: Routledge.

Franks, A. (2008). Palmers' kiss: Shakespeare, school drama and semiotics. In C. Jewitt & G. R. Kress (Eds.), *Multimodal literacy* (pp. 155–172). New York, NY: Peter Lang Publishing.

Freire, P. (1970/2007). *Pedagogy of the oppressed.* (M. Ramos, Trans.). New York, NY: Herder & Herder.

Freire, P., & Macedo, D. (1987). *Reading the word and the world.* Westport, CT: Bergin & Garvey.

García, O. (2009). Emergent bilinguals and TESOL: What's in a name?. *TESOL Quarterly, 43*(2), 322–326.

García, O., & Kleifgen, J. A. (2010). *Educating emergent bilinguals: Policies programs, and practices for English language learners.* New York, NY: Teachers College Press.

Gee, J. P. (2004). *Situated language and learning: A critique of traditional schooling.* New York, NY: Psychology Press.

Giroux, H. A. (2011). Paulo Freire and the courage to be political. *Our Schools/Our Selves, 20*(2), 153–163. González, N., Moll, L. C., & Amanti, C. (Eds.). (2006). *Funds of knowledge: Theorizing practices in households, communities, and classrooms.* New York, NY: Routledge.

Greene, M. (1995). *Releasing the imagination: Essays on education, the arts and social change.* San Francisco, CA: Jossey-Bass.

Halliday, M. A. K. (1978). *Language as social semiotic.* London: Arnold.

Hanley, M. S., & Noblit, G. W. (2009). *Cultural responsiveness, racial identity and academic success: A review of literature.* Pittsburg, PA: Heinz Endowments.

Hetland, L. (2013). *Studio thinking 2: The real benefits of visual arts education.* New York, NY: Teachers College Press.

Hodge, R., & Kress, G. (1988). *Social semiotics.* New York, NY: Polity Press.

hooks, b. (1994). *Teaching to Transgress: Education as the Practice of Freedom.* New York: Routledge.

hooks, b. (2010). *Teaching Critical Thinking: Practical Wisdom.* New York: Routledge.

Immigration Policy Institute Fact Sheet. (2015, June). *States and districts with the highest number and share of English language learners.* Retrieved from www.migrationpolicy.org/research/states-and-districts-highest-number-and-share-english-language-learners.

Jewitt, C. (2008). Multimodality and literacy in school classrooms. *Review of Research in Education, 32*(1), 241–267.

Jewitt, C., & Kress, G. R. (2008). *Multimodal literacy.* New York, NY: Peter Lang Publishing.

Kalantzis, M., & Cope, B. (2012). *Literacies.* Cambridge: Cambridge University Press.

Kennedy Arts Center: Arts Edge—National Arts Education Network: Reading through the Arts. (2014, July). *Reading through the arts: How theater and visual arts can engage students in reading.* Retrieved from http://artsedge.kennedy-center.org/educators/how-to/supporting-individual-needs/reading-through-the-arts.aspx.

Kioko, A. (2015). *Why schools should teach young learners in home language.* Retrieved from www.britishcouncil.org/voices-magazine/why-schools-should-teach-young-learners-home-language.

Krashen, S. (1981). Second language acquisition. *Second Language Learning,* 19–39.

Kress, G. (2000). Multimodality. In *Multiliteracies: Literacy learning and the design of social futures.* (pp. 182–202). London: Routledge.

Kress, G. (2003). *Literacy in the new media age.* New York, NY: Psychology Press.

Kress, G. R., & Jewitt, C. (2008). Introduction. In C. Jewitt & G. R. Kress (Eds.), *Multimodal literacy* (pp. 1–18). New York, NY: Peter Lang Publishing.

Kress, G. R., & Van Leeuwen, T. (1996). *Reading images: The grammar of visual design.* P New York, NY: Psychology Press.

Lam, W. S. E. (2006). Re-envisioning language, literacy, and the immigrant subject in new mediascapes. *Pedagogies, 1*(3), 171–195.

Lankshear, C., & Knobel, M. (2003). *New literacies: Changing knowledge and classroom learning.* New York, NY: Open University Press.

Latta, M. M., & Chan, E. (2010). Teaching the arts to engage English Language Learners. New York, NY: Routledge.

Luke, A., & Carrington, V. (2002). Globalisation, literacy curriculum practice. In R. Fisher, M. Lewis, & G. Brooks (Eds.), *Raising standards in literacy* (pp. 231–250). London: Routledge.

Moll, L., & N. Gonzalez (2004). Engaging life: A funds-of-knowledge approach to multicultural education. In J. Banks & C. A. McGee Banks (Eds.), *Handbook of research on multicultural education, Second Edition.* San Francisco, CA: John Wiley & Sons.

Morales, J., Calvo, A., & Bialystok, E. (2013). Working memory development in monolingual and bilingual children. *Journal of Experimental Child Psychology, 114*(2), 187–202.

Moseley, C. (2010). *Atlas of the world's languages in danger* (3rd ed.). The United Nations Educational, Scientific and Cultural Organization. Paris, France.

Motha, S. (2014). *Race, empire, and English language teaching: Creating responsible and ethical anti-racist practice.* New York, NY: Teachers College Press.

Musu-Gillette, L., Robinson, J., McFarland, J., KewalRamani, A., Zhang, A., & Wilkinson-Flicker, S. (2016). Status and Trends in the Education of Racial and Ethnic Groups. (NCES 2016–007). *U.S. Department of Education, National Center for Education Statistics.* Washington, DC. Retrieved October 2, 2017 from http://nces.ed.gov/pubsearch.

New London Group. (1996). A pedagogy of multiliteracies: Designing social futures. *Harvard Educational Review 66*(1), 60–92.

New London Group. (2000). *Multiliteracies: Literacy learning and the design of social futures.* London, England: Routledge.

Nieto, S. (2000). Bringing bilingual education out of the basement. In Z. F. Beykont (Ed.), *Lifting every voice: Pedagogy and politics of bilingualism* (pp. 187–207). Cambridge: Harvard Education Publishing Group.

Nieto, S., & Bode, P. (2012). *Affirming diversity: The sociopolitical context of multicultural education* (6th Ed.). Boston, MA: Pearson.

Rowsell, J. (2013). *Working with multimodality: Rethinking literacy in a digital age.* New York, NY: Routledge.

Schroeter, S., & Wager, A. C. (2016). Blurring boundaries: Using drama to examine 17th Century witch-hunts. *Journal of Adolescent and Adult Literacy, 60*(4), 405–413.

Sefton-Green, J. (2006). Youth, technology, and media cultures. *Review of Research in Education, 30,* 279–306.

Street, B. (2003). What's "new" in new literacy studies? Critical approaches to literacy in theory and practice. *Current Issues in Comparative Education, 5*(2), 77–91.

Style, E. (1996, Fall). Curriculum as window and mirror. *Social Science Record.* Retrieved May 2, 2016, from www.nationalseedproject.org/about-us/timeline/26-latest-articles/41-curriculum-as-window-and-mirror.

Suárez-Orozco, C. (2004). Formulating identity in a globalized world. *Globalization: Culture and Education in the New Millennium, 173–202.*

United States Department of Education, National Center for Education Statistics. (2015). The Condition of Education 2015 (NCES 2015–144), English Language Learners.

Utah State Office of Education. (2013). *Critical languages: Dual language immersion education appropriations report.* Retrieved from http://le.utah.gov/interim/2016/pdf/00000674.pdf.

Valdés, G., & Figueroa, R. (1994). *Bilingualism and testing: A special case of bias.* Norwood, NJ: Ablex Publishing Corporation.

Valenzuela, A. (2016). *Growing critically conscious teachers: A social justice curriculum for educators of Latina/o youth.* New York, NY: Teachers College Press.

Valenzuela, C. (2017). Sonic borderland literacies: A re/mix of culturally relevant education. In A. Wager, V. Poey, & B. Berriz (Eds.), *Art as voice: Creating access for emergent bilingual learners.* Journal of Pedagogy, Pluralism, and Practice, Special Issue 2017.

Vaznis, J. (2011). US finds statewide problems in schools: Says English learners not adequately served. *Boston Globe,* Retrieved from September 17, 2011. www.bostonglobe.com/metro/2011/09/17/finds-statewide-problems-schools.

Vygotsky, L. S. (1962). *Thought and language.* Cambridge, MA: MIT Press.

Vygotsky, L. S. (1978). *Mind in society: The development of higher psychological processes.* Cambridge, MA: Harvard University Press.

Vygotsky, L. S. (1987). Thinking and speech. In R. W. Rieber & A. S. Carton (Eds.), *The collected works of L.S. Vygotsky, Volume 1: Problems of general psychology* (pp. 39–285). New York, NY: Plenum Press. (Original work published 1934).

Wager, A., Belliveau, G., Beck, J., & Lea, G. (2009). Exploring drama as an additional language through research-based theatre. *Scenario: Journal for Drama and Theatre in Foreign and Second Language Education 3*(2), 50–64.

Wager, A., Poey, V., & Berriz, B. (Eds.). (2017). Art as voice: Creating access for emergent bilingual families and communities [Special issue]. Journal of Pedagogy, Pluralism, and Practice, 9(1).

Wright, W. E. (2015). *Foundations for teaching English language learners: Research, theory, policy, and practice* (2nd ed.). Philadelphia, PA: Caslon.

Walk the Talk

Breathing Life into Theories with Families, Schools, and Communities

WALK THE TALK—CANTASTORIA

In September 2015, artists of AgitArte and Papel Machete collaborated with El Puente and self-taught quilter Sylvia Hernandez (Brooklyn Quilt Girl) to develop and present a Cantastoria (picture story-telling) using a quilt that traces the history and development of the Prison Industrial Complex (PIC) from slavery to mass incarceration and the killing of black and Latinx men and women by police in the United States (Figure I.1). The bilingual piece includes an adaptation of the

FIGURE I.1 Industrial Prison Complex

Industrial Prison Complex

FIGURE I.2 ErikMcGregorPhotography

Photo by Erik McGregor

song "Lamento De Concepción" by Afroboricua composer Tite Curet Alonso and was first performed with El Puente's For the Movement Youth Theater Collective in the community of Los Sures (Southside of Williamsburg, Brooklyn), a predominantly Latinx and Spanish-speaking community (Figure I.2). Many creative and intentional choices such as Conga drums, spoken word, call and response, and storytelling using imagery were made in developing the piece to allow the communities most impacted by police violence and the PIC to locate themselves within the performance. The Cantastoria toured with the book, When We Fight, We Win! to over 20 cities in the US and Puerto Rico.

2

HERITAGE LANGUAGES AS A VALUABLE ASSET FOR MULTILINGUAL CHILDREN IN US SCHOOLS AND BEYOND

We Can't Afford to Lose Them!

Shabaash M. Kemeh

Introduction

The US is a microcosm of diverse cultures of the world. The presence of huge immigrant populations in this nation from many countries has indirectly contributed to the increase in diverse students in US schools today. This phenomenon has also brought up challenges for improving the academic performance of emergent bilinguals which has surged to 56% in the public school system (Gandara & Hopkins, 2010). The adoption of different multilingual education programs, although controversial in the eyes of some politicians and citizenry, appears to be the best solution (Agudelo, 2008; Hornberger, 2007). Studies have shown that multilingual education has several benefits for students, society, and the nation. It boosts linguistic and cognitive skills, academic knowledge, self- confidence, self-esteem, creativity, motivation, collaboration, and identity of emergent bilinguals (Benson, 2013; Lopez, 2007). More importantly, it gives students the heritage language and cultural competency skills they need to interact with family, relatives, and community members of their country of origin. It has the promise to promote equity and social justice in schools, communities, and the nation. Also, attaining bilingual and bicultural literacy are marketable assets for our current and future society (Agudelo, 2008; Cummins, 2000; EFA Global Monitoring Report, 2005; Mohanty, 2007).

Today there are obstacles to multilingualism for second-generation children due to immigrant families preferring English as the primary language of instruction. For example, Castaneda (2017) reported from research findings that many immigrant families from Latin America want their children to be taught in English and not Spanish. This same mentality is held by some elites, poor, and working-class immigrant families from Africa, Asia, Europe, and South America.

They equate western languages, such as English, to prestige, affluence, and power in society (Darder, in press). This trend has shown that many US-born children of immigrants, the second generation, speaks only English at home (Portes & Zhou, 2005). As a result, within the US, community-based heritage languages are gradually disappearing within immigrant homes (Heritage Language Task Force Report, 2009). Considering the numerous merits enshrined in multilingual education and the need to halt the demise of heritage language, there is a sense of urgency for policy makers, families, and educators to be proactive in placing it at the center of US public education.

As an educator and a parent of second-generation children, my wife and I have worked together for more than a decade to raise our two US-born daughters in their heritage language Ewe. In this chapter I chronicle our success story: how the arts increased proficiency of both heritage language and English, as well as highlighting the sociocultural benefits. I draw awareness to strategies and resources from our own repertoire and other successful school case studies and re-kindle hope for all stakeholders in multilingual education, especially for teachers to become more involved in efforts to preserve the heritage language. Finally, I share some useful resources that teachers can use to supplement multilingual education. All this, I hope, will promote the general good of emergent bilingual students, parents, and the nation.

Current literature in the field shows that there are alternative terms for heritage language: community language, community-based heritage language, home language, and mother tongue (Keleher, 2010; Lui, Musica, Koscak, Vinogradova, & Lopez, 2011; Said-Mohand, 2011). I will use the terms heritage language and home language interchangeably because they connect more profoundly with my narrative around ancestral language, identity, culture, and bilingualism.

My Roots and Cultural Philosophy

I was born and bred in a modest African home in a small town in Ghana in the Volta Region. I was shaped by the traditions of my home, kinship, ethnicity, and the larger societal values. My home language, Ewe, was the first gift given to me by my parents. It has since become an indelible identity mark. My parents, grandparents, relatives, and the entire community were instrumental in teaching me social skills, storytelling, music, dance, traditional games, values, and beliefs. They also taught me family and community history from the unwritten curriculum of their heritage. My elementary school, college and university education added further dimensions to my acculturation both in traditional and western values. For instance, during the course of my formal education, I was oriented to Christian religious beliefs which are intrinsic to western values. Therefore, I had to attend church regularly, follow some prescribed table etiquette, clothing styles, and food habits. I also had the opportunity to study African arts and traditions including literature, religion, marriage, traditional rule, child-rearing, language, and festivals at different stages in the core curriculum. Occasionally, I participated in traditional drumming, singing, dancing, and festival events which were organized by the school authorities at local and district levels. These experiences had played a major role in my ability to take a critical stance in discerning, analyzing, and utilizing what is ideal in both cultures to navigate life. My spouse has a similar mindset because she was also brought up and equipped with western and African values. I arrived in the US in the 1990s to pursue post-graduate studies. She joined me a few years later for the same reason.

Our first daughter was born during the intensive debate of bilingual education programs in US schools. Prior to her birth, I used to spend a lot of time mulling over which language to use in raising our child. My intuition kept flashing, "Remember your roots!" When our daughter was born, we gave her a Ghanaian name Akpene. This literarily means *Thanks to God*. Three years later her sister Akofa was also born. Her name means *Contentment* in the Ewe language. The key question for us then became: How are we going to achieve our ambitious home language agenda for our daughters as they develop proficiency in English? The narrative that follows unpacks our process.

A No English Policy at Home – This might seem draconian to an outsider, but that was our resolve. From day one, we demonstrated our commitment to speak only our heritage language to our daughters at home. We also informed family and friends who speak this language in the US, Canada, and our home country, about our policy. We requested them to adhere to it whenever they called. Unfortunately, their Ghanaian grandparents were not alive when they were born. Therefore, we were honored to have their adopted American English-speaking grandparents, Grandpa Fred and Grandma Prilly, be part and parcel of our family. They supported us in raising the children in both cultures because they also believed that it was the right thing to do.

Grandma Prilly is my colleague and mentor at the same university. Her husband Fred had lived in Ghana in the 1960s with his parents and sister. His father was the supervisor of Peace Corps geologists then. This unique Ghanaian nexus and my workplace relationship with Prilly made me a member of this loving family long before my wife arrived in the US.

The role of traditional games and arts. Our goal in this endeavor was to raise these children to speak their home language fluently. We identified and performed childhood games, songs, and dances from our culture. Every evening, especially on weekends, we reserved time for doing these creative activities. There was no formal schedule or curriculum to follow. When they were babies we used to sing lullabies for them. Later we taught them how to sing songs, and told them African stories. They learned how to do some of our traditional dances like Gahu, and Bobobo. We had a collection of CDs and DVDs of both traditional and high-life music featuring Ghanaian musicians and dancers. Highlife is a genre of music that originated in Ghana but is popular in many West African countries. It is a blend of traditional music with western instrumentation.

The best DVD resource we used for the dances and songs was *Dance-Drumming Ceremonies of Ghana* (Younge & Badu-Younge, 2011). The following are some examples of our activity sessions:

Ananse stories. I told them an Ananse story followed by discussing characters and morals in the story. These kinds of engagements allowed us to share information with the girls about our traditional family structures, values, good behavior, family history, and the current events in Ghana. The stories also stirred up their fantasies about Ghana and spawned their ability to speak their home language.

Gahu traditional dance. This is a social dance of Ewe speakers in the south-eastern part of the Volta Region. First, I discussed the history and purpose of the dances with them. Next, we watched the video together followed by learning the dances. These were special moments for us to share our stories with them about how we used to do those dances at school when we were growing up. The girls really enjoyed hearing such personal stories and asked critical questions to get to the bottom of a story that surprised them. For example, how did mom become a lead Gahu dancer in her school? How could you sing and dance at the same time?

Books in heritage language. Besides teaching Akpene and Akofa to be orally literate in our home language, we felt it was vital for them to read it as well. We used books like *Srom Gba* (Sedco, 1997), *Xlem Kpo* (Sedco, 1997), and *Yiyi Nuti Gli Adewo* (Nyaku, 1997). I guided them to read the books followed by discussions, spelling drills, and simple sentence constructions.

These activities fostered their mastery of the home language.

Moving from Home to the School Environment

Akpene, our first daughter, began preschool at the age of three in a nearby Catholic school. The diversity of the student population in the school at the time was negligible. On the first day of school, I made a request to meet with her preschool teacher. I candidly informed her that we do not speak English at home with our daughter. As a result, she would not be able to speak or understand instructions in English like her classmates whose primary language is English. The teacher was warmly receptive. She gave me an overview of the curriculum activities she had planned for the class and the role she expected parents to play.

During Akpene's preschool year, we were active in her school life on many fronts and honored invitations for parent-teacher conferences. These events enabled us to receive firsthand information about the academic progress, social and emotional growth of our daughter, including her challenges. For example, the teacher's concern in the first semester was our daughter's inability to socialize with her playmates. She gave us suggestions regarding what we could do with her at home, and what she would also do to support her. She encouraged us to let her play more of our traditional games with children of family friends and community. On her part, she planned to supplement our socialization efforts for Akpene through more group sing-along songs, games, finger play, and nursery rhyme activities in her class. This teacher was actively supporting our daughter becoming bilingual and multilingual through strategies recommended by researchers (Espinosa, 2008; Halgunseth, 2010; Tabor, 2008). For example, the teacher demonstrated sincere acknowledgement of Akpene's language and socialization dilemma. She did her best to create a congenial learning environment that was safe for her. She also facilitated many fun activities that allowed lively free movement, self-expression, listening, talking, and group interactions among the preschoolers. She even read favorite children's books to Akpene and her buddies. These enhanced Akpene's social skills as well as her communication skills in English.

The preschool year ended on an optimistic note for Akpene. We had no major complaints about her learning abilities. Her social behavior and engagement in learning were gradually improving vis-à-vis her ability to communicate in English. The teacher maintained her open-line of communication with us formally and informally as we also continued our dedication to support classroom and school activities. By the time Akpene had reached grade 2, her academic progress as well as her English fluency was being acknowledged by the teachers. Our younger daughter, Akofa, had the privilege to be exposed to some aspects of classroom and school culture prior to her formal acceptance as a preschooler in the same school. She used to accompany us to take her sister to and from school. She also attended many classroom and school events with us. There was an occasion when Akofa joined me to do a "show and tell" about Ghanaian culture in her sister's kindergarten class at the invitation of the teacher. She won the hearts of the students and teachers for her wonderful performance of some Ghanaian games and songs that I had taught the class. Akofa loved school just like her sister. She had already acquired a degree of communication in English before she started formal schooling. By the time she graduated from pre-4, she was able to speak English and read picturebooks above her reading level.

With a solid foundation now, the girls moved to a public school where there was an encouraging number of children who were African Americans, Haitians, Asians, and Latinos. This multicultural school climate enabled our daughters to have higher levels of exposure to people from different cultures, socioeconomic backgrounds, and religion. Both continued to shine in many classroom learning and school events. They received compliments from teachers for their competencies in English—reading, speaking, listening, and writing. When the girls were in grades 1 and 4, district mandates required them to transfer schools yet again.

It did not take long for the girls to bounce back to their usual love for studies, service, and camaraderie at their new school. These are the common denominators of school life for them in spite of the fact that they have their own unique personalities. Teachers at the new school contributed further to consolidating their identity and dignity by publicly valuing their culture and heritage language in a variety of ways. Most significantly, the seeds were sewn for this from the start, in their preschool education where teachers supported their culture and the home language. They encouraged this in informal ways. For instance, as mentioned earlier I was honored to be invited by Akpene's kindergarten teacher to do a "show and tell" about Ghanaian culture in her class. My assistant cultural ambassador for this presentation was Akofa. The students learned children's songs and games in our home language besides other cultural activities. I also taught the whole class some basic Ewe expressions such as "Efoa?" ("How are you?" in English). I modeled this heritage language activity through role-play with Akpene and her sister in front of the class before engaging the rest of the students. At the second school, I initiated an afterschool readers' theatre program that I had done on Ghana using an Ananse story. This was another indication of open endorsement of their culture and language. All theatre ensemble members, including my daughters, learned how to sing some Ghanaians songs that were integrated into the readers theatre performance. They also took delight in elucidating the process of preparing some native foods that were in the readers theatre script to their fellow participants and coached them to say the names of the different foods correctly through codeswitching. At the third school, teachers also demonstrated a similar positive attitude towards supporting the girls' culture and language. For example, the music teacher, who is white, learned several African songs including songs from Ghana. She continues to teach these songs to students in her music class. One particular song that thrilled Akofa was "Afokpa vuvu to la to ne ma fli." It is a song in Ewe about buying a pair of shoes from a cobbler. According to Akofa, she was filled with pride when the teacher asked her to explain the meaning of the song to others. She felt valued for the recognition given to her by the teacher. There were other instances in the social studies class where the girls were sometimes called upon to share their knowledge when the teacher happened to be teaching a lesson related to Ghana. At every phase of schooling, in all three schools, our endeavor to have our daughters maintain the home language has been supported. At the same time, our daughters' academic promise continued to crystalize. Nonetheless, there were a couple of supplemental things we had tapped to buttress their English language skills outside the classroom environment. These were interactions with their grandparents, school playground games, more exposure to the arts and books, church programs, and general family social activities.

The Role of Community

Consensus among several researchers in the field state that if a child is simultaneously exposed to heritage language and a second language consistently, he or she is likely to speak both fluently by age 6 and 7 (Espinosa, 2008; Halgunseth, 2010; Kuhl, 2004; Tabors, 2008). In our case we speak Ewe to the girls while their grandparents speak English to them. I recall vividly how their grandparents interacted with them through mundane conversations, all kinds of children's games, and songs during their infant and toddler years. They also gave them age and culturally appropriate toys, stuffed animals, and books. For example, *Martin's Big Words: The Life of Dr. Martin Luther King, Jr., Barack Obama: A Biography for Children,* and *Nelson Mandela's Favorite Folktales.* Reading books with them expanded their worldview on issues of fairness, social justice, poverty, politics, community service, dignity, and high self-esteem. These positive outcomes happened through every-day conversations and raising questions with them about the lives of these icons.

Their savvy grandparents did more beyond simply giving books and toys to them. They engaged them in fun, participatory activities whenever they came to visit. As the girls continued to develop their verbal communication skills, Grandma introduced them to hand puppets. She did several role-plays with them around everyday childhood experiences using the puppets. This was another phenomenal bilingual teaching strategy through the arts that benefited my daughters in learn-ing English as their second language. The grandparents also had humorous ways of sharing their respective rich autobiographical stories. They sometimes shared family stories, photos, and adventures that they had taken to different countries inclusive of Ghana and France. The girls often listened attentively during these conversations and asked questions in their emergent English out of curiosity to know more. The grandparents created space for the girls also to share stories about their school experiences, family in Ghana, favorite books, and vacations. Grandpa, the tech wizard, also engaged the girls' interest at an early age in many cool gadg-ets such as his latest smart phone, iPad, Kindle, and camera.

Around ages 4 and 7, their love for words and spelling became apparent and I bought the film *Akeelah and the Bee* (Atchison, 2006), recommended to me by a colleague. We watched it frequently followed by discussions in our home language around issues of determination, constructive attitude for learning, and spelling strategies. Honestly, there are advantages for immigrant parents when they have a social network of colleagues at the workplace or in the community.

Many elementary schools in the city often have school children assemble out-side before and after school. During this time, we, like most parents, just lingered while the kids played. We observed that Akpene, who used to be shy during the first semester in preschool, was gradually opening up. The physical activities and the playground chats enabled her to start developing more vocabulary in English for self-expression. Her younger sister's immersion in these games started earlier. Consequently, she made more rapid progress in English language acquisition than her sister. We also welcomed play dates which enabled our daughters to develop real friendships and to hone their English-speaking skills. For example, they have Haitian, Hindi, Spanish, Portuguese, and native English-speaking friends. Thus, English has become the common medium of communication for all of them.

Our children watched TV programs on the PBS channel such as *Reading Rain-bow, Mr. Roger's Neighborhood, Word World, Super Why, Sid the Science Kid, Sesame Street, and The Wiggles.* Their favorites on Nickelodeon channel were *Dora the Explorer* and *Go, Diego! Go.* We also had CDs with songs in English and other languages at home. These songs were played during family leisure time, when out shopping or visiting friends. We realized that watching these programs and listening to the songs on CDs enabled them to increase their English language skills. A couple of CDs which provided this impetus for them most were *Raffi, Playing for Change: Songs Around the World*, and *African Playground*.

In fall 2008 I approached our local Boys and Girls Club to create a readers theatre program. The first production was an adaptation of a Ghanaian story titled *Ananse and the Birds*. This and another readers theatre play were performed at the school that my daughters were attending. The former was shown to the general public during the school's annual Multicultural Festival featuring Africa as the theme for the year. Theatre provides many benefits to participants. These include self-confidence, understanding and appreciation of people from diverse cultures, critical thinking, cooperation, problems solving, and development of communication skills (McCaslin, 2006; Sharma, 2016). I attribute my daughters' passion for reading, public speaking, and writing to these experiences. Teachers and families who observed the theatre process and performances also acknowledged that students gained similar benefits in addition to enriched cultural knowledge about the people in Ghana.

Family time outside the home was another route we had taken to uphold our efforts to make our daughters multilingual. We were fond of going to popular places like The Children's Museum, the Museum of Science, movie theaters, and public parks with the girls and grandparents. These environments were ideal for experiential learning for them. For example, when they visited the "Do It Yourself" exhibit in the Museum of Science, they learned how to explore pressure from a bed of four thousand nails. First, they read the instructions before engaging in the activity. They also learned about flying in an airplane through simulation at "Arthur & Friends" exhibit. On other occasions, we would go to amusement parks with some Ghanaian family friends and their children. In Boston, Worcester, Framingham, and Lowell areas, African communities often have social events such as weddings and birthday parties on weekends. The church which our family attends is predominantly African. The congregation is comprised of Nigerians, Ghanaians, Togolese, and Kenyans. There are Sunday school programs for the study of scriptures, reading, singing, dancing, and other recreational activities. English is the "lingua franca," so to speak, for this community. However, there are a few Ewe speakers in this congregation from Ghana and Togo. This enables us to widen our circle of speaking our native language with other families. It has also become an annual tradition for us to go on a family vacation to Canada to visit their aunt and cousins who communicate with them in our home language almost daily via phone. So Ewe is still the medium of communication in the household during vacation. The myriad of interactions the girls have with different people, including extended family members, in all these places have been a plus for expanding their communication skills in both Ewe and English.

Lessons Learned from the Multilingual Adventure

According to Cummin's theory of Common Underlying Proficiency (CUP), there is interdependence between first and second language learning. When a child is learning one language, he or she is capable of acquiring skills and metalinguistic knowledge that can be functional in another language. This theory favors learning one's heritage language as well as a second language (Cummins, 2000). Further research indicates that second language education has benefits for literacy, social, and cognitive development that are vital for academic learning (Espinosa, 2008; Halgunseth, 2010; Roseberry-Mckibbin & Brice, 2005). By comparing and contrasting what Cummins, Halgunseth, and fellow researchers have postulated, I realized that we succeeded in achieving our goals. First, our daughters can speak our heritage language fluently. They have also acquired the cultural pride and identity which we had wanted to instill in them.

In summer 2015 we took them to Ghana for the first time to visit their relatives. They described the experience in one word, "Awesome!" They truly felt a sense of belonging. They were able to fit in well with their numerous cousins as they played games and conversed with them in our home language. Our families affectionately embraced the girls as their true progeny because they could speak the home language fluently. Second, the academic performances of both girls at school have been rewarding, as Akpene has been a member of the National Junior Honors Society. She has also been endorsed to take honors courses in ninth grade at the local high school. Akofa has an interest in writing. Current national affairs motivated her to write a letter to President Obama when she was in grade 4. She asked the President to explain to her the Obamacare Health Program and the benefits for children. Teacher feedback during parent- teacher conferences often shows that she is talented in subjects like Music, Language Arts, and Math.

Moving Forward for Action

Our story is real. It provides solid backing to claims that multilingualism promotes high academic performance. The onus, therefore, falls on teachers of language minority children in our public schools to support families in their efforts to maintain heritage language at home while exploring creative approaches that can enhance multilingual education in schools. Lucas, Henze, and Donato (2004) indicate that teachers' ability to value students' language and cultures highly is one of the keys to success within the best bilingual schools in the country. They also recommend that teachers should encourage students to develop their primary language skills and to use extracurricular activities that motivate emergent bilinguals to become more interested in both their home language and second language acquisition.

These findings resonate with me in many ways. The preschool teacher laid the foundation for my daughters' formal education by including our language and culture. She also understood that the developmental process of language learning takes place both at home and in relationship with peers (Lantolf & Thorne, 2007;Vygotsky, 1978. Our own active involvement in her class and general school affairs strengthened the bond we had with her and all the teachers. By respecting the students' language and culture, our partnership with her paved the way for creating a safe and supportive learning environment for the girls.This also affected their academic progress in the years that followed.When teachers create this ideal environment for students and permit parents to visit the classroom to share their culture and heritage language, bilingual learning becomes more effective (Copple & Bredekamp, 2009; Halgunseth, 2010).

Teachers' roles for creating extracurricular opportunities for students especially through artistic engagements provide motivation for learning.They also help students develop critical thinking, communication, collaboration, problem solving, literacy skills, and cultural literacy (Maley & Duff, 2005; Wright, 2003). Since interactions or communicative competence are essential for language acquisition, the arts are a great asset for multilingual teachers.This narrative has demonstrated various ways that the arts were used to enhance bilingual learning by our daughters. Teachers can examine and adapt some of them for bilingual instruction in their classrooms.

Conclusion

There are several factors which contribute to the demise or lack of interest in heritage languages. Halgunseth (2010) pinpoints some of those factors when she recalls:

> In the 1970s, my early childhood provider advised my Mexican American mother to stop speaking Spanish with me at home.They were concerned because, as a 2 year old, I was not verbal as my peers.Worried she was causing me harm, my mother immediately stopped speaking to me in Spanish.
>
> *(p. 1)*

For almost five decades, Halgunseth's experience is still with us. Many minority language children in our schools continue to see their heritage language, which is knowledge and power, disappear. Once that is gone, their identity—that special ethereal connection to family and ethnicity—is also lost forever. This is the basis for deciding to speak with the teacher of my daughter on the first day she went to preschool. It worked. That was self-advocacy. It is important for teachers to encourage parents to utilize this asset, too. I hope this chapter appeals to multilingual education teachers to re-dedicate themselves to the use of the arts and culture to galvanize students' commitment to home and second language learning in schools. Our heritage language is a pearl that we cannot afford to lose. I agree with Zentella (1998) who says, "When you raise bilingual children, you're not only improving their lives, you're furthering the hopes and dreams of many parents for the future of their children" p. 10. This poignant message is for all language minority children, parents, and teachers in this nation. Re-embracing the home language and bilingualism must live on for the good of all!

> *Author's Note: The names used for people in this narrative were fictional to protect their anonymity. I also wish to point out that our personal narrative presented in this chapter was not documented in any journal by me for research purposes. It was entirely an authentic, organic recall process when I decided to share the story with the public in this domain. My daughters were involved as co-creators of the text by way of critique and validation. Through frequent sessions of informal conversation in our home language, they helped me to identify specific activities, artifacts, resources, chronological contexts, experiences, and outcomes which fostered their multilingual acquisition.*

Resources for Teachers

Atchison, D. (Writer/Director). (2006). *Akeelah and the bee* [DVD]. Los Angeles, CA: Lion Gate Films.
The director depicts in this widescreen movie an 11-year-old girl's love for words which triggers her passion for spelling bee. The movie highlights what it takes to be a winner.
Burke, A. F., & O'Sullivan, J. C. (2002). *Stage by Stage: A Handbook for Using Drama in the Second Language Classroom*. Portsmouth, NH: Heinemann
These practical drama activities are used to enhance language learning for the novice.
Cavoukian, R. (1996). *The Singable Song Collections* [CD]. Nashville, TN: Rounder Records.
The songs cover themes including children, family, home, people, community, work, services, social skills, nature, and the animal world.
Johnson, M., & Buono, E. (2009). *Playing for Change: Songs Around the World* [CD]. Beverly Hills, CA: Hear Music.
Artists from around the world are featured singing about themes on war, peace, social justice, love, and humanity. Musicians include Bono, Bob Marley, and many more from South Africa, US, Ghana, Congo, India, Israel, and Spain. The sound tracks that are in English aid kids to increase their vocabulary and speaking skills.
Maley, A., & Duff, A. (2005). *Drama Techniques* (3rd ed.). Cambridge: Cambridge University Press.
This is a wonderful resource book of communication for language teachers of practical activities that can be adapted for any grade level.
Mandela, N. (2007). *Nelson Mandela's Favorite African Folktales*. New York, NY: W. W. Norton & Company.
Mandela collects several Zulu folktales and trickster animal stories from different African countries that teach about cultural values and morals to young children.
Nyaku, F. K. (1997). *Yiyi nuti gli adewo*. Accra, Ghana: Sedco Publishing.
Ananse (spider) stories for reading or telling to children in the Ewe language. Young children learn about the culture and hone their listening, reading, and speaking skills.
Putumayo Kids (2003). *African Playground* [CD]. New York, NY: Putumayo World Music.
This is a collection of fun, upbeat songs for children featuring artists from several African countries like Nigeria, Senegal, South Africa, Uganda, and Madagascar. Most of

the songs are sung in the heritage languages of the artists and some of the tracks are also in English. It is a great resource for engaging kids in conversation about diversity and the value of language in African cultures.

Rappaport, D. (2001). *Martin's big words: The Life of Dr. Martin Luther King, Jr.* New York, NY: NY: Hyperion Books for Children.

This beautifully illustrated book by Bryan Collier reveals Martin's upbringing in a segregated society, his aspirations, education and civil rights activities for social justice.

Sedco (1997). *Srom gba* (Rev. ed.). Accra, Ghana: Sedco Publishing.

This primer or a beginner's book in the Ewe language contains the alphabet. The text and illustrations are about everyday things in the child's life at home and community.

Sedco (1997). *Xlem kpo: Agbale gbato* (Rev ed.). Accra, Ghana: Sedco Publishing.

Activities, illustrations and text focus on the child, home, family, community, and work. Its scope for speaking, reading, and writing in the Ewe language is higher than the primer.

Scheneider, J. J., Crumpler, T. P., & Rogers, T. (2006). *Process drama and multiple literacies: Addressing social, cultural, and ethical issues.* Portsmouth, NH: Heinemann

Drama strategies that can foster thinking, listening, speaking, and writing are included.

Younge, P. (Writer), & Younge, P., & Badu-Younge, Z. (Producers/Directors). (2011). *Dance- drumming ceremonies of Ghana* [DVD]. Athens, OH: Azaguno.

This collection of 10 DVDs depicts traditional dances, songs, and ceremonies from different ethnic groups including the Ewes in Ghana in authentic settings.

Wright, S. (2003). *The Arts, Young Children and Learning.* Boston, MA: Pearson Education.

Theories and the benefits of all the arts are followed by very user friendly practical activities for all grade levels.

Website/Online Resources

A bilingual site for educators and families of emergent bilinguals by Colorin Colorado. www.colorincolorado.org/guides-toolkits

Bilingual Teaching Tools: www.bilingualteachingtools.com/

Bilingual and ESL education website for teachers: www.kaplanco.com/product/ 46599/latin-playground-cd?c=22

ESL and Bilingual programs: Mother Goose time preschool curriculum: www.kaplanco.com/product/46599/latin-playground-cd?c=22**Emergent   bilinguals toolkit**: www.ncela.us/

Putumayo Latin playground CDs for children featuring various musicians www.amazon.com/Latin-Playground-Putumayo-Presents/dp/B000066RKP

Schools with bilingual education models: www.aps.edu/language-and-cultural-equity/schools-and-alternative-language-service-als- *models/schools-with-bilingual-education-models*

Spanish/Bilingual/ELL/Materials: www.kaplanco.com/shop/spanish-bilingual-ell- *materials*

References

Atchison, D. (Writer/Director). (2006). Akeelah & the bee [DVD]. Los Angeles, CA: Lion Gate Films.

Agudelo, J. (2008). *Losing heritage language.* Retrieved from http://eslprog.kean.edu:8080/ default.asp?PageID=282.

Benson, J. (October 2013). Bilingual education holds cognitive and health benefits. *Huff-post Latino Voices*. Retrieved from www.huffingtonpost.com/2013/10/05/bilingual-education_n_4049170.html.

Castaneda, L. (2017). Spanish fluency in the US is decreasing with each generation. Retrieved from https://www.usatoday.com/story/life/2017/09/10/spanish-fluency-u-s-decreases-each-generation/636773001/

Copple, C., & Bredekamp, S. (2009). *Developmentally appropriate practice in early childhood programs: Serving children from birth through age 8* (3rd ed.). Washington, DC: NAEYC.

Cummins, J. (2000). Language, power, and pedagogy: Bilingual children in the crossfire. Clevendon, UK: Multilingual Matters

Darder, A. (In press). Cultural hegemony, language, and the politics of forgetting: Inter-rogating restrictive language policies. In P. Orelus (Ed.), *Affirming language diversity in schools and society: Beyond linguistic apartheid*.

EFA Global Monitoring Report Team (2005). *Education for all*. Retrieved from http://unesdoc.unesco.org/images/0013/001373/137333e.pdf.

Espinosa, L. (2008, January). *Challenging common myths about young English language learners*. Foundation for Child Development Policy Brief, Advancing PK-3. Retrieved from http://fcd-us.org/sites/default/files/MythsOfTeachingELLsEspinosa.pdf.

Gandara, P., & Hopkins, M. (2010). The changing linguistic landscape of the United States. In P. Gandara, & M. Hopkins (Eds.), *Forbidden language: English learners and restrictive language policies* (pp. 7–33). New York, NY: Teachers College Press.

Halgunseth, L. (2010). *How children learn a second language*. Retrieved from www.education.com/reference/article/how-children-learn-second-language/.

Heritage Language Task Force Report. (2009). *Report of the task force on the preserva-tion of heritage skills in Maryland*. Retrieved from http://msa.maryland.gov/msa/mdmanual/26excom/defunct/html/23language.html.

Hornberger, N. H. (2007). Nichols to NCLB: Local and global perspective on US language education policy. In O. Garcia, T. Skutnabb-Kangas, & M. E. Torres-Guzman (Eds.), *Imagining multilingual schools: Languages in education and globalization* (pp. 223–237). Buf-falo, NY: Multilingual Matters.

Keleher, A. (2010). *What is a heritage language?* Retrieved from www.cal.org/heritage/pdfs/briefs/What -is-a-Heritage-Language.pdf.

Kuhl, P. K. (2004). Early language acquisition: Cracking the speech code. *Nature Reviews Neuroscience, 5*(11), 831–843.

Lantolf, J. P., & Thorne, S. L. (2007). Sociocultural theory and second language learning. In B. VanPattorn, & J. Williams (Eds.), *Theories in second language acquisition: An introduction* (pp. 201–224). Mahwah, NJ: Lawrence Erlbaum Associates.

Lopez, L. E. (2007). Cultural diversity, multilingualism, and indigenous education in Latin America. In O. Garcia, T. Skutnabb-Kangas, & M. E. Torres- Guzman (Eds.), *Imagining multilingual schools: Languages in education and globalization* (pp. 2238–261). Buffalo, NY: Multilingual Matters.

Lucas, T., Henze, R., & Donato, R. (2004). The best multilingual schools. In O. S. Ana (Ed.), *Tongue tied: The lives of multilingual children in public education* (pp. 201–221). New York, NY: Rowman & Littlefield Publishers.

Lui, N., Musica, A., Koscak, S., Vinogradova, P., & Lopez, J. (2011). *Challenges and needs of community based heritage language programs and how they are addressed*. Retrieved from www.american.edu/cas/education/bilingual/upload/challenges-and-needs-of-community-based-heritage-language-programs.pdf.

Maley, A., & Duff, A. (2005). *Drama techniques* (3rd ed.). Cambridge, MA: Cambridge University Press.

McCaslin, N. (2006). *Creative drama in the classroom and beyond* (8th ed.). New York, NY: Allyn & Bacon.

Nyaku, F.K. (1997). Yiyi nuti gli adewo. Accra, Ghana: Sedco, Publishing.

Mohanty, A. K. (2007). Multilingualism of the unequals and predicaments of education in India: Mother tongue or other tongue. In O. Garcia, T. Skutnabb-Kangas & M. E. Torres-Guzman (Eds.), *Imagining multilingual schools: Languages in education and globalization* (pp. 262–283). Buffalo, NY: Multilingual Matters.

Portes, A., & Zhou M. (2005). The new second generation and its variants. In M. Suarez-Orozco, C. Suarez-Orozco, & D. Q. Hilliard (Eds.), *The new immigration: An interdisciplinary reader*. London: Routledge.

Roseberry-McKibbin, C., & Brice, A. (2005). What's "normal," what's not: Acquiring English as a second language. *American Speech-Language-Hearing Association*. Retrieved from www.readingrockets.org/article/whats-normal-whats-not-acquiring-english-second-language.

Sedco (1997). Srom gba (Rev. ed.). Accra, Ghana: Sedco Publishing.

Sedco (1997). Xlem kpo: Agbale gbato (Rev. ed.). Accra, Ghana: Sedco Publishing

Said-Mohand, A. (2011). *The teaching of Spanish as a heritage language: Overview of what we need to know as educators*. Retrieved from www.ugr.es/~portalin/articulos/PL_numero16/AIXA%20SAID-MOHAND.pdf.

Tabors, P. (2008). *One child: Two languages: A guide for early childhood educators of children learning English as a second language* (2nd ed). Baltimore, MD: Paul H. Brookes.

Wright, S. (2003). *The arts, young children, and learning*. Boston, MA: Pearson Education.

Younge, P. (Writer), & Younge, P., Badu-Younge, Z. (Producers/Directors. (2011). Dance drumming ceremonies, of Ghana [DVD]. Athens, OH: Azaguno

Vygotsky, L. S. (1978). Mind in society: The development of higher psychological processes (Rev ed.). Cambridge, MA: Harvard University Press.

Zentella, A. C. (1998). *How to raise a bilingual child*. Retrieved from www.potowski.org/sites/potowski.org/files/media/Zentella_manual_0.pdf.

3

PREPARING IDEOLOGICALLY CLEAR BILINGUAL TEACHERS TO RECOGNIZE LINGUISTIC GENIUSES[1]

Cristina Alfaro and Lilia I. Bartolomé

In Prince Royce's lyrical rendering of *Stand by Me* (Royce, 2010; King, Stoller, & Leiber, 1961), which was originally brought to fame by singer, Ben E. King in 1961, the singer linguistically transforms the English language song to highlight his creative and dexterous multilingual abilities. Prince Royce is a popular contemporary bachata[2] singer from New York who broke into the Latin pop mainstream in 2010. How Royce masterfully mixes a rhythm-and-blues classic with bachata sounds while combining Spanish and English to honor his Dominican and New York roots is artistically and eloquently displayed in his YouTube video (https://youtu.be/foyH-TEs9D0) (Top Stop Music, 2010). Born Geoffrey Royce Rojas, Prince Royce modernizes an old classic using codeswitching as the artistic heuristic. For example, as evident in his YouTube video, instead of singing the original English only lyrics, "No, I won't be afraid, oh, I won't be afraid," he alternatively sings, "Miedo no, no tendré, oh, I won't, no me asustare" (Royce, 2010; King et al., 1961).

Beyond the musical ingenuity, Royce accomplishes two important things: He uses codeswitching to affirm his own bilingual identity and to represent the linguistic reality of many bilinguals, thereby positioning codeswitching as an acceptable and artistic form of cultural expression and linguistic practice. He also legitimizes in music the linguistic aptitudes that are representative of the linguistic creativity that characterizes many multilingual Latina/o students in today's classrooms.

The previous example of the creative power of codeswitching signals the need for educators to recognize that lower-class multilingual Latina/o students bring numerous linguistic strengths to the classroom. We use the term *multilingual* to identify Latina/o students because it captures the reality that these students arrive in school speaking much more than two languages; they are adept at numerous standard and nonstandard varieties of English and Spanish, and they employ diverse, innovative, and creative language-mixing strategies (García, in press). In fact, language mixture is a central feature of Latina/o speech in the United States; in research on the subject, the terms *language mixing* and *codeswitching* are typically treated as synonymous. Codeswitching refers to the "mixing, by bilinguals (or multilinguals), of two or more languages in discourse, often with no change of interlocutor or topic. Such mixing may take place at any level of linguistic structure, but its occurrence within the confines of a single sentence, constituent, or even word, has attracted most linguists' attention" (Poplack, 2001).

Codeswitching constitutes one type of "translanguaging." Ofelia García (2009a, 2009b, 2013, 2014a, in press) employs the term *translanguaging* to refer to the creative ways bilinguals use two or more languages to make meaning and maximize their communicative potential. Bilinguals often move seamlessly between Spanish, English, and standard and nonstandard vernaculars of both languages. According to García (2009a), translanguaging is an umbrella term that encompasses codeswitching and other multilingual language practices. *Translanguaging* refers to the numerous creative ways that multilinguals manipulate language to make meaning and maximize their communicative potential (Williams, 1997). Multilinguals often move fluidly between Spanish and English and standard and nonstandard vernaculars. For example, a well-established body of research highlights how effectively these students translate and interpret for their families in various formal and official contexts (e.g., medical, educational, legal), which constitutes one type of translanguaging practice (García, 2009a, 2009b; García & Sylvan, 2011; Valdes, 2003).

Translanguaging thus is seen as "multiple discursive practices in which bilinguals engage in order to make sense of their bi/multilingual worlds" (García, 2009a, p. 45). Codeswitching represents another type of translanguaging. The theoretical orientation of translanguaging and the discipline of sociolinguistics both purport that a preference for certain language varieties over others' and denigration of certain practices such as codeswitching reflects social biases rather than linguistic realities (García, 2009b, 2013, 2014a; Kloss, 1977; Macedo, 2006; Peñalosa, 1981; Toribio, 2004; Wardhaugh, 1998; Williams, 1997). In fact, the metaphoric definition, "a language is a dialect with an army and a navy" (attributed to the late, renowned sociolinguist, Max Weinreich), and the fact that linguists find it difficult—if not impossible—to distinguish a language from a dialect using purely linguistic measures points to the highly political and ideological ways in which we view language variation. In other words, a standard language is also a dialect—it just happens to be the dialect of the dominant culture in a society (Kloss, 1977). Thus, any distinctions in terms of desirability or superiority of a standard language over a dialect are purely social, political, and ideological in nature.

Taken together, both bodies of work—the translanguaging research and the sociolinguistic literature on codeswitching—strongly suggest that multilingual Latina/o students can be considered linguistic geniuses. Informed by such bodies of work and that of numerous other scholars in the field (Bialystok, 1991, 2011;

Flores, 2005; García, 2009a; García & Sylvan, 2011; Kharkhurin & Wei, 2015; Sternberg, 1998; Valdés, 2003), we define *linguistic geniuses* as communicatively competent students who can discern their audience's speaking ability and use of language(s) and spontaneously employ their own linguistic and creative repertoires to receive, process, communicate, and deliver information. Thus, linguistic geniuses are capable of effectively communicating in one or more languages or a mixture of languages to complete a communicative task or to creatively deliver a message. Given the complexity of mental operations involved in codeswitching, multilingual students effectively and efficiently engage in a constant state of linguistic multitasking as they use their working memory to hold representations of two or more language systems long enough to complete communicative, academic, and creative tasks.

Hence, we consider multilingual Latina/o students linguistic geniuses who possess the cognitive and linguistic skills to deal with novel tasks as well as varied linguistic situational demands by resolving conflicts between their languages in a variety of communicative contexts. In the field of education, codeswitching and the use of nonstandard English and languages other than English among lower-class multilingual students, especially Latinas/os, have generally been misperceived as a deficiency that should be repaired (Flores & Rosa, 2015; García, 2014a; Peñalosa, 1980, 1981).

Thus, if educators can wean themselves from linguicist[3] views of Latina/o students and their nonstandard language practices and embrace a more objective and sociolinguistic understanding of Latina/o students' remarkable multilingual skills and knowledge, they can begin to pedagogically unleash these linguistic geniuses, helping them to build on their impressive communicative skills to better achieve in school and to critically appropriate standard academic varieties of English and Spanish.

In this chapter, we propose that bilingual educators develop the necessary ideological clarity[4] to unapologetically recognize the linguistic strengths and academic potential of lower-class multilingual Latina/o students in order to honor and build on their strengths. We recognize the need to prepare bilingual teachers in conventional technical instructional and classroom management skills and in standard Spanish and English language teaching strategies. However, we maintain that teachers should also examine the ideological dimensions of their work in order to interrogate false and misleading linguicist views of codeswitching and other nonstandard language practices in order to recognize the intrinsic worth of their multilingual students' existing linguistic and communicative knowledge and skills. It behooves prospective and practicing teachers who work with students from lower-class linguistic minoritized groups to learn how linguicist ideologies can manifest even in bilingual classroom contexts unless they make concerted intervention efforts to neutralize such ideologies and practices (Flores & Rosa, 2015). That is, no matter how effective a particular bilingual education model has proven to be or how promising a particular instructional method is, we believe that even these models and methods can be damaging to students if educators do not understand the power of potentially discriminatory dominant culture linguistic ideologies that may sabotage their best intentions (Bartolomé, 1994).

As we see it, bilingual teacher education programs and professional development must include the study of ideology and how it pertains to bilingual education, especially of lower-class multilingual Latina/o students. This necessarily includes acquisition of basic sociolinguistic knowledge of linguistic variation in general and of codeswitching practices in particular. We believe that bilingual educators who develop a sociolinguistic understanding of the various ways language intersects and interacts with multiple social forces are more likely to recognize and interrogate deficit language ideologies and practices and to recognize that their students are already impressive language users and communicators who arrive at school with tremendous potential to achieve and acquire academic language varieties.

Codeswitching as a Means for Untying Tongues

As bilingual educators, we like to believe that lower-class multilingual Latina/o students are largely sheltered from bias, mistreatment, and cross-cultural misunderstanding in bilingual classrooms where their native language is used for instructional purposes. However, despite the success of many bilingual and dual-language programs, the research suggests that social class and linguistic bias—especially around the issue of codeswitching—do show up in bilingual classrooms (Alfaro & Bartolomé, 2016; Cervantes-Soon, 2014; Hernández, 2015; Macedo & Bartolomé, 1999; Valdes, 1998). In fact, given bilingual educators' commitment to producing bilingual students who are fully academically proficient in the primary language, we often obligate our students to refrain from codeswitching in the classroom, in effect tongue-tying them (Delpit, 2008; Montaño, Ulanoff, Quintanar-Sarellana, & Aoki, 2005). The expectation is that primary language teachers must purposefully model standard English and Spanish using a strict separation model because students come to the classroom speaking mixed, "uneducated" nonstandard varieties that need to be corrected (García, 2014b; Flores & Rosa, 2015). Since we know that one's primary language is inextricably linked to identity then it becomes clear that when we reject students' primary languages, we end up rejecting the students themselves as well as the speech communities from which they come (Darder, 2012; Macedo, 2006; Norton, 2010).

Although nonstandard Spanish and English varieties take many forms and linguistic minoritized students come to school with different speaking styles or registers, in this chapter, we examine codeswitching—one type of language practice with a long history of being incorrectly denigrated. In fact, a rich body of literature on Spanish-English codeswitching dates back to the 1970s and recently scholars such as Antonio Martinez, Jeff McSwan, Peter Sayer, Deborah Palmer, and Guadalupe Valdés have taken it up again and reflect various theoretical schools of thought.

Codeswitching was first extensively researched in the 1970s and 1980s, particularly among Chicanos in the Southwest and Puerto Ricans in the Northeast (Amastae & Elías-Olivares, 1980; Gingras, 1971; Hernández-Chávez, Cohen, & Betramo, 1975; Peñalosa, 1980, 1981; Poplack, 1980; Timm, 1975). This earlier research yielded interesting results that the more recent studies have confirmed, one example being that the main motivation to codeswitch is not primarily the speaker's inability to come up with the right word in a particular language. Instead, codeswitching is a communicative skill that demands a high level of bilingualism and linguistic competence; it is rule-governed and requires command of the syntactic (i.e., grammar at the level of the sentence) systems of both languages.

Codeswitching does not indicate a confused mind or deficiencies in cognition. A person may switch for various reasons: (1) because of the situation (situational codeswitching), (2) because the topic has changed, (3) because a monolingual has joined the conversation, or (4) because a topic or issue is normally experienced in one of the two languages. Finally, and importantly, codeswitching can also be used for metaphorical purposes (metaphorical codeswitching). For example, the speaker may wish to communicate solidarity with the interlocutor or elicit a particular mood, such as nostalgia. In fact, codeswitching can be used to denote who is considered part of the in-group and who is considered an outsider (Wardhaugh & Fuller, 2015).

Thus, "[c]ode-switching serves to not only enhance communication in the teaching/learning process but can also help maintain and develop the languages of a bilingual" (Huerta-Macias & Quintero, 1992, p. 86). Additionally, it can serve purposes such as ease of expression, clarification, creating a sense of belonging, socializing, creating, emphasizing, and making a path for linguistic proficiency. Consequently and key to our discussion in this chapter, the literature suggests that students who are free to codeswitch as a valid means of expression are better positioned than constrained students are to discuss content matter and demonstrate their knowledge. They encounter fewer language barriers and are allowed to demonstrate greater speech fluidity (Pollard, 2002).

Also, despite the wealth of research confirming that high levels of bilingual or multilingual proficiency allow for codeswitching, even Latinas/os themselves and bilingual educators continue to hold negative beliefs that codeswitching signals incomplete bilingual proficiency, laziness in the thinking-speaking process, and "impure" language use (Fitts, 2006; McCollum, 1999; Palmer, 2008; Ramirez & Milk, 1986). These negative beliefs can, unfortunately, translate into discriminatory practices that devalue students who speak these low-status language varieties and employ codeswitching. As mentioned previously, the phenomenon of codeswitching denotes sophisticated language use. It occurs frequently because it is likely to take place anywhere two language groups come into contact (e.g., *Franglais* [French and English in Quebec], *Fragnol* [French and Spanish in Argentina], *Spanglish* [Spanish and English in the United States], and *Tex-Mex* [English and Mexican Spanish in Texas] Wardhaugh & Fuller, 2015).

It is also important for teachers to understand that, as far as linguists are concerned, nonstandard and standard languages are innately equal linguistically because no language is inherently inferior or superior (Haugen, 1966; Kloss, 1977; Wardhaugh, 1998; Wardhaugh & Fuller, 2015). All languages—standards and nonstandards—follow linguistic rules (syntax), have a sound system (phonology), use particular words (lexicon), and mark words in particular ways (morphology). Sociolinguists are also quick to say that when we refer to a language—English, for example—we are not speaking of a single homogeneous entity but a conglomeration of regional and social dialects and personal and group styles. It would be more accurate, for example, to speak of "Englishes," given the many different varieties of English that are spoken across the globe (Canagarajah, 2013; Delpit, 2008; Wardhaugh & Fuller, 2015).

Multilingual Latina/o students readily engage multiple linguistic codes and resources at their disposal to process, communicate, and deliver information. It is valuable to remember that bilinguals typically outperform monolinguals on cognitive flexibility tasks (Foy & Mann, 2014) resulting from their linguistic abilities and linguistic multitasking experience. For example, Bialystok (2011) examined the executive functions (working memory, inhibition, and shifting) of bilinguals and their monolingual counterparts. Not surprisingly, the bilinguals outperformed the monolingual children. Bialystok hypothesizes that positive results on cognitive competencies are in part attributed to the fact that multilingualism requires children to be in a constant state of linguistic multitasking, to use working memory, to hold representations of two language systems long enough to complete a task, to inhibit information from the competing language, and to shift attention between stimuli. In this respect, codeswitching is a representation of cognitive and linguistic competence whereby students can make profound connections to the content by creating deeper meanings through language mixing to enable cognitive development with superior precision and communication in their academic work. Bhatia and Ritchie (2008) add that:

> A bilingual's organization of the verbal repertoire in his/her mind is very different from that of monolinguals. When a monolingual decides to speak, his/her brain does not have to make complex decisions concerning language choice, as does the bilingual. Such a decision-making process for a monolingual is restricted at most to the choice of a limited number of varieties/styles (for instance, informal versus formal)
>
> *(p. 7).*

Furthermore, recent research on codeswitching suggests a positive correlation between habitual codeswitching and higher scores on tests of cognitive creativity. A recent study by Kharkhurin and Wei (2015) suggests that codeswitching practice has a positive impact on creativity; their study contributes to sociolinguistic research on "bilingual creativity"—"creative linguistic processes [that] are the result of competence in two or more languages" (p. 154). Their research on 157 multilingual university students reveals that students who self-identified as "habitual codeswitchers" scored higher than "nonhabitual codeswitchers" on the ATTA Assessment of Creativity, which tests for four divergent thinking traits: fluency (the production of quantities of ideas), originality (the ability to produce uncommon ideas), elaboration (the ability to embellish ideas with details), and flexibility (the ability to process information or objects in different ways given the same stimulus).

Kharkhurin and Wei's research strongly suggests that multilinguals who codeswitch frequently showed greater innovative capacity than their counterparts who do not habitually codeswitch. The authors conclude by calling for additional research investigating the relationship between codeswitching and creativity. Such research on the creative benefits of codeswitching (i.e., the advantages of allowing multilingual Latina/o students to employ their full multilingual and linguistic creative abilities) holds great promise for envisioning how to create psychologically healthy learning environments in which lower-class linguistic minoritized students are encouraged to demonstrate learning via their extraordinary communicative repertoires.

In the bilingual classroom, negative beliefs about and teacher reactions to codeswitching can potentially wound students, particularly in dual-language programs, where a key goal is to maintain and develop students' native languages while teaching them to appropriate Standard English and develop their biliteracy skills. Language-learning processes should allow for and build on students' codeswitching practices. Thus, we maintain that it is imperative to increase prospective and practicing bilingual teachers' sociolinguistic understanding so as to discover pedagogical strategies to honor and build on the repertoire of language skills such as codeswitching that lower-class, multilingual Latina/o students bring into the classroom.

In the following section, we explore possible classroom instructional approaches and strategies that tap and build on students' linguistic competence which includes codeswitching practices. First, we introduce the reader to a Cultural Wealth Model that highlights various types of cultural capital that lower-class, multilingual Latina/o students often possess and we pay particular attention to linguistic capital. Second, we highlight key research that examines Latina/o student linguistic capital in the form of codeswitching in one bilingual second grade and one sixth-grade English mainstream classroom. Third, we conclude the section with a brief discussion regarding classroom practice implications particularly around formal planned instruction and capitalizing on spontaneous "teachable moments."

A Cultural Wealth Model: Recognizing Linguistic Giftedness

Groundbreaking research that challenges worn-out deficit and linguicist views of multilingual Latina/o working-class students and embraces a "cultural wealth" view of these students offers us fresh hope that the cultural and linguistic capital along with other forms of nonmonetary capital our students bring to school will be acknowledged by their teachers (Alfaro & Bartolomé, 2016; Darder, 2012; Pérez Huber, 2009; Solórzano & Villalpando, 1998; Solórzano & Yosso, 2001; Yosso, 2005). Yosso (2005) identifies six forms of cultural wealth and given our focus in this chapter, we focus on linguistic capital.[5] *Linguistic capital* refers to intellectual and social skills attained through communication experiences in more than one language and/or style, such as translating and interpreting abilities, creative storytelling, and other oral culture skills. These skills require skillful language negotiation that draws on multiple linguistic profiles and successfully exerts the appropriate type of communication for the given context. Because the linguistic capital that students bring to the classroom are sources of knowledge, they can and do serve as springboards to new learning. Therefore, pedagogical practices that reflect a cultural wealth orientation should encompass the inclusion of students' linguistic capital, including codeswitching practices in the classroom.

Recent research studies using a cultural wealth model theoretical framework have begun identifying the characteristics of linguistic cultural wealth. In fact, a growing number of studies that examine Spanish/English codeswitching and the use of Spanglish to teach conventional academic skills strongly support this additive model (Martinez, 2010; Martinez, Orellana, Pacheco, & Carbone, 2008; Sayer, 2013, 2008). Many of these studies capture linguistic minoritized students' strengths and skills as translators and interpreters and have begun to examine how these skills and abilities link positively to their schoolwork (García, 2009a and b; Faulstich, Orellana, Dorner, & Pulido, 2003; Faulstich, Reynolds, Dorner, & Meza, 2003; Martinez et al., 2008).

For example, Martinez's (2010) research on sixth-grade Mexican American students' codeswitching included a component that asked students to focus on and explain their codeswitching practices, which resulted in their increased metalinguistic awareness. Martinez reports that Spanglish functions as a semiotic tool that enables multilingual Latino students to accomplish important state-required language standards, such as clarifying and/or reiterating utterances, quoting and reporting speech, joking and teasing, establishing solidarity and intimacy, shifting voices for different audiences, and communicating subtle nuances of meaning.

Martinez (2010) and the classroom teacher tapped into the students' growing metalinguistic awareness to help them transfer their codeswitching skills, such as shifting voices for different audiences and communicating subtle nuances in meaning, to their academic writing. Based on his findings, Martinez concludes that "leveraging the skills embedded in students' use of Spanglish could radically transform how students view the relationship between everyday and academic knowledge, and thereby have a transformative impact on their academic literacy learning" (p. 146).

Sayer (2013) reports comparable findings in his research in an English/Spanish transitional bilingual second-grade classroom where the teacher encouraged students to use all their linguistic resources during classroom instruction. The teacher, a Tex-Mex speaker herself, allowed students to codeswitch, use archaic forms of Spanish, and speak rural varieties of Mexican Spanish without castigating them. She celebrated their multilingual skills and allowed them to use their mixed-language vernacular to communicate and to demonstrate their learning in the classroom. Sayer recommends that teachers

> recognize a need to contest language ideologies that favor dominant languages [and] . . . develop translanguaging instruction that (1) teaches the standard language form through the vernacular; (2) uses the vernacular to mediate academic content; and (3) imparts lessons that instill ethnolinguistic consciousness and pride.
>
> *(p. 85)*

We similarly encourage bilingual educators to devise a pedagogy that encourages linguistic minoritized students to tap into and proudly display their linguistic wealth in the classroom and to build on it as a strategy for appropriating standard academic discourses in both target languages.

Bilingual teacher educators must take an informed sociolinguistic view of the linguistic resources that linguistic minoritized students bring to the classroom and consciously and critically take into account their "linguistic funds of knowledge" (Sayer, 2013). These connections between students' vernaculars and academic language, as Martinez (2010) writes, "constitute potentially transformative points of leverage for academic literacy, teaching, and learning" (p. 145). Moreover, as Flores and Rosa (2015) brilliantly argue, teachers require an alternative pedagogical approach that celebrates the dynamic linguistic practices of linguistic minoritized students while raising their awareness about issues of language and power. They write:

> This approach would also empower teachers to move beyond pedagogies geared toward responding to students' purported linguistic deficiencies or "gaps" and . . . provide these students with tools to challenge the range of inequalities with which they are faced. This is a powerful shift from teaching students to follow rules of appropriateness to working with them as they struggle to imagine and enact alternative, more inclusive realities.
>
> *(p. 168)*

Teachers can plan formal lessons on codeswitching much like the classroom teacher and the researcher did in the Martinez (2010) study. In addition, teachers can also be vigilant in order to get the most from these spontaneous codeswitching "teachable moments" and teachers need to be clear regarding their knowledge about sociolinguistics in general and the phenomenon of codeswitching in particular. We have found in our teacher preparation practice that allowing teachers to articulate clear and coherent language philosophies reflective of their learning around the normality of language variation and the appropriateness of codeswitching and other translanguaging practices enables them to maximize their students' linguistic giftedness in both naturally occurring contexts and during formal instruction. In naturally occurring settings teachers must commit to observing the flow of how students use their funds of knowledge and diverse linguistic repertoires in order to effectively work with the *instant-by-instant* language shifts that authentically happen when students are making sense of concepts covered in a lesson or unit of study. These on the spot moves—"the translanguaging *corriente*" as Garcia, Johnson, and Seltzer (2017) refer to it, constitute moments when students' spontaneous creativity have the space to develop and evolve.

In the case of formal instruction, teachers can explicitly create classroom spaces where students are encouraged to demonstrate their linguistic prowess. Teachers well-grounded in their sociolinguistics knowledge can strategically work to create learning contexts and specific lessons and activities that encourage multilingual linguistics to confidently display their communicative dexterity and talent. The following are a few possibilities for purposely creating linguistic wealth learning contexts:

- Create opportunities where the teacher and students discuss their linguistic resources to unveil the realities of when and why we codeswitch in our language use;
- Discuss the importance of using "standard language" for academic projects and for knowing and using the codes of power;
- Create intentional and strategic lessons where students are encouraged to use their diverse linguistic repertoires in artistic ways;
- Develop an understanding within your classroom setting that the multilingual students are each other's best linguistic resources;
- Develop a classroom environment that values content over form when the focus is on learning new concepts. That is, in these learning contexts, teacher and students focus on demonstrating knowledge regardless of language variety or form employed;
- Celebrate students' linguistic creativity and explicitly celebrate them as linguistic geniuses.

An example of one bilingual dual language teacher's strategic creation of lessons to encourage students to use their diverse linguistic and creative resources comes to mind. Mrs. Blanco teaches a sixth-grade English social studies and language arts class in a Freirean-influenced dual language school in Southern California approximately eight minutes from the United States-Mexico border. The majority of her students are Mexican American whose parents desire their children to become fluently bilingual and biliterate. When you walk into Mrs. Blanco's classroom you immediately sense the students' powerful confidence with respect to their academic ability and their diverse linguistic repertoires. Mrs. Blanco strategically creates specific lessons where students are encouraged to use their diverse linguistic and artistic resources to convey their understanding of social issues through creative writing (poetry) and collaborative group performances (music, art, and dance).

For example, in one class session that one of the authors, Alfaro, observed, students engaged in a social studies and language arts activity on patterns of migration. At the end of their unit of study, students in groups of four presented essays, skits, poetry, music with original lyrics, and dances to express their understanding and problems posing issues while engaging both English and Spanish languages in creative and powerful ways.

Following is an example of what one group orally presented from their written work. They followed up with a musical and dance performance.

> Migration, Immigration, Documented, Undocumented:
> —*¿Porqué estamos aquí?*
>
> "You know that people come to the United States, con el deseo de trabajar duro, to make a better life. I know, and we know, that there is a huge cost to this, frecuentemente tenemos que olvidarnos de nuestra cultura, idioma, y a veces hasta de nuestro orgullo de ser Mexicano." What does this all mean—¿porqué estamos aquí?
>
> *(why are we here?)*

During this oral presentation of written work one student played the claves (pair of musical wooden sticks) and another one strummed the guitar as the four students alternated articulating their stances and also eloquently rotated languages to add emphasis, feeling, and creativity to their message, similar to what many young artists do in the twenty-first century as our example of Prince Royce at the beginning of this chapter exemplifies. During the students' oral and musical presentations, in addition to their innovation and creativity, Mrs. Blanco assessed students' comprehension and critical thinking skills about the social studies topic—migration. In addition, she assessed language arts objectives—oral and written language, discourse demands, syntax demands, and lexical demands—thus meeting social studies and language arts state standards (Alfaro, Durán, Hunt, & Aragón, 2015). It was evident to Alfaro that Ms. Blanco places her students' historical and cultural backgrounds, languages, creativity, voices, perspectives, and their emerging linguistic and cultural formations at the center of her teaching. Mrs. Blanco's knowledge of the cultural and pedagogical value of codeswitching allowed her to create learning contexts where her multilingual students could confidently show off their skills and knowledge as linguistic geniuses.

Conclusion

Given the projected growth of the cultural and linguistic diversity of students in US public schools, it is critical that bilingual educators factor social class and cultural diversity into their view of language variation and better understand how "invisible" social class and language bias can undermine their best efforts with students from the economically poorest populations. Clearly, more research is needed to help teacher educators better prepare bilingual teachers to develop greater sociolinguistic awareness in order to recognize and nurture their students' linguistic capital, as well as developing counter-hegemonic practices via a cultural wealth orientation that views and treats Latina/o students as the linguistic geniuses that they are or have the potential to become. A fundamental challenge, in our opinion, is to teach dominant culture "school language" varieties in intellectually honest and bias-free ways (Alfaro & Bartolomé, 2016; Faltis & Valdés, 2016). Lower-class multilingual Latina/o students must learn to appropriate new language varieties in additive, enriching, creative, and self-empowering ways. Teaching standard academic discourses in both English and Spanish cannot be accomplished without first taking a detour through linguistic minoritized students' vernaculars.

In conclusion, we find it appropriate to close this chapter with a quote that describes one well-recognized linguistic genius: Juan Felipe Herrera, the former US Poet Laureate (2015–2017). His work illustrates the need for new ways of encouraging lower-class multilingual students to find their voice by capitalizing on their entire linguistic repertoires to powerfully communicate with their varied audiences. In his poetry, Herrera eloquently expresses the connection between the arts, culture, and languages: "Words have sounds, and sounds have emotional and artistic textures and ways of using them that are contingent on culture" (Herrera, Voice Your Language Conference, 2016). Herrera credits many of his critical educational moments to Mrs. Sampson, his most influential elementary school teacher, who inspired him by praising him and pointing out that, "You have a beautiful voice." Since he did not speak English at the time, a classmate translated for him: "Dice que tienes una voz bonita." Today, Mrs. Sampson's message can be seen to convey respect for language diversity, honoring students' linguistic and artistic talents and the cultural wealth they bring to the classroom.

We conclude with this insightful quote from Mrs. Sampson, Herrera's elementary school teacher in which she highlights the urgent need for classroom teachers to honor lower-class Latina/o multilingual students' linguistic abilities and skills:

> Teachers, encourage your students to find their voice! You have a wonderful opportunity to nurture your students' creative, cultural, and linguistic talents. I urge you to seek the talents within your classroom and always learn from your students. You may have the next Juan Felipe Herrera, U.S. Poet Laureate, in your classroom. Don't miss that opportunity. Rethink your pedagogy to ensure that all of your students' voices, language, and cultural backgrounds are valued, honored, and nurtured.
>
> *(Sampson, Voice Your Language Conference, 2016)*

Notes

1 In this chapter, the authors expand upon the 19th Annual *La Cosecha* Dual Language conference presentation, *The Hidden Class Structure* in Two-Way Bilingual Classrooms, given by Lilia I. Bartolomé on November 21, 2014.
2 *Bachata* refers to a popular guitar genre that originated in the Dominican Republic and contains African, Indigenous, and European music influences.

3 Phillipson (1992) says linguicism refers "exclusively to ideologies and structures where language is the means for effecting or maintaining an unequal allocation of power and resources" (p. 55). He states that linguicism is "in operation if a teacher stigmatizes the local dialect spoken by the children and this has consequences of a structural kind, that is, there is an unequal division of power and resources as a result" (p. 55).

4 Bartolomé (2002) explains that ideological clarity refers to the ongoing and never-ending process that requires individuals to compare and contrast their explanations of the existing social order with those propagated by the dominant society. The expectation is that, by consciously juxtaposing ideologies, teachers will understand if, when, and how their belief systems uncritically reflect those of the dominant society and support unfair and inequitable conditions (p. 168).

5 Yosso, (2005) outlines the six forms of the Cultural Wealth Model: (1) aspirational capital, (2) linguistic capital, (3) familial capital, (4) social capital, (5) navigational capital, and (6) resistance capital.

References

Alfaro, C., & Bartolomé, L. I. (2016). La claridad ideológica del maestro bilingüe: Un reto en la educación bilingüe de calidad. In M. Guerrero, L. Soltero-González, C. Guerrero, & K. Escamilla (Eds). Abreindo brecha: Antología crítica de la educación bilingüe de doble inmersión (pp. 95–117). DLeNM: Fuentes Press.

Alfaro, C., Durán, R., Hunt, A., & Aragón, M. J. (2015). Steps toward unifying dual language programs, common core state standards, and critical pedagogy. *Association of Mexican American Educators Open Issue. 8*(2), 17–30.

Amastae, J., & Elías-Olivares, L. (Eds.) (1980). *Spanish in the US: Sociolinguistic aspects.* Cambridge: Cambridge University Press.

Bartolomé, L. I. (1994). Beyond the methods fetish: Toward a humanizing pedagogy. *Harvard Educational Review, 64*(2), 173–194.

Bartolomé, L. I. (2002). Creating an equal playing field: Teachers as advocates, cultural border crossers, and cultural brokers. In Z. Beykont (Ed.), *The power of culture: Teaching across language differences* (pp. 167–191). Cambridge, MA: Harvard Education Publishing Group.

Bartolomé, L. I. (2014). The hidden class structure in two-way bilingual classrooms. In *Keynote Address Presented to the 19th Annual La Cosecha Dual Language Conference*, Santa Fe, New Mexico, November 20–21..

Bhatia, T. K., & Ritchie, W. C., (2008). The bilingual mind and linguistic creativity. *Journal of Creative Communication 3*(1), 5–21. Bialystok, E. (1991). Metalinguistic dimensions of bilingual language proficiency. In E. Bialystok (Ed.), *Language processing in bilingual children* (pp. 113–140). Cambridge: Cambridge University Press.

Bialystok, E. (2011). Coordination of executive functions in monolingual and bilingual children. *Journal of Experimental Child Psychology, 110,* 461–468.

Canagarajah, S. (2013). *Translingual practice: Global Englishes and cosmopolitan relations.* London: Routledge.

Cervantes-Soon, C. G. (2014). A critical look at dual language immersion in the new Latin@ diaspora. *Bilingual Research Journal: The Journal of the National Association for Bilingual Education, 37*(1), 64–82.

Darder, A. (2012). *Culture and power in the classroom: Educational foundations for the schooling of bicultural students.* New York, NY: Paradigm Publishers.

Delpit, L. (2008). *The skin that we speak: Thoughts on language and culture in the classroom.* New York, NY: New York Press.

Faltis, C., & Valdés G. (2016). Preparing teachers for advocacy and for teaching in linguistically diverse classrooms: A vade mecum for teacher educators. In D. Gitomer, & C. Bell (Eds.), *5th Edition of the handbook on teaching* (pp. 549–592). Washington, D.C.: AERA.

Faulstich Orellana, M., Dorner, L., & Pulido, L. (2003). Accessing assets: Immigrant youths' work as family translators and "para-phrasers." *Social Problems, 50*(4), 505–524.

Faulstich Orellana, M., Reynolds, J., Dorner, L., & Meza, M. (2003). In other words: Translating or "para-phrasing" as a family literacy practice in immigrant households. *Reading Research Quarterly, 38*(1), 12–34.

Fitts, S. (2006). Reconstructing the status quo: Linguistic interaction in a dual-language school. *Bilingual Research Journal, 29*(2), 337–365.

Flores, B. M. (2005). The intellectual presence of the deficit view of Spanish-speaking children in the educational literature during the 20th century. In P. Pedraza & M. Rivera (Eds.), *Latino education: An agenda for community action research* (pp. 75–98). Mahwah, NJ: Lawrence Erlbaum Associates.

Flores, N., & Rosa, J. (2015). Undoing appropriateness: Raciolinguistic ideologies and language diversity in education. *Harvard Educational Review, 85*(2), 149–171.

Foy, J. G., & Mann, V. A. (2014). Bilingual children show advantages in nonverbal auditory executive function task. *International Journal of Bilingualism, 18*(6), 717–729.

García, O. (2009a). *Bilingual education in the 21st century: A global perspective.* Oxford: Wiley-Blackwell.

García, O. (2009b). Education, multilingualism and translanguaging in the 21st century. In A. K. Mohanty, M. Panda, R. Phillipson and T. Skutnabb-Kangas (Eds.), *Multilingual education for social justice: Globalising the local.* New Delhi: Orient BlackSwan.

García, O. (2013). From Diglossia to Transglossia: Bilingual and multilingual classrooms in the 21st century. In C. Abello-Contesse, P. M. Chandler, M. D. López-Jiménez, & R. Chacón- Beltran (Eds.), *Bilingual and multilingual education in the 21st century: Building on experience* (pp. 155–175). Bristol, UK: Multilingual Matters.

García, O. (2014a). U.S. Spanish and education: Global and local intersections. *Review of Research in Education: Language Policy, Politics, and Diversity in Education, 38*(1), 58–80.

García, O. (2014b). Countering the dual: Transglossia, dynamic bilingualism and translanguaging in education. In R. Rubdy & L. Alsagoff (Eds.), *The global-local interface, language choice and hybridity* (pp. 100–118). Bristol, UK: Multilingual Matters.

García, O. (in press). Decolonizing foreign, second, heritage, and first languages: Implications for education. In Donaldo Macedo (Ed.), *Decolonizing foreign language education: The misteaching of English and other colonial languages.* New York, NY: Routledge.

Garcia, O., Johnson, S., & Seltzer, K. (2017). *The translanguaging classroom: Leveraging student bilingualism for learning.* Philadelphia, PA: Caslon Inc.

García, O., & Sylvan, C. E. (2011). Pedagogies and practices in multilingual classrooms: Singularities in pluralities. *Modern Language Journal, 95*(3), 385–400.

Gingras, R. C. (1971). *A critical review of standard procedures for studying Spanish-English bilinguals.* Retrieved from ERIC database (ED 110206)

Haugen, E. (1966). *Language conflict and language planning.* Cambridge, MA: Harvard University Publishing.

Hernández, A. M. (2015). Language status in dual immersion: The dynamics between English and Spanish in peer interaction. *Journal of Immersion and Content-Based Language Education 3*(1), 102–126.

Hernández-Chávez, E., Cohen, A. D., & Betramo, A. F. (Eds.) (1975). *El lenguaje de los chicanos: Regional and social characteristics of language used by Mexican Americans.* Arlington, VA: Center for Applied Linguistics.

Herrera, J. F. (2016, February). *Voice your language conference.* San Diego, CA.

Huerta-Macias, A., & Quintero, E. (1992). Code-switching, bilingualism, and biliteracy: A case study. *Bilingual Research Journal, 16*(3–4), 69–90.

Kharkhurin, A. L., & Wei, L. (2015). The role of code-switching in bilingual creativity. *International Journal of Bilingual Education and Bilingualism, 18*(2), 153–169.

King, B. E., Stoller, M., & Leiber, J. (1961). Stand by me [Recorded by P. Royce, 2010]. On *Stand by Me* [MP3 file]. Delray Beach, FL: Top Stop Studios.

Kloss, H. (1977). *The American bilingual tradition.* Rowley, MA: Newbury House.

Macedo, D. (2006). *Literacies of power* (2nd edition). Boulder, CO: Westview Press.

Macedo, D., & Bartolomé, L. I. (1999). *Dancing with bigotry: Beyond the politics of tolerance.* New York, NY: Palgrave.

Martinez, R. A. (2010). Spanglish as literacy tool: Toward an understanding of the potential role of Spanish-English code-switching in the development of academic literacy. *Research in the Teaching of English, 45*(2), 124–149.

Martinez, R. A., Orellana, F., Pacheco, M., & Carbone, P. (2008). Found in translation: Connecting translating experiences to academic writing. *Language Arts, 85*(6), 421–431.

McCollum, P. (1999). Learning to value English: Cultural capital in a two-way bilingual program. *Bilingual Research Journal, 23*(2 & 3), 113–134.

Montaño, T., Ulanoff, S. H., Quintanar-Sarellana, R., & Aoki, L. (2005). The debilingualization of California's prospective bilingual teachers. *Social Justice, 32*(3), 103–121.

Norton, B. (2010). Language and identity. In N. H. Hornberger & S. L. McKay (Eds.), *Sociolinguistics and language education* (pp. 349–397). Tonawanda, NY: Multilingual Matters.

Palmer, D. (2008). Building and destroying students' "academic identities": The power of discourse in a two-way immersion classroom. *Qualitative Studies in Education, 21*(6), 647–667.

Peñalosa, F. (1980). *Chicano sociolinguistics: A brief introduction.* Rowley, MA: Newbury House Publishers.

Peñalosa, F. (1981). *Introduction to the sociology of language.* Rowley, MA: Newbury House Publishers. Pérez Huber, L. (2009). Challenging racist nativist framing: Acknowledging the community cultural wealth of undocumented Chicana college students to reframe the immigration debate. *Harvard Educational Review, 79*(4), 704–729.

Phillipson, R. (1992). Linguistic imperialism and linguicism. In *Linguistic imperialism* (pp. 50–57). Oxford: Oxford University Press.

Pollard, S. (2002). The benefit of code switching within a bilingual education program. *Department of Hispanic Studies,* 1–101.

Poplack, S. (1980). Sometimes I'll start a sentence in Spanish Y TERMINO EN ESPANOL: Toward a typology of codeswitching. *Linguistics* 18(7/8), 581–618.

Poplack, S. (2001). Code-switching (Linguistic). In N. Smelser, & P. Baltes (Eds.), *International encyclopedia of the social and behavioral sciences* (pp. 2062–2065). Amsterdam, Netherlands: Elsevier Science Ltd.

Ramirez, A. G., & Milk, R. D. (1986). Notions of grammaticality among teachers of bilingual pupils. *TESOL Quarterly, 30*(3), 495–513.

Royce, P. (2010). *Stand by me.* On *Prince Royce* [digital file]. Florida: Top Stop Music.

Sampson. (2016, February). *Voice your language conference.* San Diego, CA.

Sayer, P. (2008). Demystifying language mixing: Spanglish in school. *Journal of Latinos and Education, 7*(2), 94–112.

Sayer, P. (2013). Translanguaging, TexMex, and bilingual pedagogy: Emergent bilinguals learning through the vernacular. *TESOL Quarterly, 47*(1), 63–88.

Solórzano, D., & Villalpando, O. (1998). Critical race theory, marginality and the experience of students of color in higher education. In T. Mitchell & C. A. Torres (Eds.), *Sociology of education: Emerging perspectives* (pp. 181–210). Albany, NY: State University of New York Press.

Solórzano, D., & Yosso, T. J. (2001). Maintaining social justice hopes within academic realities: A Freirean approach to critical race/LatCrit pedagogy. *Denver University Law Review, 78*(4), 595–621.

Sternberg, R. J. (1998). Abilities are forms of developing expertise. *Educational Researcher, 27*(3), 11–20.

[Top Stop Music]. (2010, January 25). *Prince Royce—Stand By Me (Music Video)* [Video File]. Retrieved from https://youtu.be/foyH-TEs9D0.

Toribio, A. M. (2004). Spanish/English speech practices: Bringing chaos to order. *International Journal of Bilingual Education and Bilingualism, 7*(2 & 3), 133–154.

Timm, L. A. (1975). Spanish-English code switching: El Porqué and how-not-to. *Romance Philology, 28*, 473–482.

Valdes, G. (1998). Dual-language immersion programs: A cautionary note concerning the education of language-minority students. *Harvard Educational Review, 67*(3), 391–429.

Valdes, G. (2003). *Expanding definitions of giftedness: The case of young interpreters from immigrant communities.* Mahwah, NJ: Routledge.

Wardhaugh, R. (1998). *An introduction to sociolinguistics* (3rd ed.). Malden, MA: Blackwell.

Wardhaugh, R., & Fuller, M. (2015). *An introduction to sociolinguistics* (7th ed.). Malden, MA: Wiley Blackwell.

Williams, C. (1997). *Bilingual teaching in further education: Taking stock.* Addysgu, Bangor, Wales: Welsh Language Board.

Yosso, T. J. (2005). Whose culture has capital? A critical race theory discussion of community cultural wealth. *Race, Ethnicity, and Education, 8*(1), 69–91.

4

INCLUSIVE TEACHING FOR BILINGUAL AND MULTILINGUAL LEARNERS

Collage as Ornithology

Mariana Souto-Manning and Jessica Martell

In US classrooms and schools, children who are learning the dominant American English language and developing bilingually or multilingually are often expected to engage in "grade-level" academic work and display "academic language skills" (Hill & Miller, 2013). They are compared with their English-dominant peers, under the presumption that proficiency in English serves as an indicator of cognitive development and academic aptitude. They are closely watched, scaled, and rated. They are sorted almost immediately upon enrolling in school, not even having the chance to develop linguistically in a new realm. This is a problem as both "grade level" and "academic language skills" are ethnocentric constructions, which effectively serve to disempower children, disregarding their ways with words (Heath, 1983) and favoring a dominant way of being and knowing.

As a social construction, the concept of grade level serves to continue normalizing education in ethnocentric and biased ways. It upholds racist ideas (Kendi, 2016) as it continues to fail many children, positioning them as being "at risk" for failure. This is especially the case for children who are adding dominant American English to their linguistic repertoires as they are developing bilingually or multilingually; they are asked to perform in one language only, not being able to engage their rich linguistic experiences and practices in school. They are evaluated and valuated according to the dominant language of power (what Delpit [1988] labeled the language "of those who have power"), i.e., dominant American English (Paris, 2009). Furthermore, they are expected to display such dominant language knowledge in written format; after all, written language, a second-order symbolic system (Meier, 2004) or second-order symbolism (Vygotsky, 1978, p. 111), tends to be overprivileged in schools (Genishi & Dyson, 2009; Souto-Manning & Martell, 2016).

This favoring of dominant American English and of written language in US schooling often results in the marginalization of multilingual children. As a result, multilingual children often feel incapable as learners and their peers may come to see and paradigmatically construct them as deficient (Souto-Manning, 2013; Yoon, 2008). Seeking to trouble such deficit perspectives, which continue to position capable children as needing to be remedied, we propose collage as a way of making curriculum inclusive (Souto-Manning & Martell, 2016), as a way of re-mediating learning tasks and environments (Gutiérrez, Morales, & Martinez, 2009).

Collage as Translinguistic Symbolic Representation

In this chapter, we share a situated representation of how collage can serve as a way to represent what children know visually, signifying their knowledges, experiences, and perspectives. To do so, we critically employ Universal Design for Learning (National Center for Universal Design for Learning, 2012) as a framework for re-mediating learning, explaining how collage can be (re)positioned specifically in science, providing multiple means of engagement, representation, action, and expression in ornithology (the study of birds). We also explain how collage allows (emergent) bilingual and multilingual children (García & Kleifgen, 2010) to engage in learning across languages and to negotiate successful student and scientist identities. Collages afford a more inclusive and translinguistically relevant way of making meaning.

We position collage as a worthy and legitimate medium for academic communication across language codes, blurring the arts and science divide (Cahnmann, Souto-Manning, Wooten, & Dice, 2009) in the early childhood classroom. Collage is a powerful communicative tool because it serves as a primary symbol of representation, as Vygotsky (1978) explained. That is, a feature of written language

> is that it is second-order symbolism, which gradually becomes direct symbolism. This means that written language consists of a system of signs that designate the sounds and words of spoken language, which, in turn, are signs for real entities and relations. Gradually this intermediate link, spoken language, disappears, and written language is converted into a system of signs that directly symbolize the entities and relations between them. It seems clear that mastery of such a complex sign system cannot be accomplished in a purely mechanical and external manner (p. 106).

From this perspective, children who are adding language(s) to their communicative repertoires are negotiating two second-order processes: (1) from their home and community language practices to the language practices (over)valued in schools (in this case, dominant American English) and (2) from oral to written language. Alternatively, they may be negotiating a third-order process in writing (from their rich and varied language repertoires to oral dominant American English to written dominant American English).

Through the critical re-mediation of the Universal Design for Learning (UDL) framework, collages can expand the ways in which young children engage, represent, act, and express their knowledge of science and identities as scientists (National Center for Universal Design for Learning, 2012). In such a manner, collages allow children adding dominant American English to their linguistic repertoires to competently engage in academic learning—moving beyond the need to write in dominant American English (second-order symbolism) toward pictorially representing their knowledge (first-order symbolism). Daniel Meier (2004) explained, "the prehistory of written language follows this course: Undifferentiated marks grow into scribbles and other symbolizing marks, then into figures and pictures, and finally into signs" (p. 14). While signs (such as letters) are language-specific (for example, /j/ sounds different in English and Spanish), figures and pictures are likely to provide translinguistic ways to make meaning (Souto-Manning & Martell, 2016). Thus, they are likely to provide a more accurate measure of learning, clearer windows into learning processes. Collage is thus a translinguistic symbolic system of representation, affording the possibility of communicating meaning across languages.

Theoretical Perspectives

In 1983, Clifford Geertz declared the need for the boundaries between the sciences and the humanities to be blurred in research. Here, we employ a critical theoretical perspective (Freire, 1970)—troubling what is and seeking to transform our pedagogical perspectives—to fully include the voices and perspectives of young children who are multilingual learners. To do so, we blur the boundaries between the academic subjects of science and art, re-mediating these fields and allowing for inclusive and culturally relevant learning to take place. We challenge the idea of learning as the mere transmission of knowledge (positioning ourselves against what Freire (1970) labeled the banking approach to education) and engage students in negotiating learning experientially (Dewey, 1938). We embrace the role of teachers as learners and invite our students to step into the role of teaching. It is from this perspective that we approach and re-mediate UDL in culturally relevant ways.

A re-mediation framework allows us to shift the blame from individual students, who are often and have historically been seen as being filled with deficits needing to be remediated. This framework allows us to move away from the "central strategy in addressing the academic needs of students who differ from the dominant norm" (Gutiérrez et al., 2009, p. 227), including those labeled as "English language learners." It rejects "[d]eficit notions about the cognitive potential of individuals from nondominant communities [that] have persisted in social science inquiry, particularly where literacy is concerned" (p. 212). Instead of seeing individual students (or groups of students) as problems, re-mediation calls for the reorganization of learning via a new mediation of students' multiple worlds, communities, knowledges, experiences, and identities, resulting in "meaningful learning in robust ecologies" (p. 236).

In employing re-mediation, we seek to unveil the power of reorganizing learning, social relationships, and artifacts being used. This is an imperative as "multiple cultures are present in every classroom, and that whenever culture-using creatures interact, they create between them a hybrid subculture, appropriate to the culture it mediates" (Cole, 1998, p. 300). Gutiérrez and colleagues proposed that "mediational artifacts" can serve to "exploit the existing hybridity, help to create particular social environments of development in which students begin to reimagine who they are and what they might be able to accomplish, academically and beyond" (p. 237). We thus employed collage as "mediational artifacts," pedagogically re-mediating culturally relevant teaching and more traditional (and restrictive) education concepts, such as academic literacy. Utilizing these perspectives, we shifted the focus from fixing students to rethinking teaching and learning.

Culturally Relevant Teaching

> Culturally relevant pedagogy rests on three criteria or propositions: (a) Students must experience academic success; (b) students must develop and/or maintain cultural competence; and (c) students must develop a critical consciousness through which they challenge the status quo of the current social order.
>
> *(Ladson-Billings, 1995, p. 160)*

Ladson-Billings (1995) explained that despite inequities in schools and societies, "students must develop academic skills" (p. 160); this requires helping them experience academic success in authentic ways, having high academic expectations and high standards (note that this does not mean that education must be standardized; quite the contrary). She also proposed that experiencing academic success does not negate one's cultural and linguistic background. In fact, she underscored that "students must maintain some cultural integrity" (p. 160) as they develop academically. From such a perspective, culture can thus serve "as a vehicle for learning" (p. 161). Beyond academic achievement and cultural competence, students should "develop a broader sociopolitical consciousness that allows them to critique the cultural norms, values, mores, and institutions that produce and maintain social inequities" (p. 162).

Academic Literacy: Understanding and Expanding the Concept

Academic literacy is often posited as an important concept for multilingual students, often labeled "English Language Learners" (Gibbons, 2009). Yet, it is often framed as something that needs to be acquired by "English Language Learners"— from a banking approach to education (Freire, 1970), which purports that teaching is the deposit of knowledge into human brains akin to the deposit of money into banks. From a culturally relevant perspective, academic literacy must be challenged and include the culturally grounded linguistic practices in which diverse communities engage—especially those who have been historically minoritized (McCarty, 2002). Content area literacy includes speaking, reading, and writing (communicating in general) within a specific academic realm. With the Common Core State Standards and the ensuing push for informational texts in elementary classrooms, content area literacy has dominated much of the curriculum. Yet, apart from firsthand experiences, such informational texts honor certain cultures over others and invariably exclude children from culturally and linguistically minoritized backgrounds.

Methodology and Data Sources

Through a collaborative research partnership over the course of one academic year, we (a teacher educator and public school teacher in New York City) engaged in documenting a puzzling pattern (specifically, how children always selected the same partners to share their work in science) and troubling it through our pedagogical actions within the context of a second-grade dual language classroom in New York City. Instead of allowing children to self-segregate according to language (Spanish-dominant children sharing with Spanish-dominant children and English-dominant children sharing with English-dominant children), we sought to disrupt this by engaging in a study of New York birds, fostering a new learning environment where inquiry and art allowed students to learn translinguistically and construct academic competence beyond knowledge of and mastery in dominant American English.

Students were encouraged to engage in expansive ways of recording observational data in their journals, and then, after studying the characteristics of particular New York birds through the Audubon New York *For the Birds!* (http://ny.audubon. org/education/birds) program, they each created a collage, which represented their learning translinguistically. During the *For the Birds!* program (over the course of eight weeks), we collected student artifacts, took field notes, and engaged in openended interviews with students, seeking to understand their experiences in the *For the Birds!* program, as budding ornithologists. Within this context, collage became a language of disruption, troubling the concept of academic "competence as linguistic alignment" (Souto-Manning, 2013, p. 305) and allowing students to communicate across languages while reaching learning standards in a variety of academic areas—all while developing as competent ornithologists (Mills, 2014).

The Case of Ornithology: Studying Birds in Our Immediate Context

Ornithology is the branch of zoology that studies birds. In the elementary grades, it is located under the umbrella of science. Seeking to make science more accessible to the children she taught, Jessica fundraised through a crowd-sourced website and brought the *For the Birds!* program to all second grades at her school. The special thing about this program was that it made visible how science is all around the city of New York. Specifically, it invited children to knowledgeably inquire, observe, and document birds in their natural habitat. As they observed these birds, the children focused on size, shape, color pattern, and behavior of local birds identified in the Audubon guide *For the Birds!*

Audubon New York's For the Birds!

Audubon New York's *For the Birds!* is an elementary education program that teaches environmental awareness and appreciation of nature through the study of birds, with an intensive study of birds indigenous to New York City and New York State. Over the course of eight weeks, second-grade students in Jessica's dual language (Spanish/English) class in a New York City public school learned about their local, natural environment through classroom lessons, outdoor field trips to Central Park and Riverside Park, and engaged in a conservation project that enhanced bird habitat in Riverside Park, the public park closest to the school. Students also took neighborhood walks so they could learn firsthand (through observation and engagement); talked about what they were learning authentically (asking real questions, sharing insights and observations, documenting what they saw); and compared different species of birds (for example, pigeons/perching birds they saw everywhere vs. eagles/raptors they rarely saw flying high up in the sky).

Each week, Jessica's second-grade students worked with two volunteers from Audubon New York. They learned facts about birds, which included how to identify birds, bird habitats, as well as environmental issues that affect birds. Jessica had high expectations for her students. She wanted them to excel in science and to do so she sought to make science engaging, motivating, and affectively appealing. She also wanted students to develop competence with city and neighborhood resources as they acquired school knowledge. She engaged students so that they could make observations and explore local habitats, in addition to developing academic language and science literacy. Finally, she supported students' evolving critical consciousness—by problematizing environmental injustices and the pictorial representation of birds, which often only included males. The students learned how to be "birders" (ornithologists) as well as bird stewards and activists who were learning science in culturally relevant ways (Ladson-Billings, 1995).

Scientific writing, documentation, and reading skills were developed as students participated in this program. Students were eager to document what they learned about weekly, regardless of whether (1) their writing was at grade level or not and (2) they were writing (in English and/or in Spanish) or employing artistic means of representation, such as drawing. They also sought out informational texts (including picturebooks) about birds and their natural habitats. To enhance engagement, access, and representation, the arts were integrated into the project. For example, students visited the New York Historical Society's exhibit, *Audubon's Aviary*, where they had the opportunity to view original paintings of John James

Audubon. They were inspired by Audubon's paintings and were able to connect with enthusiasm due to the work they had done beforehand. Bringing together their firsthand observation skills and their observations of the paintings by Audubon, students created their own pieces of art, collages of birds they had observed.

Because collages were rich but did not restrict students to written words, they served as a symbolic representation that crossed languages, being positioned as translinguistic symbolic representations. Through translinguistic symbolic representations, such as collages, students adding English and Spanish to their communicative repertoires were able to engage in learning that was purposeful, interesting, and motivating. Jessica's purposeful re-mediation of the "ecology of learning" resulting in "a rich learning ecology" afforded all of her students the real opportunity to "expand their repertoires of practice through the conscious and strategic use of a range of theoretical and material tools" (Gutiérrez et al., 2009, p. 227). Her students were able to represent what they were learning, science content, in ways different than the traditional "write a report" assignment. They were able to learn through doing, strategically expressing what they knew and meeting New York State learning standards in Math, Science, and English Language Arts (ELA). They engaged in a universally-designed learning experience that integrated math, science, social studies, art, reading, and writing, blurring disciplinary lines through collages. Here we share an example in hopes of shedding light onto the power and possibilities of using art, specifically collage, to enhance science learning, making it more inclusive, meaningful, and relevant.

Art in Science Learning

In the collage below, a multilingual learner (primary speaker of Spanish, adding English to her communicative repertoire) represented her knowledge of common New York urban birds pictorially. The collage portrayed by Figure 4.1 represents a blue jay. The blue jay, as captured by the collage, is between 9 and 12 inches (or 23 to 30 centimeters) long. The child's collage represents how the blue jay is grayish on its throat, chest, and belly. The crest is featured in the collage, as are the bars on its tail. Its bill, legs, and feet, although purportedly black, the child purposefully represented it with charcoal paper to capture the observations that the bird's legs were not shiny black, but lusterless: a true "a New York bird," as another child voiced.

The blue jay is positioned close to a tree, which signifies multiple characteristics of blue jays. First, it communicates how the blue jay buries seeds to eat later . . . and sometimes never finds them. They are "esparcidores de semillas" (seed spreaders) and the seeds and nuts they spread sometimes grow into tress. It also signifies how the blue jay eats mostly seeds, nuts, and fruit, being mostly a vegetarian (although classified as an omnivore). Finally, the tree also represents the place where blue jays nest (in trees).

The blue jay's scientific name, *Cyanocita Cristata*, contains a Latin word similar to Spanish (crestado is similar to cristata, Eng: crested). Because the child was a

FIGURE 4.1   Collage of Blue Jay (*Cyanocita Cristata*), a Common NYC Urban Species

primary speaker of Spanish, you can see how the blue jay's crest in the collage is accentuated. It is not a surprise that the blue jay was a bird portrayed by a number of the children in Jessica's class; the children saw several of them—after all, it is loud and colorful; it is also clearly discernible. The children spotted blue jays in each of their bird watching visits to Central Park and Riverside Park. There was also one blue jay that would regularly visit the tree outside the classroom window, in an area called "the reading garden."

This specific symbolic representation captures a blue jay in mid-air, representing an aerial chase observed (which can signal courtship). While not scientifically accurate, this collage demonstrates knowledge of blue jay characteristics, physiology, and habitat (key domains for bird study). Because the images of Audubon's birds they had accessed at the New York Historical Society were "true to size," the children in Jessica's class attempted to be "true to size" in their collages.

Opportunities to observe firsthand and engage allowed students to go from observation to first-order symbolic representation (Vygotsky, 1978), as evidenced by this situated representation and by many other collages composed by Jessica's second graders. In Jessica's second grade, students learned through observing, expanding their repertoire of experiences, and developing knowledge. They developed as scientists and came to see themselves capably as ornithologists who observed the behavior and physiology of common urban species not only in school excursions, but with their families during weekends and breaks (as reported by the children and families). This was not because there was an expectation that their families would complete some sort of out-of-school task, but a real representation of the power of re-mediating teaching and learning in ways that are culturally relevant and universally designed (grounded on UDL tenets). The children in Jessica's second grade also became advocates for bird habitat conservation—all while using art as a way of capturing, representing, and communicating what they came to know.

Conclusion

Collage offers powerful implications to the teaching of (emergent) bilingual and multilingual students. It offers a medium through which they can negotiate and project competent identities in academic areas such as science. Through collages, students can take more risks communicating their learning, communicate across languages, and come to regard their peers as capable, challenging the hierarchy associated with dominant American English as the language of power—or the language of those who have power (Delpit, 1998). The arts—in this case, collage—can serve as an entryway to learning science, motivating children to represent their knowledge in linguistically inclusive ways and to negotiate competent scientist identities, individually and socially. Finally, the arts offer powerful pedagogical ways for breaking down language hierarchies in learning—or at least encourage children to communicate—across languages.

References

Cahnmann-Taylor, M., Souto-Manning, M., Wooten, J., & Dice, J. (2009). The art & science of educational inquiry: Analysis of performance-based focus groups with novice bilingual teachers. *Teachers College Record, 111*(11), 2535–2559.

Cole, M. (1998). Can cultural psychology help us think about diversity? *Mind, Culture, and Activity, 5*(4), 291–304.

Delpit, L. (1988). The silenced dialogue: Power and pedagogy in educating other people's children. *Harvard Educational Review, 58*(3), 280–298.

Dewey, J. (1938). *Experience and education.* New York, NY: Collier Books.

Freire, P. (1970). *Pedagogy of the oppressed.* New York, NY: Continuum.

García, O., & Kleifgen, J. (2010). *Educating emergent bilinguals: Policies, programs and practices for English language learners.* New York, NY: Teachers College Press.

Geertz, C. (1983). *Local knowledge: Further essays in interpretive anthropology.* New York, NY: Basic Books.

Gibbons, P. (2009). *English learners, academic literacy, and thinking: Learning in the challenge zone.* Portsmouth, NH: Heinemann.

Gutiérrez, K., Morales, P. L., & Martinez, D. (2009). Re-mediating literacy: Culture, difference, and learning for students from nondominant communities. *Review of Research in Education, 33*, 212–245.

Genishi, C., & Dyson, A. H. (2009). *Children, language, and literacy: Diverse learners in diverse times.* New York, NY, and Washington, DC: Teachers College Press and National Association for the Education of Young Children.

Heath, S. B. (1983). *Ways with words: Language, life, and work in communities and classrooms.* New York, NY: Cambridge University Press.

Hill, J., & Miller, K. (2013). *Classroom instruction that works with English language learners.* New York, NY: ASCD.

Kendi, I. (2016). *Stamped from the beginning: The definitive history of racist ideas in America.* New York, NY: Nation Books.

Ladson-Billings, G. (1995). "But that's just good teaching!" The case for culturally relevant pedagogy. *Theory Into Practice, 34*(3), 159–165.

McCarty, T. (2002). *A place to be Navajo: Rough Rock and the struggle for self-determination in Indigenous schooling.* New York, NY: Routledge.

Meier, D. (2004). *The young child's memory for words: Developing first and second language and literacy.* New York, NY: Teachers College Press.

Mills, H. (2014). *Learning for real: Teaching content and literacy across the curriculum.* Portsmouth, NH: Heinemann.

National Center for Universal Design for Learning. (2012). *Universal design for learning guidelines.* Retrieved from www.udlcenter.org/aboutudl/udlguidelines_theorypractice.

Paris, D. (2009). "They're in my culture, they speak the same way": African American Language in multiethnic high schools. *Harvard Educational Review, 79*(3), 428–447.

Souto-Manning, M. (2013). Competence as linguistic alignment: Linguistic diversities, affinity groups, and the politics of educational success. *Linguistics and Education, 24*(3), 305–315.

Souto-Manning, M., & Martell, J. (2016). *Reading, writing, and talk: Inclusive teaching strategies for diverse learners.* New York, NY: Teachers College Press.

Vygotsky, L. S. (1978). *Mind in society: The development of higher psychological processes.* Cambridge, MA: Harvard University Press.

Yoon, B. (2008). Uninvited guests: The influence of teachers' roles and pedagogies on the positioning of English language learners in the regular classroom. *American Educational Research Journal, 45*(2), 495–522.

5

FAMILY ART BACKPACKS

Building Family-School Connections Through Art and Story

Dorea Kleker and Mika K. Phinney

> *Tonight Farha is the teacher. She stands at the head of a full table, holding a book titled, Rangoli: Discovering the Art of Indian Tradition (Ananth & Jain, 2011). "I show them the pictures and tell them about Diwali." She is at Family Art Night where, along with her mother, she is teaching her peers and their families about rangoli, an Indian art form where patterns are created on the ground with colored sand, colored rice, flour, or flower petals (see Figure 5.1 and 5.2).*
>
> *The cafeteria is full. Mothers, fathers, students, toddlers, and teenage siblings have come to be part of Art Night. Five tables are set up with art activities. Each table is manned by a student and one of their parents. Students are leading teaching demonstrations of their creations: rangoli, a Guatemalan spin drum, drawing and chalk art, a piñata ornament, and mixed-media collage, all of which were inspired by the Family Art Backpacks.*

Farha is a fifth-grade student at Newling Elementary, a culturally and linguistically diverse urban, arts-integrated, Title I elementary school of approximately 900 students in northern California. At Newling, emergent bilingual learners account for 85% of the school population; while Spanish is the predominant language spoken by students and their families, Punjabi, Tagalog, Urdu, Hindi, Arabic, French, and Cantonese are among the 20 languages present. There are bilingual Spanish/English classrooms at each grade level.

In 2012, Newling Elementary was the recipient of a federal School Improvement Grant (SIG). SIG grants are funds from the US Department of Education which are eventually granted to local agencies that demonstrate the greatest need, to raise the achievement in their lowest performing schools. Schools choose a model and create a 3-year plan that shows a strong commitment to use the funds to provide adequate resources to students. At Newling Elementary, grant money was used to create a whole-school model based in the deeply held belief that all students deserve an equitable education.

FIGURE 5.1 Farha and her mother demonstrate rangoli at Family Art Night

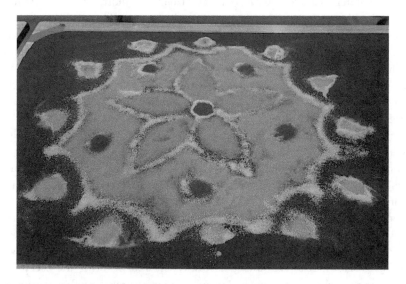

FIGURE 5.2 Completed rangoli

A rotation schedule was developed to give each grade level one day a week of enrichment classes in the arts, sciences, computer lab, and library. While students rotated through the classes, classroom teachers received a full day of professional development in a variety of areas, including the arts. Additional staff was hired to teach visual and performing arts (dance and drama) classes. A well-known literacy coach was hired to provide regular professional development in Language Arts. Support staff and a variety of outside consultants provided additional trainings. The arts are often something students are "rewarded" with upon meeting arbitrary benchmark scores. With this rotation schedule, the arts were not a reward but were used to transform the learning environment for all students by fostering student engagement, attendance, and motivation to learn, and improving school culture and climate (Stevenson, Landon, & Brazell, 2013).

Newling Elementary School's arts-integrated approach had resulted in significant gains by students, marked by an increase in attendance, test scores, and the school's Academic Performance Index (API) score. However, the arts were generally experiences directed and facilitated by SIG-funded arts teachers. As the funding came to a close, the Family Art Backpacks were developed as a cost-effective, sustainable way of maintaining the equity that the arts had provided.

What are the Family Art Backpacks?

Developed through collaboration between Dorea Kleker, an instructor at the University of Arizona, and Mika K. Phinney, who at the time was Newling Elementary's art specialist, the Family Art Backpacks were adapted from the Family Story Backpacks, a transportable curriculum to facilitate the sharing of stories within children's families (Acevedo, Kleker, Pangle, & Short, 2016). The Family Art Backpacks are designed to provide accessible and equitable arts and literature-based experiences within classroom and home settings. These experiences create new contexts from which to build family-school relationships and partnerships, facilitate connections across families, and promote learning from and with families. What we had not anticipated were the myriad ways in which the backpacks and families' art practices would support and enrich both students' home languages and their acquisition of English.

Each of the backpacks is designed around one of ten art themes (paper sculpture, dance, weaving, music, mixed media, etc.) and contains 3–4 fiction and nonfiction picturebooks in which the characters use the art form as part of their daily lives or the art form is featured significantly in the illustrations. The backpacks also include a fabric world map, open-ended art invitations, basic art materials, and a response journal in which families can share their own stories through writing, drawing, photos, and/or a variety of creative methods. Students are able to check out the backpacks for a week and use them with family members in any way they choose to share stories and artistic talents. When students bring the backpacks back into their classrooms, time and space is designated for the public sharing of how the backpacks were used in their homes, the stories they learned about their families, and the art that they created.

The backpacks were not designed to be traditional "reading" backpacks where students were required to read all of the books and write responses, but rather to engage students and their families in richer multimodal literacy experiences. The books were carefully chosen to represent a variety of cultures, languages, genres, formats, and text structures. We intentionally sought out high quality, multicultural books that allowed students and their families to find points of connection while also encouraging an exploration of cultures different from their own (Bishop, 1990; Botelho & Rudman, 2009). While we incorporated input from families at an informational meeting, the final backpack themes were ultimately dependent upon the availability of high-quality, multicultural, multilingual books.

For example, the Weaving backpack (see Figure 5.3) contains: *Abuela's Weave* (Castaneda, 1995), a book available in both Spanish and English, about a young girl and her grandmother in Guatemala; *A Long Piece of String* (Wondriska, 2010), a wordless book about the many shapes, forms, and functions of a simple piece of string; *The Roses in my Carpets* (Khan & Himler, 1998), a book set in a refugee camp in Afghanistan; and *Songs from the Loom: A Navajo Girl Learns to Weave* (Roessel, 1995), a nonfiction book set in a Navajo community. Each set of books contains a wordless book and a bilingual book when available so that all families—regardless of their home language and/or reading abilities—can access the theme

FIGURE 5.3   Weaving backpack contents

and have the opportunity to make connections between the stories in the books and their own family stories and artistic practices.

Each backpack also contains a response journal, a binder that includes a bilingual cover sheet of ideas for family responses, an optional art invitation with basic supplies, and blank pages for responses. There is no "right" way to use the backpacks or respond to them. Instead, families are encouraged to respond in any way they choose, through any format or medium. The responses, many of which include drawings and photographs of families' art creations, remain in the binder and continue to travel with the backpack as it journeys to the next home. Students are encouraged to "read" other students' journal responses. In this way, responses are being shared across students, classrooms, and households.

In the classroom, students are asked to talk about how and with whom they used the backpack and to share their response(s) and/or artifact(s). Once responses are shared at school, any accompanying artifacts are displayed in the classroom as well as in a variety of settings around the school. As families are invited to respond in any language and through any medium, these multimodal "texts" serve as an acknowledgement and celebration of the multiple cultures, languages, literacies, and artistic practices of both students and their families.

Modes of Inquiry: Unpacking Student and Family Voices

In April 2015, the program was introduced as a pilot to Newling Elementary's parent group, *Platicas*, and to Mika's visual arts classes for grades 3–5. Twelve backpacks (four themes, three backpacks of each theme), were offered for checkout from the art classroom. Over a six-week period, 54 students and families checked out backpacks. Participation was entirely optional; many students decided to participate only after seeing how their classmates had used the backpacks.

The success of the pilot led to the official project roll out in October 2015, with 40 backpacks (10 themes, four backpacks of each theme). Classroom teachers could choose to sign up for a five-week session with the understanding that participation required a clear demonstration of enthusiasm about the project, a space in the classroom allotted for display of artifacts, and a 15–20 minute sharing session facilitated by Mika each week. Thirty-four classrooms and approximately 500 students and their families checked out and used the backpacks during the school year.

In order to understand how students and their families were using and responding to the backpacks, we gathered and analyzed journal entries from families, photos of the artifacts families created, field notes and audio recordings of students sharing and discussing their families' responses within their classrooms, and interviews and small focus group discussions with both students and parents. These were debriefed regularly.

Students and families chose to engage with the backpacks in a wide variety of ways, and we offer the following vignettes and student voices to share the diversity of written, oral, and artifactual responses to the backpacks. Borrowing the term from Jackson and Mazzei (2012), we have chosen to "think with theory," integrating the professional literature throughout the vignettes to analyze the role the backpacks have played in supporting students' emergent bilingualism.

Using Art and Language to Compare and Contrast Personal Cultural Traditions

Farha, the fifth grader we met at the start of this chapter, has taken home a backpack and comes to class ready to share her family's cultural traditions through an elaborately detailed diorama depicting her family during Diwali (see Figure 5.4).

Brandon, also a fifth grader, is inspired by the Storytelling backpack to share his family's stories around Christmas, creating a small paper *piñata* ornament with his mother (see Figure 5.6). Both Farha and Brandon decide to include written descriptions in their response journals (see Figures 5.5 and 5.7).

Culturally relevant and sustaining pedagogy positions families' languages and cultural practices as educational expertise (Garcia, 2009); therefore, students are

FIGURE 5.4 Artifact—Farha's Diwali diorama

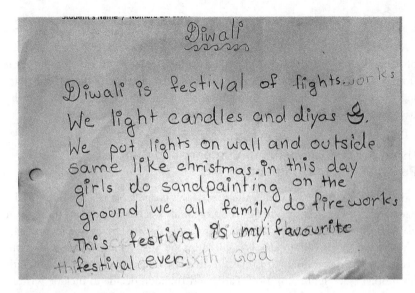

FIGURE 5.5 Response journal—Farha's description of Diwali

FIGURE 5.6 Artifact—Brandon's piñata

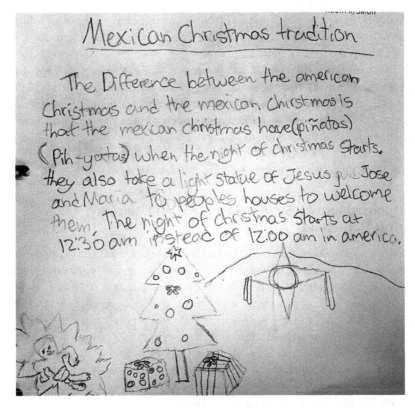

The difference between the american Christmas and the mexican chirstmas is that the mexican christmas have (piñatas) (Pih-yatas) when the night of christmas starts. they also take a light statue of Jesus and Jose and Maria to peoples houses to welcome them. The night of christmas starts at 12:30 am instead of 12:00 am in america.

FIGURE 5.7 Response journal—Brandon's description of Mexican Christmas traditions

invited to respond in the journals in any way, with any other family members, and in any language(s) they choose. Students know that they will be asked to share their responses and thus decide how best to describe what they did with the backpacks—the conversations held with family members, the family stories that were shared, and/or the artifact(s) that were created. In addition to drawings, students often integrate what they know about academic texts and a variety of text structures into their written responses. Response journals have included speech and thought bubbles, comics, diagrams with labels, directions, lists of materials, compare and contrast essays, and graphic organizers.

In the previous examples, both Farha and Brandon make the decision to compare and contrast personal cultural traditions between their countries of origin and their current homes in the US, drawing from the transnational contexts that shape their lived experiences. In order to translate and represent the stories shared by their families in their home languages (Punjabi/Spanish) into English, they incorporate what they know about nonfiction text structures into their responses. New vocabulary—*piñata, rangoli, Diwali*—is introduced through the description of the artifacts and practices connected to each of the holidays; Brandon even includes a pronunciation guide for others who might not speak or read Spanish.

Emergent bilinguals' cultural knowledge and language abilities are important resources in enabling their academic engagement across the curriculum (Cummins et al., 2006). While the backpack themes did not specifically focus on festivals and holidays, the invitation to respond freely created a space for students to make meaningful connections, to affirm and invest their identities in their learning, and to engage a wide range of strategies to ensure that these identities were both clear and accessible to their teachers and classmates.

Response Journals: Sharing Language and Culture Across Households

The journal responses remain in the backpacks as they travel across homes; students and families read each other's texts, often finding new points of connection from which to tell their own stories. The books and bag of chalk in the Art Beneath our Feet backpack inspired one family to play a game of hopscotch and then illustrate this in their response journal. As this particular journal journeyed across subsequent households, the single drawing and description of hopscotch motivated other parents to share their own stories about the hopscotch games they played as children. In this way, both students and their families became familiar with the many different versions of this popular game such as *bebeleche* ["bem beleche"] (see Figure 5.9) and *avion* (see Figure 5.8).

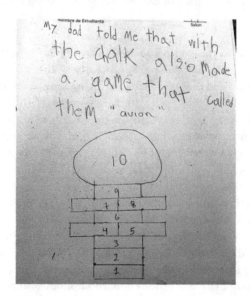

FIGURE 5.8 "Avion"—hopscotch

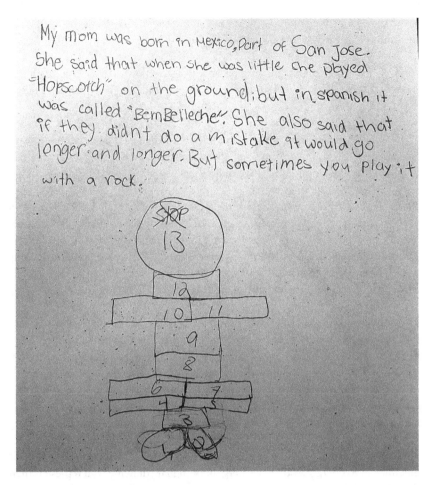

My mom was born in Mexico, Part of San Jose. She said that when she was little she played "Hopscotch" on the ground; but in spanish it was called "Bem Belleche". She also said that if they didn't do a mistake it would go longer and longer. But sometimes you play it with a rock.

FIGURE 5.9 "Bem Belleche" [Bebeleche]—hopscotch

The journals create instructional spaces for multilingual and multimodal responses, sending a message to students and their families that their home languages and cultural practices are seen and valued as resources for learning (Ntelioglou, Fannin, Montanera, & Cummins, 2014). The multitude of stories shared in these journals reach beyond individual students, classrooms, or families; they act as a springboard by which linguistic and cultural knowledge is shared across the broader school community.

Gaining Confidence: Telling Stories through Art

Although willing to share, second-grader Rafael approaches the front of the classroom with his shoulders hunched and says he's "a little shy." When Mika asks him what he did with the backpack at home he responds that he and his family looked at the books together and took turns reading the pages. Taking out the journal, he nervously explains his worries that his response does not contain writing:

Rafael: I was drawing the pictures because I didn't know how to spell the things.
Mika: Do you want to tell us the story you were thinking of as you were draw-ing this?

Despite his nervousness, he looks intently at the detailed drawing he has made (see Figure 5.10) and begins to speak; his voice and expression are clear and gain confidence as he continues to share orally:

Rafael: One day a dragon was getting apples. Then it saw an egg. Then it put it in a nest. I tried to make it a special ending, but I couldn't have no more space for it . . . a special ending, but I don't have no more space for a different dragon. I do a lot of pictures. . . . I'm really good at drawing things, and fish and . . . a lot of things.
Maria: He made a picture that tells us a story.

At a young age, Rafael already recognizes the status that writing—with accurate spelling—carries as the privileged mode of communication in school settings (Jew-itt, 2005). In this case, the blank, unlined pages of the response journal "permitted" the use of drawing, which supported Rafael both in developing the story he carried in his mind and in transforming this into something that could be shared with his classmates (Neu & Berglund, 1991). Furthermore, by inviting him to tell the story he was thinking of as he drew, Mika positions both his illustration and the oral story behind it as equally valued modes through which Rafael can share his knowledge.

Drawing can act as a bridge from one symbol system to another (Dyson, 1992; Sidelnick & Svoboda, 2000). For emergent bilinguals, drawings can represent their thoughts and ideas, support discussion of these with others, and serve as reference points to which students can turn when writing (Adoniou, 2013, 2014; Neu & Berglund, 1991). While Rafael wasn't yet ready to share his story through writ-ten letters and words, his illustration itself was the text, a reference point from which he could orally "read" and confidently discuss the story he had carefully composed with others.

Artifacts are just items until they are talked about, shared, and have stories told about them (Ray & Glover, 2008). Rafael's illustration is much more than a drawing of a dragon and apples; it is a carefully chosen artifact carrying with it his everyday experiences of being, doing, and feeling (Pahl & Roswell, 2010). Rafael's illustra-tion alone did not tell his story, yet it affords Rafael the supportive context needed to make the leap into experimenting with storytelling in English before he is fully comfortable. Through his oral description, we see the many complex thought pro-cesses behind his work. As he reminds us, there is still much more to this story.

FIGURE 5.10 Response journal—Rafael's dragon story

Art as Motivation: "I can't wait to share!"

Third-grader Yessenia is a student whose articulation difficulties have historically made her hesitant to participate in any way that would require her to produce oral language. On sharing day, Mika barely makes it inside the classroom door as Yessenia quickly approaches and exclaims, "I'm so excited, I can't wait to share!" She can barely contain herself as Mika brings the class' attention to the front of the room. She begins by leafing through a chosen book from the Art in Nature backpack, pointing out her favorite illustrations. She continues by reading her journal entry and then walks around the room proudly showing her work to her peers. The class applauds, thinking this concludes her presentation—but she is not finished. She proceeds to pull out a handmade paper flower and eagerly continues:

> I used some of my paper, then I fold it then I cut it, then I roll it, then I put glue. Then I cut it, like this part of the leaf, then I folded it. . . . [demonstrating to others] I even did something else. . . . I even did a butterfly. It gave me [an] idea and I wrote something here. It said [reads journal], "They are butterfly. They call them summer birds." This gave me the idea to make the butterfly and the flowers. . . . I knew that I know how to make these so I did that and I couldn't wait to show it [to] all of you.

Yessenia is eager to show off her work, receiving praise and validation from both her peers and teachers. None of the shyness or hesitancy that has typically been part of her school interactions is evident. In fact, she is confident and effusive.

The open-ended nature of the backpacks positions Yessenia as the central meaning maker, not only in designing and creating her response but also in communicating this to others on her own terms (Hanley & Noblit, 2009). Through this interactive process, she is able to share in a way that she is comfortable and even excited about. Assuming the role of teacher, her voice is empowered as she uses her experiences with the backpack to authentically demonstrate her academic knowledge: offering a book summary, quoting the book passage that served as her inspiration, and expertly offering a demonstration of how to create the artifacts she made at home.

Yessenia uses her paper butterfly and flower as representational resources to create meaning both for herself and her peers (Kress, 1997). With no specific structure imposed on the sharing, Yessenia seizes the opportunity to enact and share this meaning-making in her own way through authentic, dialogic interactions with her peers and teachers. Learning is mediated and enhanced by talk (Souto-Manning & Martell, 2016); Yessenia's story highlights that a commitment to creating space for sharing and for a variety of talk in classrooms supports oral language development and broadens the learning of all students.

Art as Literary Analysis

It's Wednesday and Mika is visiting the fifth graders in room 7 for their weekly sharing session. While students typically wait for a teacher to initiate the sharing, it quickly becomes clear that Luz is taking charge today. Mika is just saying hello to the class as Luz begins, enlisting the help of a few friends. They wheel an easel to the center of the carpet and hang up the fabric map, which has been pre-marked with clothespins.

Luz begins by sharing some of the stories she learned about her mother, moving the clothespins around the map to represent various locations:

> She lived all of these places because she traveled a lot with her dad. So she went in the northern . . . northern places in Mexico where the mountains are and she also went to Mexico City and she went down here to Guatemala.

Given that the books in the backpacks represented a variety of global regions, fabric maps were included in each backpack as a visual support for locating these regions and as a reference for where the stories take place. What we didn't anticipate were the many diverse ways in which students and families used the maps at home and at school as artifacts to teach geography lessons, learn where family members were born or had lived, and to share family stories.

Luz continues by leafing through the book *The Tin Forest* (Ward & Anderson, 2013) from the Found Objects backpack, showing the illustrations to her classmates while giving a brief yet thorough summary of the book. As she finishes her summary, she shows the class the last page of the book, in which an old man has transformed an undesirable place into a beautiful forest of found objects. She puts down the book, picks up a piece of pink paper she has brought from home, and begins reading her written summary:

> In the start, it was plain. No one wanted to live in the tin dump that was filled with tin trash, except an old man that lived in a cottage. He got an idea. He wished that there was color. A colorful jungle, there it was, his wish came true.

Luz concludes her presentation by trading her pink paper for the artifact she has made at home—*papel picado*—and offers her own unique interpretation:

> So I made papel picado that Ms. Phinney showed us how to do in 3rd grade. So, it represents how . . . it's plain right? [Holds up the papel picado to show that it has simple geometric designs cut into it] Until you flip it [she turns to the other side where lines, shapes, and colored designs have been added] and like how he wished to make a jungle.

Papel picado, a Mexican folk art decoration made by cutting intricate designs into paper, is culturally significant to Luz and something she explored two years prior in her art class. She uses this art form to respond to a story she has read, visually representing the transformation of the tin dump into the colorful forest the old man imagined; the "plain" *papel picado* (see Figure 5.11) is "transformed" into the colorful jungle with the addition of the color and design (see Figure 5.12). The meaning Luz made from the text of the book was not one easily or directly translated into an oral or written response. Through a process of transmediation

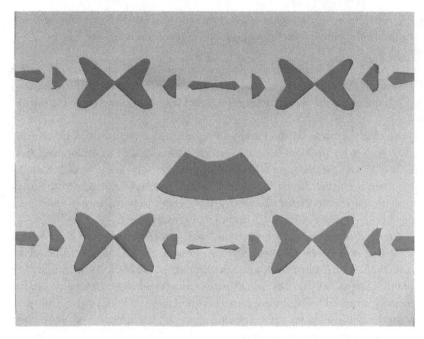

FIGURE 5.11 Papel picado "plain"

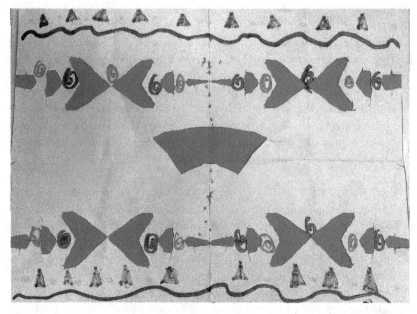

FIGURE 5.12 Papel picado "transformed"

(Leland & Harste, 1994; Cope & Kalantzis, 2008; Harste, 2013), or her conscious mode-switching from map, to book, to written summary, to oral synthesis and storytelling, and finally to the art form of *papel picado*, Luz demonstrates her deep reflective analysis of the story, something her written summary alone could not adequately represent. (Cowan & Albers, 2006). Each mode of interpretation played its own unique role in contributing to a fuller construction of meaning-making for both Luz and her audience (Jewitt, 2008).

Discussion

The Family Art Backpacks respond to Chappell and Faltis's (2013) call for increased opportunities to engage emergent bilingual youth in socially nego-tiated uses of language that relate authentically to their lives and the space to tell personal stories in ways that humanize and dignify themselves, their families, and their communities (p. 83). Rather than the common practice of focusing on what our emergent bilingual learners still need to learn, the backpacks have provided students with opportunities to share and celebrate the multiple con-texts of language and experiences they navigate, and the complex ways in which they are able to synthesize home and school learning. The freedom to respond creatively and in any language—both in the journal and through the creation of artifacts—has allowed for students to experiment with and integrate new literary and linguistic forms, structures, concepts and multiple modes of communication into their learning.

Short, Kauffman and Kahn (2000) assert that children need multiple ways of responding to literature available to them.

> In their lives outside school, learners naturally move between art, music, movement, mathematics, drama and language as ways to think about the world. They talk and write, but they also sketch, sing, play, solve problems, and dance their way to new insights. It is only in schools that students are restricted to using one sign system at a time to think.
>
> *(p. 160)*

The backpacks do not ask children to respond in a specific or standardized way but rather provide students with the opportunity to move seamlessly between multiple ways of making meaning and communicating this meaning to others.

Sharing has been central to the success of the backpacks. We must provide our emergent bilingual students the opportunity to orally share their stories and arti-facts in public spaces—and listen carefully to what they have to say about them. Through students' sharing, we have witnessed powerful family stories, innovative ways of interacting with books and maps, and a wide array of artistic talents and artifacts inspired by the backpacks. We have also seen the numerous and varied ways in which our emergent bilingual learners authentically explore, construct, negotiate, and re-negotiate meaning both at home with their families and at school with peers and teachers. When artifacts created at home are shared within the official spaces of school, families' identities, languages, traditions, and stories are recognized, celebrated, and woven into the broader academic spaces of school practices and curriculum.

For emergent bilingual students at Newling Elementary it was clear that this was something *different*. They were excited to take the backpacks home, use them with their families, and proudly share what they did and/or created when they returned to school. Inspired by the backpack contents, students and their families created elaborate responses in the form of dioramas, full-size *piñatas*, and found-object sculptures. Their journal entries were eloquent displays of the ideas, stories, and memories shared within the families. Students learned about their parents' early lives and began to see connections through their familial generations. As Brandon so expressively stated, "It's different because . . . we get to communicate with our parents and we get to know more stories that we didn't know." Luz also adds her heartfelt recommendation for others: "I would suggest to other people that they try to do this because it's a way of communicating with your family—in another way of just talking but it involves art."

Conclusion

We conclude where we began, in a packed auditorium at Family Art Night. The evening event was centered on artifacts created by students and their families, all of which were inspired by the backpacks. Our teaching artists—students and their families—proudly showcased their traditions, cultures, and enormous artistic talents as they provided teaching demonstrations and guided others in creating their own masterpieces to take home.

Even with the best and most creative of intentions, family-school interactions, especially those with emergent bilingual learners, are routinely built around telling families "how to do school at home" or how to encourage and practice more "school-like behaviors" with their children (Pope, 2001). In contrast, the open-ended nature of the backpacks allows students to share their experiences in ways that are significant to them and their families. The artifacts they created are laden with memories and histories, steeped in the everyday practice of families' lives (Pahl & Roswell, 2010). When students and families are positioned as important *sources* of knowledge and expertise rather than empty receptacles to be filled with information, skills, and strategies (Freire, 1970), they are able to draw from their own family stories, practices, and home languages to experiment with and demonstrate their learning in authentic, meaningful ways that support both their home language(s) and their acquisition of other languages.

As Paris and Alim (2017) remind us, to be culturally and linguistically sustaining requires that our pedagogies "attend to the emerging, intersectional, and dynamic ways in which they [languages and cultures] are lived and used by young people" (p. 9). By intentionally placing art within the context of the lives of students and their families, the family art backpacks build and draw from students' and families' expertise, create authentic connections with and engagement from families, and validate and encourage multiple ways of communicating and sharing this knowledge with others (Hanley & Noblit, 2009).

Family Art Backpack Book List

Art Beneath Our Feet

- *Pavement Chalk Artist: The Three-Dimensional Drawings of Julian Beever* by Julian Beever
- *Rangoli: Discovering the Art of Indian Decoration* by Anuradha Ananth, illustrated by Shailja Jain.
- *Chalk* by Bill Thomson

Mixed Media

- *Snapshots from the Wedding* by Gary Soto
- *Window* by Jeannie Baker
- *Hands Around the Library: Protecting Egypt's Treasured Books* by Susan L. Roth, illustrated by Karen Legget Abouraya
- *A Splash of Red: The Life and Art of Horace Pippin* by Jennifer Bryant, illustrated by Melissa Sweet

Dance

- *Mirror* by Suzy Lee
- *Jingle Dancer* by Cynthia Leitich Smith and Ying-Hwa Hu, illustrated by Cornelius Van Wright
- *Jose! Born to Dance: The Story of Jose Limon* by Susanna Reich, illustrated by Raul Colon

Weaving

- *The Roses in my Carpets* by Rukhsana Khan, illustrated by Ronald Himler
- *A Long Piece of String* by William Wondriska
- *Songs from the Loom: A Navajo Girl Learns to Weave* by Monty Roessel
- *Abuela's Weave / El Tapiz de Abuela* by Omar S. Castaneda, illustrated by Enrique O. Sanchez

Found Objects

- *The Tin Forest* by Helen Ward, illustrated by Wayne Anderson
- *Shadow* by Suzy Lee
- *Drummer Boy of John John* by Mark Greenwood, illustrated by Frané Lessac
- *Dream Something Big* by Dianna Hutts Aston, illustrated by Susan L. Roth

Music

- *The Conductor* by Laetitia Devernay
- *Music Everywhere!* by Maya Ajmera, photographs by Elise Hofer Derstine and Cynthia Pon
- *Grandma's Records* by Eric Velasquez
- *Hana Hashimoto, Sixth Violin* by Chieri Uegaki, illustrated by Qin Leng

Art in Nature

- *A Desert Scrapbook: Dawn to Dusk in the Sonoran Desert* by Virginia Wright-Frierson
- *Flashlight* by Lizi Boyd
- *Summer Birds: The Butterflies of Maria Merian* by Margarita Engle, illustrated by Julie Paschkis

Paper Sculpture

- *Yoko's Paper Cranes* by Rosemary Wells
- *The Piñata Maker / El Piñatero* by George Ancona
- *One Red Dot* by David A. Carter

Storytelling

- *The Magic Brush: A Story of Love, Family, and Chinese Characters* by Kat Yeh, illustrated by Huy Voun Lee
- *A Wave in Her Pocket: Stories from Trinidad* by Lynn Joseph, illustrated by Brian Pinkney
- *My Abuelita* by Tony Johnston, illustrated by Yuyi Morales
- *The Mysteries of Harris Burdick* by Chris Van Allsburg

Theatre/Acting

- *Sidewalk Circus* by Paul Fleischman, illustrated by Kevin Hawkes
- *Kamishibai Man* by Allen Say
- *Fartiste* by Kathleen Krull, illustrated by Paul Brewer and Boris Kulikov
- *Shining Star: The Anna May Wong Story* by Paula Woo, illustrated by Lin Wang

References

Acevedo, M. V., Kleker, D., Pangle, L., & Short, K. G. (2016). Thinking with teacher candidates: The transformative power of story in teacher education. In A. C. Iddings (Ed.), *Communities as Resources in Early Childhood Teacher Education (CREATE): An Ecological Reform Design for the Education of Culturally and Linguistically Diverse Students* (pp. 100–119). New York, NY: Routledge.

Adoniou, M. (2013). Drawing to support writing development in English language learners. *Language and Education, 27,* 261–277.

Adoniou, M. (2014). Drawing conclusions: What purpose do children's drawings serve? *Australian Art Education, 36*(1), 81–105.

Ananth, A., & Jain, S. (Illustrator). (2011). *Rangoli: Discovering the art of Indian decoration.* London: Frances Lincoln Children's Books.

Bishop, R. S. (1990). Mirrors, windows and sliding glass doors. *Perspectives: Choosing and Using Books for the Classroom, 6*(3), ix–xi.

Botelho, M. J., & Rudman, M. K. (2009). *Critical multicultural analysis of children's literature: Mirrors, windows, and doors.* New York, NY: Routledge.

Castaneda, O. S., & Sanchez, E. O. (Illustrator). (1995). *Abuela's Weave/El Tapiz de Abuela.* New York, NY: Lee & Low Books.

Chappell, S. V., & Faltis, C. J. (2013). *The arts and emergent bilingual youth: Building culturally responsive, critical and creative education in school and community contexts.* New York, NY: Routledge.

Cope, B., & Kalantzis, M. (2008). "Multiliteracies": New literacies, new learning. *Pedagogies: An International Journal, 4*(3), 164–195.

Cowan, K., & Albers, P. (2006). Semiotic representations: Building complex literacy practices through the arts. *The Reading Teacher, 60*(2), 124–137.

Cummins, J., Cohen, S., Leoni, L., Bajwa, M., Hanif, S., Khalid, K., & Shahar, T. (2006). A language for learning: home languages in the multilingual classroom. *Contact, 32*(2), 52–71.

Dyson, A. H. (1992). The case of the singing scientist: A performance perspective on the "stages" of school literacy. *Written Communication, 9*(1), 3–47.

Freire, P. (1970). *Pedagogy of the oppressed.* New York, NY: Herder and Herder.

García, O. (2009). Emergent bilinguals and TESOL: What's in a name? *Tesol Quarterly, 43*(2), 322–326.

Hanley, M. S., & Noblit, G. W. (2009). *Cultural responsiveness, racial identity and academic success: A review of literature.* A paper prepared for the Heinz Endowments. Retrieved from http://www.heinz.org/UserFiles/Library/Culture-Report_FINAL.pdf

Harste, J. C. (2013). Transmediation: What art affords our understanding of literacy. Oscar S. Causey Address. Paper presented at the meeting of the Literacy Research Association, Dallas, Texas.

Jackson, A. Y., & Mazzei, L. A. (2012). *Thinking with theory in qualitative research: Viewing data across multiple perspectives.* New York, NY: Routledge.

Jewitt, C. (2005). Multimodality, "reading", and "writing" for the 21st century. *Discourse: Studies in the Cultural Politics of Education, 26*(3), 315–331.

Jewitt, C. (2008). Multimodality and literacy in school classrooms. *Review of Research in Education, 32*(1), 241–267.

Khan, R., & Himler, R. (Illustrator). (2004). *The Roses in my Carpets.* Ontario: Fitzhenry and Whiteside.

Kress, G. (1997). *Before writing: Rethinking the paths to literacy.* London: Routledge.

Leland, C. H., & Harste, J. C. (1994). Multiple ways of knowing: Curriculum in a new key. *Language Arts, 71*(5), 337–345.

Neu, G. F., & Berglund, R. L. (1991). The disappearance of drawings in children's writing: A natural development or a natural disaster? *Literacy Research Report* (No. 5): Northern Illinois University.

Ntelioglou, B. Y., Fannin, J., Montanera, M., & Cummins, J. (2014). A multilingual and multimodal approach to literacy teaching and learning in urban education: A collaborative inquiry project in an inner city elementary school. *Frontiers in Psychology, 5*.

Pahl, K., & Roswell, J. (2010). *Artifactual literacies: Every object tells a story.* New York, NY: Teachers College Press.

Paris, D., & Alim, H. S. (2017). *Culturally sustaining pedagogies: Teaching and learning for justice in a changing world.* New York, NY: Teachers College Press.

Pope, D. C. (2001). *"Doing school": How we are creating a generation of stressed out, materialistic, and miseducated students.* New Haven, CT: Yale University Press.

Ray, K. W., & Glover, M. (2008). *Already ready: Nurturing writers in preschool and kindergarten.* Portsmouth, NH: Heinemann.

Roessel, M. (1995). *Songs from the loom: A Navajo girl learns to weave.* Minneapolis: Lerner Publishing Group.

Short, K. G., Kauffman, G., & Kahn, L. H. (2000). "I just need to draw": Responding to literature across multiple sign systems. *Reading Teacher, 54*(2), 160–171.

Sidelnick, M. A., & Svoboda, M. L. (2000). The bridge between drawing and writing: Hannah's story. *The Reading Teacher, 54*(2), 160–171.

Souto-Manning, M., & Martell, J. (2016). *Reading, writing, and talk: Inclusive teaching strategies for diverse learners, K-2.* New York, NY: Teachers College Press.

Stevenson, L., Landon, J., & Brazell, D. (2013). *A policy pathway: Embracing arts education to achieve title 1 goals.* Retrieved from California Alliance for Arts Education Website: www.artsed411.org/files/Embracing_Arts_Ed_to_Achieve_Title1_Goals.pdf

Ward, H., & Anderson, W. (Illustrator). (2003). *The tin forest.* London: Puffin Books.

Wondriska, W. (2010). *A long piece of string.* San Francisco, CA: Chronicle Books.

Walk the Talk

Questions for Reflection and Further Applications for Practice

Berta Rosa Berriz

How can we, as teachers, bring to life the ideas, examples and challenges presented in these first four chapters? Throughout my career as a public school teacher of emergent bilingual youth, I always say that I have never taught the same lesson twice. Guiding my creative decision making as I teach are the diverse needs of my current group of students and then a series of guiding principles, values, and experiences. This is what I love about teaching, each day offers possibilities and new learning for teacher and student alike. There are two key aspects to an enlivening practice: First is a reflective practice that cues me into my own stance and bias regarding my students and the content; then, there are the ways create inclusive and challenging structures for learning. Even in contexts of hyper segregation and the tyranny of low expectations each one of us teachers has the power to spark a fire in our learning communities a life-long aspiration for learning. Indeed, these authors shine a light on both principles and the practice.

Shabaash Kemeh tells us how family and teachers, in collaboration, create a supportive environment engaging family language and culture as a resource for academic progress. Cristina Alfaro and Lilia Bartolomé challenge us to get clear on both recognizing the linguistic capital involved in the process of tanslanguaging and other innovative forms of communication as well as the oppressive forces that attempt to stifle these social and cultural skills. Using collage as "translinguistic symbolic representation" of scientific knowledge, Jessica Martel and Mariana Souto-Manning engage students' cultural funds of knowledge while lifting or accelerating academic learning. Family Art Backpacks center the everyday lived experiences of families to enrich both languages of home and school; build relationships among families and enrich family and school interactions.

Questions for Reflection

As a teacher, what do I know about my own family history? What are the languages associated with that history? How has my own family history, language(s) and culture woven into the decisions that I make each day?

What are the ways that I get to know the families and communities where I teach? What are the structures that support co-construction of knowledge throughout the teaching and learning process? How do I name, interrogate and transform the cultural and linguistic deficit views that are pervasive throughout the educational system?

Practice for Accelerating Instruction

My Knowledge Collage: In order to accentuate that each member of the learning community brings knowledge to the academic year ahead, young scholars go home with a throw-away camera, sharing the camera and taking turns. They photograph their community and interview family members on values, wisdom, stories, and more. They create a collage with the photos and other symbolic representation of their knowledge. Once the collages are finished, I record the knowledge that each student brings to our classroom on a chart paper divided into three sections: Family/community/school. Surprisingly, school knowledge is always the least represented of these categories. We add to this chart as we move through the academic year.

   The Creatures That Live in All of the Water in the World—Reclaiming Geography Project: With an emphasis on reading, writing, and arithmetic in our schools, it is not surprising that, as a group, the class has limited knowledge of geography. This is critical, since it is through the content area where language takes on meaning and comes alive. Social studies and science are essential to building literacy. Two weeks at the beginning of the year accelerates this essential learning. We take a field trip to the aquarium in our community. Action research groups focus on the animals that live in one of the oceans, lakes, and rivers represented in the aquarium. Projecting a world map onto mural paper, students trace the continents, islands, peninsulas, labeling these and the bodies of water. Once the mural map is complete, fresh water and sea life cutouts, resulting from the field research adorn the mural. Two weeks: learning opportunity gap addressed.

   Talking Back to History: US history forms part of the content area curriculum. To affirm student critical thinking, the learning community is asked to talk back to the history just covered in each unit. On one side of the chart paper we list the most important ideas that summarize the learning. On the other side students talk critically back to that history from their own experiences.

   Here are some examples of my fifth graders talking back to the study of slavery in the US

Why did the enslaved Africans have to work so hard?	My mom works hard and they make her work harder and harder. My mom works two jobs. She has very little time to sleep.
Black people resisted slavery for justice. They fought for what is right.	We are writing letters. We want to be able to learn Spanish and end the segregation in schools.

The biography autobiography project builds a direct bridge from the biography of a character from early US history to specific moments in the biographer's life. Briefly explained here are the three major components of this project: Turning Point Moment Pop-up Books, Timeline Buddies, and Biographers' Celebration. My goal is to use reading and writing to foster a deep understanding of social studies concepts such as: everyday people's relationship to history; that family stories, beliefs, and values form part of the social, political, and economic conditions of a society and that who we are and what we do shapes history. At the same time my students will learn to read for information and determine important ideas by gathering facts that respond to their own research questions. These skills prepare scholars to think critically about the presentation of US history from a deep place of knowing.

Turning Point Moment Pop-up Books

Each student selects a character to research through reading books from the classroom and public libraries as well as on the web. Personal choice is key to motivation and engagement. Our book collection includes representation of the lives of women, native peoples, and African Americans, as well as presidents and military leaders. Biographers gather ideas guided by such questions as: What was your character's childhood like? What problems did she/he face and overcome in life? What was life like in those days? Who were their heroes or role models? What are the connections between you and the person you researched? How does she/he inspire you for your future? The research resulting from these questions become chapters in a book accompanying the artful Pop-up Book.

Students then select one event in their character's life that depicts a connection between the character and their own lives to feature in a pop-up book. Robert Shreefter, an arts educator and Associate Professor at Lesley University, guided us in the creation of a pop-up book of one moment in the life of their character. Deepening their knowledge about one event supported students in constructing timelines—a string of events in a life. Students place their biography timelines on a larger timeline of American history. They pair up with Timeline Buddies, another character who lived during the same period of time, for discussion throughout the writing process.

The Timeline Buddies added a dimension of reality to the life stories. It was as if history came to life in a conversation with a contemporary. Even if they did not know one another in "real life" the reasons that kept them apart in history—such as differences in race or class—gathered significance. For example, Phillis Wheatly and George Washington biographers were timeline buddies. In the artistry about that moment the reader gets to meet both protagonist and writer. The students took ownership of the bookmaking art.

Harriet Defends a Friend (Figure 5A.1) crystallizes both the meaning of Harriet Tubman's life for Zuhaly and her own values and aspirations. We brought the student writing to audiences in our community. The writers dressed as the characters they had researched and prepared selected quotes to speak in a fishbowl conversation at the events. We invited families, faculty, and community folks to a publishing event at our local public library that featured their pop-up book, the accompanying chapter book, and delicious food prepared by the families. The community celebration was critically important to me as it pushed through the walls imposed on my students in school.

> At age 13, Harriet's owner grew tired of making her a house servant. He sent her where she needed to work as hard as a man. One day, her owner was chasing a slave who wanted to escape. The owner had a two-pound weight in his hand. When he was going to throw it, Harriet Tubman got in the way. The weight hit her on the forehead. All these events that happened during Harriet Tubman's childhood show that she was really caring and courageous.
>
> *Zuhaly*

"One thing that I have learned about good writing is grammar. Reading aloud, I can find the grammar" (Zuhaly).

FIGURE 5A.1   Harriet Tubman Turning Point

FIGURE 5A.2   Shreefter1 I Map the Galaxy

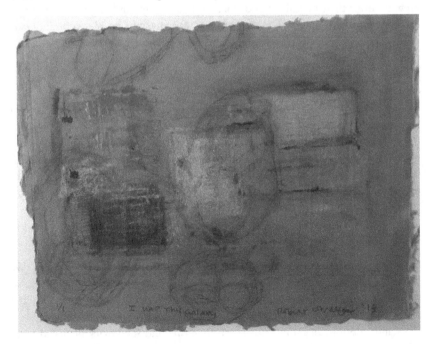

FIGURE 5A.3   Shreefter2 I Map the Galaxy

Robert Shreefter Artist Statement

This mono print with dry point etching is from a large series of prints entitled, "I Map the Galaxy" (see Figures 5A.2 and 5A.3); the pieces are loosely based on the layout of the childhood apartment I grew up in in Brooklyn, NY. This "map" is not meant to be an accurate plotting of the space. It is an artistic and emotional creation that makes the rooms repositories of certain objects, memories, moments, feelings, etc. The ink that's rolled on a plexi plate is scratched into and distressed to add depth and to convey feeling; the use of color also is meant to help delineate and contrast rooms. The fine and spidery lines of the dry point etching swirls outside and beyond the apartment. Though I made 20 or more of these, each is a distinct and separate piece that presents the space in particular ways that represents the textures, colors, and emotions of this place.

Much of my work in the present and past is about mapping. I am exploring ideas about how we in art (and writing) "map" our spaces . . . spaces we come from . . . spaces that are imbued with feeling and history, and maybe distortion; and how we are guided by our own memories and shifting vantage points of these space.

I have seen students make maps of their brains, allotting various-sized places for how they imagine what takes up space in the heads and what is "on their minds." Making maps of the heart is similar—what students see "close to their hearts" and have emotional attachment to. Making maps of the places students grew up in or their neighborhoods that are fictive maps and are created as a way to show what is important to them, what was possibly problematic. In many bookmaking projects, using secret place books, students made books of places that they felt safe or create spaces that are idealized and are places in which they would feel happy and free of worry.

The pop-up books based on a specific time in a historical figure's life are maps in their own way—maps of a moment, a place, a deed, a defining instant that helped make the person who they were and would be remembered for. In making the assignment include why this moment is important to the student him/herself, the book takes on maps/places in which the students see themselves with their own subjectivity, using their own stories and sense of what's important to them—and their own reflection of self-understandings.

Practice for Engaging Student Funds of Knowledge

Students' relationship to their cultural background supports their learning. We actively encourage this in our classroom exhibits. A central welcoming piece at the beginning of the year is a blank world map. Students go home on the first day with an enlarged map of their state or country of origin to fill with illustrations and locations of family stories, celebrations, and memories of first days of school. This Family Map project opens a year-long series of family interviews on varied topics, such as: What is sound? What are the names of rocks and minerals in your country/neighborhood? What advice would you give your child to keep for their future? The story maps bring to the classroom the first portraits of the families that make up our learning community. Soon, immigration routes, bright hummingbirds, tropical islands, and pictures of dinner tables adorn our world map. I remember a remarkable discovery. It was the first time that all of my students memorized their addresses with certainty. It was as if knowing their place in the world gave meaning to the street where they lived. The world map reminds me of how important to the success of our students it is to consider the whole before its categorical parts. This opening geographical exploration enables students find their place in the big picture of the world and begins to establish a sense of belonging to our learning community.

The quilt project uses images of family stories to nurture relationships among students. The quilt is a literacy-based integrated art experience that builds community using art and oral history. For homework, students learn important family history, such as births, weddings, and travel. Each student creates a paper collage about his or her family stories. The outcome is a paper collage of identity portraits that include cultural words and phrases and paragraphs written about each person in the group. This initiates the information gathering about the family *funds of knowledge*. It is a visual reminder, something kids can see, of how they are connected to each other. The family quilt enhances the panorama of a new classroom with the familiar images of home.

Morning Circle Meeting includes a call and response of students' names. Sometimes we whisper, sometimes we dance our family names. Here is a creative movement version. Students stand in a circle in class. Turning their backs on the circle, each child comes up with a movement to accompany their name, using both their first and last name. Returning to the circle, each child says their name with a movement. The class responds by imitating the motion while saying the name in a call and response fashion. Movement and names go around the circle, creating the Generation Name Dance of the learning community.

As the ritual call and response of names settles, others around the circle share stories about their names, nicknames, and namesakes. Miguel was named after his father's favorite uncle. Marilyn carries the name of her great-grandmother who was an important matriarch. Kevonia was called Kiki by her sister and now everyone calls her Kiki. Joshua is carrying his father's name and his sister their grandmother's name who is still in Puerto Rico. Each name is a thread on the weave of the family heritage regardless of the immigration route.

"Stepping into the Future" produces another family portrait that incorporates family values into our classroom. Toward the end of the year, students are asked to interview a family member, older sibling, or someone they admire in their community to ask advice for their future. Students request an old pair of shoes from this local hero/ine and bring it to class for an art project. There is a base for the sculpture made out of foam core board. On this surface, students create a collage that includes their future aspirations as well as advice from their elders. The shoes are artfully decorated to illustrate, and proclaim the qualities of their inspiration. With a glue gun, the shoes form a sculpture on top on the base.

Students create business cards and write an artist statement about their sculpture. I like to display these along the hall on the way to the end of the year celebration.

"El dia de mañana, you will need to connect with folks from different cultures and languages if you want to make a difference" (a father's advice to his daughter).

Note

* For critical approaches to educator reflective practice please see: Valenzuela, A. (2016). *Growing Critically Conscious Teachers: A Social Justice Curriculum for Educators of Latino/a Youth*. NY: Teachers College Press.

SECTION II

In the Heights

Lifting Potential, Expanding Possibilities

IN THE HEIGHTS—NUESTRO TRAYECTO BY YOSELIN RODRIGUEZ

Nuestro Trayecto shares my personal experience and that of many immigrants from Guatemala. The triptych (Figure II.1) shares the external and internal voices that push at each stage of this journey. Crossing the border is one of the most difficult experiences an immigrant can go through. As I've heard loved ones say, in the path you are asked to run, to be quiet, and to hide for the fear of getting caught. We are forced to leave prized possessions and come to a place where complaining is not an option. We are asked to keep quiet and work hard because that's expected of us. When we hear threats and offensive language towards us, we are to remain silent, powerless. Though fear may want to overtake, there is a voice that remains in the silence and that is one of encouragement to remind us, we are resilient. We have to keep dreaming in the stillness so that our actions may speak louder than the words said about us. But is that enough? What does it take from us to make it in this country? Is the courage to take a path of dirt and darkness of 4,000 miles enough, is it enough to "just keep working harder" and to "just keep dreaming"?

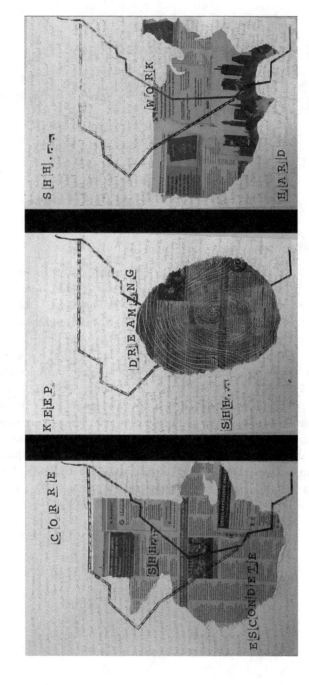

FIGURE II.1 Triptych_Immigration

6

SEEN FROM WITHIN

Photography, Culture, and Community in a Dual-Language School

Mary Beth Meehan and Julie Nora

It is a warm spring evening and the hallways of the International Charter School (ICS) are crowded. Children in formal dresses and clip-on ties stand nervously along the school's hallways, which have been turned into a gallery of color photographs and accompanying texts, written in English, Spanish, and Portuguese. Throughout the crowd, the students' families, friends, and teachers mingle together, along with members of the larger school community. Hope, a third-generation Rhode Islander, stands proudly before her self-portrait, in which she is shown amid her horseback riding trophies. Susana, who emigrated from Colombia the previous year, presents her self-portrait, in which she is wearing a helmet, lycra shorts, and rollerskates. Her writing, in Spanish and English, describes her career as a speed skater in her native country. Carlota stands before a photograph of her Cape Verdean-born grandmother, seen wiping tears from her eyes as she stands at her son's grave. Now at the exhibition, Carlota's grandmother is moved to tears again. She and Carlota embrace and speak softly in Cape Verdean Creole.

This celebration of the lives of these young people is the final exhibition of *Documenting Cultural Communities* (*DCC*), a unit embedded in the International Charter School's dual language education model and curriculum. In the project, some 60 third-grade students collaborate annually with teachers and a photographer-in-residence, to create photographs and write stories about their own cultural communities. Through the process of this work, students learn narrative photographic strategies, explore cultural concepts, and develop language learning and literacy in both primary and secondary languages—all by using their own experiences as the curriculum's primary text. This exhibition is the culmination of the 12-week project, all of which allows for the rich lives of these students to be seen from within.

The International Charter School

From the moment you enter the ICS, you hear multiple languages. A student is greeted with "Hola papi" by the receptionist, as he says good-bye to his father in Spanish and orders his lunch in English; a girl and her mother discuss an assignment with a teacher in Portuguese; in a nearby classroom, students explore multiplication strategies in Spanish. Behind the scenes, the school's population of 362 students represents ten countries of birth, with their parents being born in 19 countries. Students come from all levels of socioeconomic status, are of different races and ethnicities and countries of origin. They speak mostly Spanish, English, or Portuguese at home.

ICS is a dual-language immersion school, whose mission is to teach students in the languages of the communities it serves. Whether in the Spanish-English strand, or the Portuguese-English strand, all students spend their days immersed part-time in either their native or second languages, emerging from the school in the fifth grade reading, speaking, and writing at grade level in both. Central to this mission is the ethos of leveling the playing field for all students, helping them to appreciate and understand many other cultures, and to teach them to work collaboratively from their multiple experiences and backgrounds. All students—those from the dominant culture as well as newcomers— are encouraged to strive towards high standards of academic achievement that is rooted in inquiry about the world, themselves, and others.

Most schools are not adequately structured for emergent bilingual students. Instructional programs rarely give these students access to academic concepts and skills (Gándara, Maxwell-Jolly, & Driscoll, 2005; Lucas, 1997), delivering, instead, "dull and insipid pedagogy" (Nieto, 1996). A common reaction to less than fluent English is for teachers to expect lower level cognitive performance (Dabach, 2014; Chamot, 1989). Teachers of Latina/o students who are emergent bilinguals often consider their students to be slow learners (Moll, 1988) and usually simplify or water down the curriculum (Blanchard & Muller, 2015; García-Nevarez, Stafford & Arias, 2005; Gersten, 1994; Moll, Estrada, Diaz, & Lopes, 1980; Ramirez, 1992). Research (Arreaga-Mayer & Perdomo-Rivera, 1996; Ruiz, 1995) suggests that the result of such pedagogy is low-level student engagement, which ultimately leads to what Valdés (2001) terms *educational deadends*.

The *Documenting Cultural Communities* curriculum accomplishes multiple educational goals, fully aligned with the mission of ICS. The project validates students' cultures, engages students and their families, promotes language and literacy development, and taps into multiple literacies. In the project, each child's experience, regardless of race, culture, language proficiency, income, or parents' educational level is acknowledged, validated, celebrated, and results in a public display. Students build an understanding of culture through their *own* experiences, which are presented as *parallel* narratives that can be compared and contrasted, *without* privileging or implying a hierarchy or system of dominant/

inferior groups. Like the additive bilingualism that is integral to the dual-language model, all students benefit from maintaining and developing their own cultural identities while learning the similarities and differences of those of their peers.

Unlike a model of education in which students are required to assimilate the dominant culture, ICS recognizes that its diverse student body and family community is a rich asset that can become a relevant foundation for its curriculum. According to Valenzuela (1999),

> subtractive schooling encompasses subtractively assimilationist policies and practices that are designed to divest . . . students of their culture and language. A key consequence of these subtractive elements of schooling is the erosion of students' social capital evident in the presence and absence of academically oriented networks among immigrant and U.S.-born youth, respectively.
>
> *(p. 20)*

What Valenzuela (1999) calls "subtractive schooling" influences students' attitudes towards their own knowledge and personal competence, potentially creating a context for students to internalize an ideology of inferiority (Moll, 1999).

Dr. Julie Nora, the Director of ICS, has taught, researched, and advocated for bilingual education for the past 25 years. Nora embraces the dual language bilingual education model used at the ICS, where she has been the Director since 2003, as it emphasizes the assets that all students bring to school, including those whose first language is not English, with an intentionally diverse student population. Having personally benefited from the transformative power of education, she is passionate about issues of social justice and equity in education and works to provide such opportunities to others.

Artist-in-Residence Mary Beth Meehan began her photographic career as a photojournalist, covering immigration and urban life in Rhode Island. Now working independently, she produces long-term projects that challenge members of communities to explore the way they see themselves and each other. Her current body of work, entitled *ReSeeing*, combines image, text, and public installation, prompting conversations nationwide about how our preconceptions prevent us from seeing one another, who gets to speak for whom, and what the implications are for us, as a society.

In 1970, conceptual photographer Wendy Ewald first put cameras into the hands of children. Ewald (Ewald & Lightfoot, 2002) understood the dangers of "outsiders" taking on the role of speaking for others, and spent the next decades working to empower the children of marginalized, often misrepresented communities, to tell their own stories. Ewald understood that photography and literacy were intimately related, that one could not make photographs without the use of language, and that writing was dependent on being able to see. She identified a back-and-forth relationship—between looking, seeing, writing, and looking again—that linked the two practices and allowed them to strengthen one another.

Long an admirer of Ewald's work, Meehan developed her own teaching practice as a natural extension of her photography-based work. Concerned in particular with how immigrant communities, communities of color, and economically challenged communities were portrayed in the larger public discourse, she learned how to work within communities to help people define, refine, and share their own stories. When Meehan's son entered the ICS as a kindergartener, Meehan recognized that walking the halls of that urban school was a student body that carried within them an almost inexpressible wealth of linguistic, cultural, and worldly—as well as personal—experiences, all of which remained virtually "unseen" by the dominant community outside the school.

In DCC students' direct experiences would now become the primary data for their studies of culture. In this new project, students' own creation of primary source materials—in both photography and writing—would become the means for exploring those ideas. And verbal learning strategies—in both their native language and secondary languages—would be integral to the process. This was the start of DCC.

A New, Visual Language

The word *photography* comes from the Greek words *phōs*—meaning light, and *graphé*—meaning representation by means of lines: drawing, or writing. When Meehan steps into the third-grade classrooms to introduce the principles of narrative photography, her curriculum mines this relationship—between the development of visual literacy and the speaking, reading, and writing of verbal language. As the culture of the ICS is based on the importance of "multiliteracies"— students becoming proficient in multiple languages—DCC adds yet another language to the students' toolbox of fluencies. Meehan begins by introducing the idea that *pictures tell stories*. Her first lesson teaches students how to "read" the stories that photographs tell.

Meehan begins the very first class of the unit by projecting the work of other photographers onto a white board, on which she can draw. Starting with this image from the series *Suburbia*, by the photographer Bill Owens (1973) (see Figure 6.1), she outlines the edges of the image and identifies them as the image's "frame." She then leads the students through a very directed process of decoding this image, asking them first what they *see* inside this frame. Writing along the edge of the white board, she records what the students tell her they see: *a mother, a baby, curlers, dirty dishes in a sink, a messy kitchen.* She likens these details to the details that an author might use in a story, and, through the conversation, the students begin to understand that this frame is a primary tool a photographer uses to decide which details are important to her story. Drawing on top of the projected photograph, Meehan draws a frame only around the mother and baby. *What is different about this framing?* she asks. Students are able to understand that such a close-cropped frame would show that the woman and baby are together, but would omit the details that let a viewer know where

FIGURE 6.1 Photograph from *Suburbia*, by Bill Owens (1973) entitled "How Can I Worry About the Damn Dishes When There Are Children Dying in Vietnam". Reprinted with Permission.

Photograph by Bill Owens, from the series Suburbia

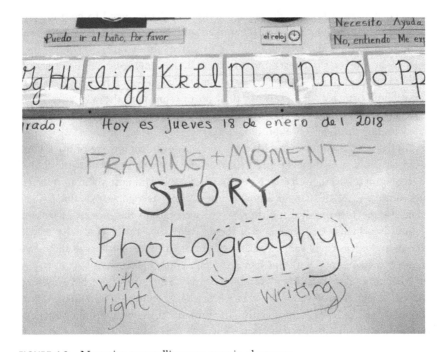

FIGURE 6.2 Narrative storytelling structure in classroom

they are standing, what is around them, and—more abstractly—why the mother may be experiencing certain feelings. Concretely, then, the students now see the frame as a powerful tool of narrative selection—that what a photographer puts inside the frame, and what he or she decides to leave out, creates context, provides meaning, and leads to story development. It is analogous to the process of writing.

Next, Meehan asks students to describe the "moment" in which the photographer took the photograph—when did he press the button on his camera? Students reply that they are seeing a moment in which the mother's face looks depressed, when her expression reveals that she may be overwhelmed with the tasks before her. Meehan asks them to imagine how the photograph would be different if the mother and baby were laughing together in the photo, yet standing within the same frame. Students are able to imagine that, in that case, the photograph might suggest that the mother and baby are able to enjoy each other's company, in spite of the mess around them. By choosing a different moment to portray, the photographer would have delivered a different narrative image, a different story. Once students realize that a photographer's choice of the "moment" she portrays is as important to story development as choosing her "framing," Meehan is able to set down a model that students will return to again and again, throughout the project: FRAMING + MOMENT = STORY (see Figure 6.2).

Students Begin to See in Pictures

In order to write a story, students need to be seated, they need to be quiet and focused, they need proficiency in a spoken and written language—they need to be able to "see" in words. In order to make photographs, however, they need to be out of their seats, moving their bodies, engaging with the action of life. For third graders, this process is new, physical—it is fun. And for students whose primary strength is not their relationship with the written word—especially in a language that they are in process of learning—this process becomes a new avenue for their self-expression.

On the next classroom visit, Meehan gives each student a piece of black construction paper, asks them to fold it in half, and cut a square out of the folded edge. She then asks them to open the sheets of paper and raise them up to their eyes. With a sense of wonder, students immediately recognize that this is their "frame"—the first physical tool they've received toward the process of making pictures (see Figure 6.3). This tool is theirs—only they can decide what it will include and what it will exclude, making them the primary authors of their own seeing. Now equipped with this frame, students climb up on chairs, get down on their bellies, explore what they see in 360 degrees. They roam the school hallways and enter the classrooms of cooperative teachers—filling their frames as they choose to, saying "click" and imitating the pressing of the button on a camera, as they indicate the moments that interest them.

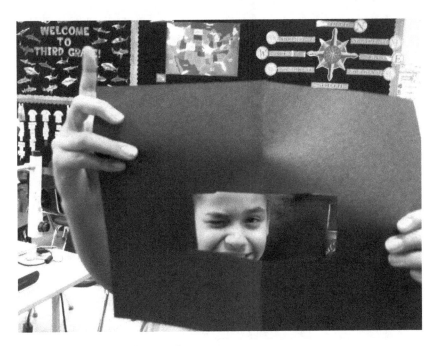

FIGURE 6.3   Student with paper frame

After the black-paper exercise, students are given their first assignment, to tell the story of their weekends, in pictures. Yet they are still not given a camera. Wanting them to solidify their familiarity with visual narrative structure before becoming distracted by the cameras, Meehan gives them a sheet of plain paper: "This is your camera for the weekend," she says. "Please draw a frame on it, and fill your frame with the details and moments that make up the story that you choose to tell." Students return on Monday with drawings that begin to reveal their understanding of the visual literacy concepts, while also beginning to show the first signs of their cultural lives (see Figures 6.4, 6.5 and 6.6). With this understanding in place, they are given real cameras to use for the duration of the project.

Photographing Their Lives

It is the middle of the school semester, and students have been photographing every weekend for two weeks. On this day, they are in the classroom, reviewing their contact sheets—printouts of the photographs they have taken. Meehan's guiding model—Framing + Moment = STORY—is written on the board. Equipped with this three-tiered evaluation process, they are able to critique their own work: *Have I been deliberate about what I put in, and what I left out, of my frame? Have I captured a clear moment? Is there anything in the frame that gets in the way of a viewer seeing this moment? Is there a story here that I want to tell?* (see figure 6.7).

FIGURE 6.4

"My Mom Makes Cachupa (A Traditional Cape Verdean Stew) and Milho, (A Sweet Drink)," by James V.

After they have reviewed their own work, Meehan projects a selection of their images onto the white board, leading a conversation that is student-directed, and takes the form of a shared conversation: "I see your brother, and I know you love your brother, but there doesn't seem to be any story here," says one student to another. "I see your mother hugging your brother, but your Dad's head is in the way," says another student. "If you had moved your feet to the left, your Dad's head wouldn't be in the way, and you would have made a stronger story."

On this day, Gabriela is poring over her many photographs—of her family at home playing dominoes, her friends at a bowling birthday party, her extended family at a wedding. James, a budding ballroom dancer, is deciding which self-portrait shows the best "moment" of himself, dancing with his mother. But Bianca is struggling. She has a few photographs of her parents, but is not excited about the project. She says she doesn't "see" any stories around her.

ICS teachers learn about students' *funds of knowledge* (Moll, 1999) through home visits, Family Message Journals (Wollman-Bonilla, 2000), and meetings with families. The teachers know that Bianca comes from a large Mexican family, and that her grandparents own and run a popular restaurant in a densely populated urban neighborhood. In order to help Bianca advance, the teachers begin to ask her about the restaurant and its significance. Bianca begins to recognize that the restaurant is a place of meaning, that important family rituals are played out there. Teachers ask her to write: *What does she sees when she is there? Why is*

FIGURE 6.5

"My Mother Working as a Waitress," by Brianna L.

FIGURE 6.6

"I'm Cleaning the Dishes and I'm Tired," by Justin P.

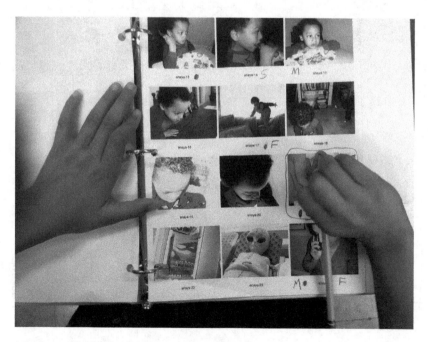

FIGURE 6.7 Student's editing notebook

it important? What languages does she hear? How does it smell? What is her favorite dish? Now that Bianca has identified a story, Meehan helps her strategize ways to photograph it. *Can you visit the restaurant over the weekend, while your grandparents are working? Can you ask for their permission to go behind the scenes, to photograph while they work? Where might you put yourself, in order to "frame" the stories that happen there?* The following week, Bianca returns with photographs that show her grandmother making tortillas, her grandfather washing the restaurant's dishes, and the patrons enjoying the fruit of her grandparents' labor (see Figure 6.8).

At another table, Kevin is editing his work. Usually quiet in the classroom and struggling to keep up with the achievements of his classmates, Kevin has assumed a place of honor in the photography project. He has produced a body of work that captures subtle moments, sophisticated compositions, and a sense of framing, composition, and mood that are startling, and consistent week to week.

Yet, in trying to tease out of Kevin the process by which he is making his work, Meehan realizes that he has no language for it, he cannot describe it to her—he just "sees" it. Together they select a series of Kevin's photographs—describing his home, his parents and siblings and large extended family (see Figures 6.9 and 6.10). Kevin then is able to begin to construct his writing—less instinctively and fluidly than he does his picture making, but he builds it nonetheless. To accompany a photo of his father and uncles eating crabs, he uses the word CRAB to create an acrostic poem: *Crabby, Really spikey claws, Awesome, Bowl of Soup.* He

FIGURE 6.8

"Mi Abuela Trabaja en un Restaurante," by Bianca L.

FIGURE 6.9

"My Uncles Together Eating Crabs," by Kevin M.

FIGURE 6.10

"My Sister Loves to Sing," by Kevin M.

uses his sister's name, JESS, to write another acrostic poem about her, in Spanish: *Juguetona y elegante; Energetica y chistosa, Siempre baila en la sala, Selena es su apodo.*

There are many links between learning the art of photography and learning a second language. Frequently students who are not fully proficient in the language they are learning do not have access to grade level content or higher order thinking. The use of visuals is key to providing them with such access. Though the making of a photograph requires cognition, it does not necessarily require language. The medium poses a visual, *nonverbal* structure with which to create a story. By identifying what they are seeing, using the frame of the camera to select the elements most important to them, and then deciding on which moment to capture, the student creates a visual narrative, a concrete instantiation of that student's personal experience. Often this photograph reflects a complex subject, rendered without words.

Revealing Their Cultures

Why is teaching cultural competence important? Research suggests (Enos, 2014) that increasing diversity in a geographic area may actually lead to more hostility than tolerance between members of different cultural groups. This work counteracts that. Again, as emphasized by the mission of cross-cultural respect at ICS, students become prepared to live in a global world in which they will interact with others from kaleidoscopically different cultures and experiences. As traditional school are pressured to focus on reading and math, as dictated by standardized assessments, at ICS the educational goals related to language and culture become more and more of a global priority.

In educational terms, students whose language and culture differ from the dominant language and culture of school are challenged with yet another set of skills and knowledge to master. To master these skills requires newcomers to move toward full participation in the sociocultural practices of a community. What contributes to high levels of engagement for students who participate in *DCC* is, in part, the fact that the students' lives and divergent cultural experiences form the basis of the project curriculum. In a constructivist manner, this project builds students' understanding of culture through their *own* experiences. As one student, Julius, was motivated to visualize himself as an astronaut, spending an entire weekend creating a spacesuit and moonscape in his bedroom, so do all *DCC* participants become engaged to show the beauty and particularities of their own lives, which necessarily reveal the cultures within which they live.

In ICS's Portuguese-English classroom, Fatima has photographed the *Festa do Divino Espirito Santo*—the Feast of the Holy Spirit, a Portuguese tradition in which Fatima's family participates. In the ceremony, the parish priest places a crown on each family member's head, and delivers a blessing. In Fatima's first set of photographs, her family is shown in a neighbor's home, where the community is assembled in the living room. The priest is placing the crown on a woman's head, while people stand around her. In the foreground of the photo stands a table with refreshments, as well as the wall separating the kitchen from the living room. The wall is illuminated by the flash from Fatima's camera (see Figure 6.11).

Referring back to the model—Framing + Moment = Story—Meehan and Fatima begin to critique this photograph. Inside the frame, Fatima has captured the crown, the priest's hands, the surrounding community. She has also shown the tops of bottles on a table, and a blank wall. The moment she has captured is a precise one— the very moment in which the priest is placing the crown on the woman's head.

Through their conversation, Fatima begins to understand that she has captured a storytelling moment, but that her framing—including the bottles, the wall, being so far from the important moment—is interfering with the storytelling potential of her photograph. Rather than see the faces of parishioners, we see the kitchen's white walls. Instead of the priest's gesture, we see the column separating the kitchen from the living room. Fatima tells Meehan that the ceremony will continue on the following week, this time in the church. Meehan, then, is able to help her prepare to re-photograph the scene. They discuss where Fatima's body might need to be in order to *fill her frame* with only storytelling elements. They emphasize how important it is that she remain focused on the moments in which the crowning will be most visible. On the following Monday, Fatima comes to school with the following photograph (see Figure 6.12):

In her new photograph, Fatima's grandfather is shown being crowned by the priest. He, the priest, and the gesture of the priest placing the crown on his head

FIGURE 6.11

"Festa do Divino Espirito Santo I," by Fatima P.

FIGURE 6.12

"Festa do Divino Espirito Santo II," by Fatima P.

now fill the frame. The emotion of the photograph is palpable. Fatima and Meehan debrief on how she achieved this new photograph:

Mary Beth Meehan:	What did you do, in this picture?
Fatima Ponceano:	I went close to the priest and my Grandpa. You can see my priest and my Grandpa, getting crowned very close.
MBM:	How is this different from your other pictures?
FP:	In my other pictures I was behind him and I wasn't so close. You could see the wall and everything.
MBM:	How did that change the story?
FP:	It changed the story because you didn't really see what was going on inside the picture that I did before; you couldn't really see the people getting crowned. You were basically looking at a wall, and people lining up.
MBM:	What are we seeing in this new picture, and how does it make the story different?
FP:	I'm up close so you can just see my Grandpa, and you're not really paying attention to everything else and there's no wall. You just see the priest and my Grandpa.
MBM:	By getting closer, what happened for us, as viewers?

FP: You get to see what's *actually* going on, what I'm trying to take the picture of.

MBM: Do you think it changed the mood?

FP: Yes. You can tell that when he's closing his eyes he's focusing, and every-
           one else is quiet—it's like a quiet mood.

MBM: What's he focusing on?

FP: The priest, and praying.

MBM: What does the crown mean?

FP: I think it means that you're entering Jesus's home, and you're inside his
           church. You're inside his home and you're getting blessed by him.

MBM: How did you make this picture?

FP: In this moment my whole family was getting crowned. By the time I got
           crowned I had to run all the way down—well, I didn't run. I speed-
           walked to our seats, I grabbed the camera, and I went really close, and
           made sure it was a perfect moment.

In Fatima's case, coming from a traditional Portuguese family living in the US, the
family's cultural markers are clearly seen, and quite simple to describe. Yet, most
often, cultural markers are not so discrete. It is important to note that, in thinking
about the concepts of culture, students are not asked to objectify themselves or
their families based on easy stereotypes: Mexican, American, Brazilian, White, etc.
They are asked instead to consider the fluidity with which individuals inhabit and
move within various cultures, and are taught to look at all areas of their lives. By
making narrative photographs that tell the stories of their lives, they are able to
then identify the concrete places in which culture appears—whether that be at
a religious ceremony, in a sporting arena, or on the street. The photograph made
by Carolina, as follows, shows the various cultures in which she resides. Born in
Brazil, she is now squarely situated in an American lifestyle, from her getting ready
for her First Communion to her Hannah Montana bedspread (see Figure 6.13).

In the course of the project, as it is constructed around ideas of culture, it is often
the children with close immigrant backgrounds who have a rich wealth of personal
material to share. Whereas an assimilation model of schooling would exclude those
children's experiences from the classroom, with *DCC* those experiences take center
stage. Ironically, then, it is often the children from within the dominant culture who
find it hard to identify the ways in which culture appears in their lives. This allows for
a complex and nuanced conversation between teachers and students, in which they
realize that all human beings live within the cultural constructs of sports, food, religion, recreation, and so on. Angus, whose family has lived in the US for many generations, began the project questioning whether his life showed any aspects of culture
at all. But his mother is a gardener, and his family keeps chickens, which he came to
understand as part of the culture of his home. Thus, his self-portrait, which he titled in
English and Spanish, shows him at home with his favorite chicken (see Figure 6.14).

Writer and educator Ron Berger has advocated extensively for the development of a "culture of quality" and "ethic of excellence" in schools. He writes

FIGURE 6.13

"My First Communion Dress," by Carolina S.

FIGURE 6.14

"Chicken with a Crossbeak/Pollo Con un Pico de Cruz," a self portrait by Angus A.

about the importance of constructive critique, revision, and high performance standards as the basis for student learning, growth, and, ultimately, self respect (Berger, 2003). In working with a resident teaching artist, third graders at the International Charter School are exposed to a level of visual rigor that borrows directly from professional standards. They are given multiple opportunities, over the course of six weeks, to re-photograph their subjects, using new knowledge and strategies. Most importantly, they receive the message that they *can* succeed in making storytelling photographs, and are given ample chances to improve as they do so. Their sense of accomplishment is always significant.

Images and Words, Working Together

Once students have made a portfolio of images that they feel satisfy the model of Framing + Moment = Story, they turn their attention to their own writing. Classroom teachers now have a font of student-driven inspiration to draw out the students' language development, by helping them to decode their own images. They begin by referencing the students' first reading of images—back to the first exercise decoding the photograph by Bill Owens, and ask the students to name what they see, inside their frames: *What do you see? Who is in the picture? Where is this person standing?* Teachers then ask students to consider the moment that they have captured: *What is happening in this photograph? What moment does it show? Why did you choose this moment?* With these prompts next to their own photographs, students are then able to begin to render verbally, and in written form—two separate pieces written in two languages—the complex meaning of a familiar scene in their lives. Bilingualism is enabled through a common visual starting point.

For Caroline, she really wanted to photograph her mother at work. Never before allowed inside the factory where her mother and aunt fabricate boxes (Figure 6.15), Caroline used the photography project as a way to gain access to the space, to have agency over her own interests, and to investigate an aspect of her life about which she'd always been curious. With Meehan's encouragement, she got in touch with her mother's boss, explained her project, and obtained permission to photograph inside the facility. When she returned to school on Monday, she had made a photograph of her mother and aunt, in front of a table piled with pink boxes that they had fabricated. In reviewing her photographs for the week, Caroline knew she had made an important picture, and was determined to write about it, with the goal of the piece being in the final exhibition. But she didn't know where to begin.

Faced with the blank page, many students with emerging language proficiency become anxious. They envision their final writing on the wall at the exhibition and can't imagine how to get there. And yet, the presence of the photograph motivates them to find the right words, to express the meaning that they see. In order to facilitate those first writing steps, teachers begin with a "word blast." They ask students to simply look at their photograph and write down any word that comes to their minds. Now working in Google Chrome, the teachers can see

FIGURE 6.15

"My Mother and Auntie at Work Making Boxes," by Caroline L.

the writing that each student is producing in real time, and can make suggestions as they go.

In Caroline's first word blast, her teacher was able to give her encouragement and guidance about how to bring her writing to a more complete fruition of Caroline's ideas and then help her with spelling errors (see Figure 6.16).

Caroline was then able to go back into her document, and draw the words and phrases from her word blast into more complete sentences.

Once the basics of the photographs have been established, teachers then ask the students to move into more abstract, complex analyses of their photographs, asking such questions as: *How do the people pictured feel? What is the mood of the photograph—how does it make you feel? Why is this scene important to you?* Teachers are then able to bring in all of the students' senses, asking them to further expand their awareness and consider: *As you were photographing, what sounds or languages did you hear? What else could you see outside the frame that you chose? Could you smell food cooking? If you sampled that food, how did it taste?* And lastly, but by no means less importantly: *How does this image reflect your culture?*

In Caroline's case, she clearly wanted to focus on her own success in gaining access to her mother's workplace, and wanted to write about the person who gave her permission to photograph there. Still working in Google Drive, Caroline's teacher was able to give encouragement for her progress in expressing her ideas, but still noticed that there was an element of meaning missing from Caroline's

box's	boxes for cancer
for cancer	hard work
hard work	focused
focust	trying really good
trying realy good	doing work
doing work	not fooling around
not fouling arouwnd	making sure doing it correct
making sher doing it corect	doing the correct thing
doing the corect thing	working hard together

Caroline,
Let's work on this together. I am wondering if you want to choose a different style of writing for this photograph. The story here is so great, and I don't think a word blast tells us enough information . . . What do you think?
—Ms. Brooke

FIGURE 6.16   Teacher uses online tool to give writing feedback to student

written narrative. She points her in this direction with a written prompt, asking Caroline to finish this sentence: *I wanted to take photographs at Interpack* (her mother's workplace) *because. . . .* Working in her document, Caroline is able to answer this question: *Interpack is an important place for me because most of my family works there* (see Figure 6.17).

Making Meaning, in Multiple Languages

The first building block of any type of language—written, oral, or visual—is the ability to articulate meaning. While our favorite poets or fiction writers can look at an object or gesture and see larger, more universal or metaphoric significance, some children—indeed, many of us— have difficulty seeing the moments of our ordinary lives as meaningful. Through the process of *DCC*, third-grade students are able to begin to recognize, isolate, describe, and share small moments of their daily lives. They may have eaten cachupa with their families countless times, but now they are able to "see" that ordinary activity as a ritual that has value, that describes the people they love, the culture they come from, and their feelings about the world they inhabit.

Andre and his parents had emigrated to Rhode Island from Portugal only months before the beginning of the DCC project, which meant that his facility in English was just beginning. Yet, while immersed in his Portuguese-driven classes, he was able to share with his teacher (a native Portuguese speaker from Brazil) his feelings of ambivalence about leaving friends and family behind. In very rudimentary English, Andre described to his teachers that, in Portugal, he was surrounded by friends and family, but their family lacked work and income. "In America," he said, "we have no people, but we have money." His quiet photograph, then, of his parents seated alone at their dinner table in Rhode Island, became a metaphor

Interpack Box nFactory
By, Caroline Lemus

Dear Ana,

Thank you for letting me take pictures at Interpack. I know that kids aren't supposed to go in there because it can be dangerous, but I was lucky because you let me go and take pictures. You are a good manager because of how you took me on a tour of Interpack. I also like the way you talk to the people in the factory. Thank you for letting me do all my work at Interpack. I wanted to take photographs at Interpack beacausecause I wanted

Caroline,
I made some changes and added in a new sentence for you to write from. Great work so far!
—Ms. Brooke

Interpack Box nFactory
By, Caroline Lemus

Dear Ana,

Thank you for letting me take pictures at Interpack. I know that kids aren't supposed to go in there because it can be dangerous, but I was lucky because you let me go and take pictures. You are a good manager because of how you took me on a tour of Interpack. I also like the way you talk to the people in the factory. Thank you for letting me do all my work at Interpack. I wanted to take photographs at Interpack because I wanted to I learn about the machines and how they use them. There are so many different machines and I can't keep track of all of them. Interpack is an important place for me because most of my family works there.

Thanks Again,
Caroline Lemus

FIGURE 6.17 Teacher corresponds with student to give feedback on writing

through which Andre could explore his feelings of loneliness here in the US, and his feelings of separation from his friends and family back home, in Portugal (see Figure 6.18). By embroidering this small detail of his life with his growing visual and verbal skills, Andre and his fellow DCC students are truly able to elevate such moments into powerful reflections on what it means and how it feels to be a third-grade student at this time and place. It is this elevation of the ordinary that often brings the viewers of the students' final work to tears.

FIGURE 6.18

"Family Dinner in Rhode Island," by Andre B.

FIGURE 6.19   "My Mom at Work Selling Cosmetics," by Isaias S.

Back at our opening celebration, a young boy stands in a three-piece suit in front of his photographs. With him are his mother and grandmother, who speak to him in Cape Verdean Creole. In one photo, we see his mother photographed from above, sitting at a table covered with an embroidered cloth very common to Cape Verdean households. Next to her is a plate of home-made meat pies. In her hands are a pen and notecards related to her work, as a salesperson for Avon cosmetics (see Figure 6.19).

The student has written his text in the form of a letter to her. He writes (Figure 6.20):

Dear Mom,

When I look at this picture I think about how dedicated you are to your work. I have learned from you to be deticated. Just looking at this picture. I remember the first day of Avon work, you had no idea what to do but then your freind, Carmen, helped you. Now are so good, you have taught other people how to do it. Right next to you is a plate of food made by Mamanina my great-grandma she lives right down the street and she allways cooks for the whole family. I think you love eatting her CaChupa the best especially after all your work. Thank you mom for working hard to give our family a good example. I think your very special.

Love your son Isaias Semedo*

FIGURE 6.20 Student writing a letter to his mother to accompany his photograph

FIGURE 6.21   "Isaias for President," a self portrait by Isaias S.

In the next photo, the same boy is seen in a self-portrait wearing a formal suit—the same one he is now wearing to his exhibition. In the photograph, he is posing as the President of the United States.

In his written piece, Isaias describes that he has a dream to become the President, and would use his presidential power to enact gun-control legislation, to make the country "safer for everyone" (see Figure 6.21). At his final exhibition, his mother and grandmother stand examining the boy's photographs, and reading his writing. Soon, his mother is in tears. She tells us that she didn't know he was aware of how hard she was working, or the sacrifices that she had made for him—in immigrating to this country, in taking multiple jobs so that he could eventually go to college. In each of the nine years of the *DCC* project, families gain a new, often surprising or even revelatory window into their children's minds, lives, and experiences. At times parents even get a new understanding of themselves, as parents, through the eyes and words of their children. As one parent said, "through this project we get to see them see us." As Isaias stands with his mother and grandmother in front of his work, it is as though, thanks to the work of *DCC*, the boy is truly *seen from within*—even to the people who know and love him the best.

Conclusion: Preparation for a Life of Global Awareness

In the best possible way, education can be a key element to the "governing of the self" (Popkewitz, 1998), or the development of an inner discipline with which

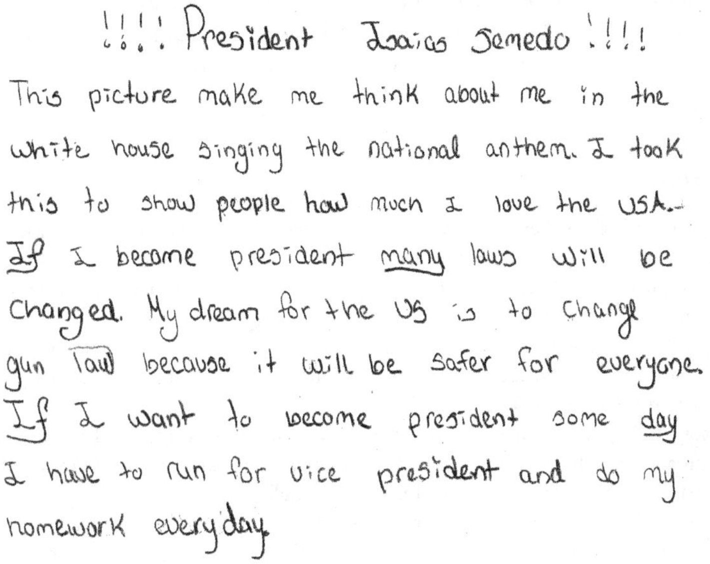

¡¡¡¡ President Isaias Semedo ¡¡¡¡

This picture make me think about me in the white house singing the national anthem. I took this to show people how much I love the USA. If I become president many laws will be changed. My dream for the US is to change gun law because it will be safer for everyone. If I want to become president some day I have to run for vice president and do my homework everyday

FIGURE 6.22 "Isaias for President" accompanying text

individuals can navigate their social worlds. Social betterment is dependent on the development of individuals who can control their own circumstances and environment (Vygotsky, 1978; Dewey, 1972). The goal of education within this framework is to develop the student's natural talents to the maximum (Dewey, 1972). By engaging in activities that are of interest to each and every student, these young learners can influence change and eventually become agents of change for social organization (Glassman, 2001).

In our increasingly "flat" world, where geographical divisions are becoming less relevant (Friedman, 2005), our students need the skills to be competitive in a global context, which includes being able to engage in cultural exchanges across the earth. Yet schools in the US are not keeping pace with preparing students for increased globalization (Suárez-Orozco & Sattin, 2007). DCC has the dual effect of having students' own cultures and histories validated and celebrated, and giving them the hands-on experience of documenting and exploring the cultural present. By documenting their own cultural communities and sharing them with their classmates, third-grade students are able to gain key cross-cultural understandings, encouraging tolerance and empathy, and emphasizing the awareness of similarities and differences in human life over value judgments driven by the dominant culture.

In the current era of education reform, there is an increased focus on student performance on standardized tests measured only in English and narrowly focusing on math and reading. The onus of developing the skills that our children need in an increasingly globally connected world, such as multilingualism, cross-cultural competence, and collaboration, is placed entirely on individual schools and educators. *DCC* is one example of how one school attempts to do this. As we see with Isaias, all students and their families have dreams of how schools will help them reach their full human potential. As educators, we are obliged to help them get there.

References

Arreaga-Mayer, C., & Perdomo-Rivera, P. D. (1996). Ecobehavioral analysis of instruction for at risk language-minority students. *The Elementary School Journal, 96*, 245–258.

Berger, Ron. (2003). *An ethic of excellence, building a culture of craftsmanship with students*. Portsmouth, NH: Heinemann Publishing.

Blanchard S., & Muller C. (2015). Gatekeepers of the American dream: How teachers' perceptions shape the academic outcomes of immigrant and language-minority students. *Social Science Research, 51*, 262–275.

Chamot, A. U., & O'Malley, J. M. (1989). The cognitive academic language learning approach. In P. Rigg & V. Allen (Eds.), *When they don't all speak English* (pp. 108–125). Urbana, IL: National Council of Teachers of English.

Dabach, D. (2014). "I am not a shelter!" Stigma and social boundaries in teachers' accounts of students' experience in separate "sheltered" English learner classrooms. *Journal of Education for Students Placed at Risk, 19*, 98–124.

Dewey, J. (1972). *Experience and education*. New York, NY: The Macmillan Company.

Enos, R. D. (2014). The causal effect of prolonged intergroup contact on exclusionary attitudes: a test using public transportation in homogeneous communities. Working Paper, Harvard University.

Ewald, W., & Lightfoot, A. (2002). *I wanna take me a picture*. Boston, MA: Beacon Press.

Friedman, T. (2005). *The world is flat: A brief history of the 21st century*. New York, NY: Farrar, Straus, & Giroux.

Gándara, P., Maxwell-Jolly J., & Driscoll A. (2005). *Listening to teachers of English language learners: A survey of California teachers*. Berkeley, CA: Policy Analysis for California Education.

García-Nevarez, A. G., Stafford M. E., & Arias B. (2005). Arizona elementary teachers' attitudes toward English language learners and the use of Spanish in classroom instruction. *Bilingual Research Journal, 29*, 295–317.

Gersten, R. M., & Woodward, J. (1994). The language minority student and special education: Issues, themes, and paradoxes. *Exceptional Children, 60*, 310–322.

Glassman, M. (2001). Dewey and Vygotsky: Society, experience, and inquiry in educational practice. *Educational Researcher, 30*(4), 3–14.

Lucas, T. (1997). *Into, through and beyond secondary school: Critical transitions for immigrant youths*. Washington, DC & McHenry, IL: Center for Applied Linguistics & Delta Systems Co.

Moll, L. (1988). Some key issues on teaching Latino students. *Language Arts, 65*, 465–472.

Moll, L. (1999). The diversity of schooling: A cultural historical approach. In M. de la Luz Reyes & J. J. Halcón (Eds.), *The best for our children: Critical perspectives on literacy for Latino students* (pp. 13–28). New York, NY: Teachers College Press.

Moll, L., Estrada, E., Díaz, E., & Lopes, L. M. (1980). The organization of bilingual lessons: Implications for schooling. *The Quarterly Newsletter of the Laboratory for Comparative Human Cognition, 2*(3), 53–58.

Nieto, S. (1996). *Affirming diversity*. New York, NY: Longman.

Owens, B. (1973). *Suburbia*. San Francisco, CA: Straight Arrow Books.

Popkewitz, T. (1998). Dewey, Vygotsky, and the social administration of the individual: constructivist pedagogy as systems of ideas in historical spaces. *American Educational Research Journal*, 35(4), 535–570.

Ramirez, J. D. (1992). Longitudinal study of structured English immersion strategy, early-exit and late-exit transitional bilingual education program for language-minority children (executive summary). *Bilingual Research Journal, 16*, 1–62.

Ruiz, N. (1995). The social construction of ability and disability: II. Optimal and at risk lessons in a bilingual special education classroom. *Journal of Learning Disabilities, 28*, 491–502.

Suárez-Orozco, M., & Sattin, C. (2007). Wanted: Global citizens. *Educational Leadership*, April, 2007, 58–62.

Valdes, G. (2001). *Learning and not learning English*. New York, NY: Teachers College Press.

Valenzuela, A. (1999). *Subtractive schooling: U.S.-Mexican youth and the politics of caring*. Albany, NY: State University of New York Press.

Vygotsky, L. S. (1978). *Mind in society: The development of higher psychological processes*. Cambridge, MA: Harvard University Press.

7

MEETING THE NEEDS OF AND GIVING VOICE TO LINGUISTICALLY DIVERSE CHILDREN THROUGH MULTIMODAL AND ART-BASED ASSESSMENTS

Whitney J. Lawrence and Janelle B. Mathis

Today, more than ever, it is imperative to explore and connect the literacy practices privileged in school with those valued in the homes and local communities of our students. As literacies continue to be redefined and what it means to be literate in the 21st century is refined accordingly, we turn to research in the arts (Albers & Harste, 2007; Greene, 1995; Sanders, 2010) and multimodality (Kress, 2010; New London Group, 2000; Pahl & Rowsell, 2010; Towndrow, Nelson, & Yusuf, 2013) for alternate approaches to assessments, ones that may afford children from diverse backgrounds the opportunity to make meaning and communicate in forms outside of those deemed appropriate by the people in power. The term *multimodal assessment* in this chapter refers to assessments that take into account the different forms and modes in which children communicate and make meaning in all contexts of their lives. The focus of multimodal assessments is on the design, form, and demonstration of understanding on a topic or concept. In a multimodal assessment, children engage in what Siegel (1995) refers to as "transmediation," or "the act of translating meanings from one sign system to another" (p. 455) and what Kress (2010) calls "transduction," or the movement of meaning across modes (p. 125). For example, one may take a traditional writing assignment and move it to a painting. For the purpose of this paper, the authors have chosen to use the term transmediation.

Integrating art may seem like the impossible in a time when standardization and accountability have taken over. However, a multimodal, arts-based approach makes teaching in the standards-based world richer and provides us with deep insight into our children as meaning makers and communicators that will assist us in ensuring that our children are prepared to meet the challenges of the world in which they live. To uncover multimodal assessments' potential in providing such insight, this chapter shares multimodal strategies that integrate the arts and afford children from linguistically and culturally diverse backgrounds opportunities to make meanings more complex than what language might afford and communicate these meanings, however abstract, to those around them.

Each story, told from the perspective of Whitney, whose classroom was the context for these learning experiences, models the curricular negotiations made to ensure that we simultaneously met the linguistic and cultural needs of our children for engaged interactions as well as the demands of the state standards. Additionally, we detail the learning experiences that framed the students' engagements, to make explicit ways educators can reclaim their autonomy and create spaces that are inclusive of all students. These stories uncover the way multimodal assessments invite children from linguistically diverse backgrounds to communicate and demonstrate their learning, the ultimate purpose of assessments.

The Context and the Students

This investigation took place at a suburban elementary school located in the Southwest, Circle Field Elementary. The local neighborhood is comprised of older homes integrated with a number of apartment complexes. The local school is diverse with a 36% mobility rate. At the time of the study, the school had approximately 700 students, with about 80% participating in the free or reduced lunch program. All four of the fourth-grade students in this investigation receive or have received services from the English as a Second Language program. This campus does not offer a bilingual or dual language program. Two receive pull-out services, while the other two remain in the regular education classroom. Three of the four are labeled "limited English proficient" (LEP), and all four are labeled "at-risk," according to labels defined by the state.

Ianali

Ianali moved from Brazil nine months ago, and she came only knowing "hello." She was very reserved, but instantly became friends with Gabrielle. After meeting her the first day, I came home and ordered six bilingual Portuguese/English picturebooks for her to have to read in class, supporting her home language of Portuguese. I bought her flashcards to assist with the noticing and naming of content area topics, such as shapes, money, animals, etc. For the first three months, we used my cell phone to translate the learning experiences for her. Four girls in class would take turns being her "helper" and would use my phone to answer questions, share ideas, or clarify anything with Ianali. By December, Ianali was speaking in full sentences and writing narrative and expository essays comparable to English-speaking students in our class. Her stepfather and I stay in frequent contact about Ianali. Ianali's mother has concerns about being away from their family and culture and considered moving back at the semester's end. But after seeing how well Ianali was adjusting and making friends, her mother decided to stay.

Gabrielle

Gabrielle's family moved from Mexico when Gabrielle was five, and Spanish is predominately spoken at home. Her dad owns Mexican restaurants in the local community where this investigation took place. Gabrielle has shown signs of struggle in the area of literacy since kindergarten. In first grade, her teacher attempted to retain her, but her parents wanted Gabrielle to move on. In third grade, she was retained after scoring poorly on standardized assessments. After having Gabrielle for about a month, I inquired of previous teachers about patterns I was noticing in Gabrielle's literacy practices. Some patterns, when she engaged in traditional literacy practices such as writing an essay or reading texts, centered around the alphabetic principle, indicated a disability. I also noticed early on that Gabrielle was able to communicate and demonstrate learning at a deep level in nontraditional forms, pointing to her ability to make meaning and communicate.

Stella

Stella's grandparents are from Tonga, a small island north of New Zealand. Both of her parents graduated from the local community high school, and at home a mix of English and Tongan are spoken. I had Stella's sister the previous year and had an established relationship with her mom. The arts, especially music, art, and dance are an important part of their Tongan culture. Stella is a first-year monitor, meaning she no longer participates in the services provided by the school system. Stella typically hangs out with the other Tongan students at lunch and recess and wears clothes and jewelry that indicate how much she values her Tongan roots. I attend church services, dance performances, and birthday parties with Stella's family.

Katelynn

Katelynn's family is from Laos and Thailand. Her grandmother moved to the states and opened a Thai restaurant in the local community. Katelynn is a storyteller and enjoys sharing stories about her family and culture with the class. Often read-alouds are paused for a story by Katelynn. She often talks, writes, and shares stories about going to temples to worship or celebrate. When given a choice in topic explorations, Katelynn typically engages in topics connected to her personal culture, experiences, and life. Katelynn is a multimodal meaning maker, but she struggles to communicate or demonstrate her learning in traditional forms. Specifically, language that shows up on standardized assessments is confusing to Katelynn, and her interpretation of what is being asked is not always accurate.

Multimodal Assessments

Our children are growing up in a world where meaning-making and communicating are multimodal events. Simply being able to read conventional signs in fixed systems will no longer prepare them for the world they face (Sanders & Albers, 2010; Trilling & Fadel, 2009). Children must be equipped with the cognitive capabilities to read gestures, images, music, language, and many other sign systems. Children also need the tools to synthesize information and communicate complex ideas in a variety of forms. This section illustrates the way multimodal assessments take emphasis off of language and expand it to communicative practices, opening a space for children to communicate and make meaning in modes that build on the semiotic resources reflective of their world outside of school and the world they face. Each story is embedded within a learning experience grounded in our work towards global citizenship. In Figure 7.1, I have provided a summary of the literacy learning goals, student response projects that serve as data, and guiding questions that assisted in interpretation of mastery for each learning experience. Guiding questions are used to analyze student work, assess mastery, and guide future teaching and learning. These questions assist in assessing mastery of the content area skills which are aligned with state assessments.

Collage Summaries

Often in society the heroes that are glorified are those with fame or power, making it easy to overlook the everyday acts of bravery that deserve as much attention as those glorified by society. We began the unit by brainstorming a list of heroes in the fight for equality among African Americans. Of course, Rosa Parks, Martin Luther King Jr., and "that girl that went to an all white school" were mentioned. This surface level understanding of Black History made this unit even more relevant. I asked students if they had heard of Langston Hughes, Duke Ellington, Florence Mills, or Ella Fitzgerald. Two students had heard of Langston Hughes and that was it. I told the children that these were unsung heroes, ones who paved the way for Martin, Rosa, and Ruby. The students spent five weeks exploring art, music, and literature's influences on equal rights; exploring people, places, and events of the Harlem Renaissance; and investigating someone from this era that inspired them.

We explored the work of artist Romare Bearden. The students read *Me and Uncle Romie* by Jerome Lagarrigue in small groups, and I read aloud *My Hands Sing the Blues: Romare Bearden's Childhood Journey* by Jeanne Walker Harvey. We studied collage art by watching YouTube videos and reading digital how-to articles. The students then made meaning of Romare Bearden's work using the Digging Deeply into Art (see end of chapter). In one instance, we analyzed *The Dove*, a collage by Bearden, portraying a bustling New York City street. We discussed the disproportioned scales of images, hidden political messages, and how the first layer carried its own meaning in the story and served as the setting. Additionally, we used this art to analyze the way Romare Bearden synthesized information to share a story or idea.

The students spent three weeks reading picturebooks and images, watching documentaries, listening to music, and researching topics of interest. At the end of the unit, the students created a collage, one that shared an important story or idea about the Harlem Renaissance. The story or idea to be shared was their

Learning Goals:
Make inferences using text evidence for support.
Summarize and synthesize information from a wide range of sources in a logical and coherent order.
Make connections between diverse texts, across a wide range of genres, using own experiences, thematic links, and to the world at large.
Compose an expository essay with a central idea and supporting details.

Data Collection:
Collage with short museum summary; collage with expository essay

Guiding Questions for Interpretation of Mastery:
Learning goals one:
  Were conclusions drawn that were not explicitly stated?
  What evidence was provided to support these inferences?
  Did the conclusions show the reader's ability to uncover hidden messages provided by the author? If so, how?
  Do these inferences show the reader's ability to critically read texts?
Learning goals two:
  Were multiple sources utilized to draw information?
  Was the reader focused on the main ideas and main events?
  Is the summary presented in a logical and coherent order?
  Did the reader go beyond a surface level of restating information? What new knowledge was taken away from this learning experience?
Learning goals three:
  Were connections made at a local and global level?
  Are connections relevant and do they add to the information presented?
  Were both similarities and differences across texts noted?
Learning goals four:
  Is there a clear central idea?
  What details support this idea?
  Is the essay presented in a coherent and logical order?

FIGURE 7.1 Content Assessed in Literacy Experiences

choice, but they needed to consider the first layer, as it would represent the setting, or context, of their story or idea. Considering the elements of collage art, students created their collages, communicating their understanding of this historical era and the unsung heroes whose acts of bravery inspired us. Such an approach to visual art is "multiphasic," or one where multiple individual elements "overlap, collide, or merge together" to create new meaning (Albers, 2007, p. 138). Examples from Gabrielle and Ianali are provided:

Student Artwork

Student Summary

Black Lives Matter

Black lives matter is a movement right now, but it was also important during the Harlem Renaissance. Adelaide Hall was important because she sang and danced in Harlem, proving that blacks could sing and dance just as well as whites. She and others, like Ella Fitzgerald, Duke Ellington, Josephine Baker, and Florence Mills, all proved that black lives do matter.

FIGURE 7.2 Harlem Renaissance Collage and Summaries

Student Artwork

Student Summary

Lena and Cab

Lena Horne and Cab Calloway were important people during the Harlem Renaissance. They proved that black people can do anything that white people. They proved that they are equal to the white people.

FIGURE 7.2 (Continued)

As the students were working on their collages, Gabrielle found a current *Time Magazine* with the words "Black Lives Matter" and ran up to me excitedly to share that a current magazine says "Black Lives Matter." When I asked her what she thought of that she replied, "Black lives matter now just like they did during the Harlem Renaissance." Gabrielle was able to connect issues of the present with issues of the past and made this the theme of her collage.

The multiphasic pieces created by Gabrielle and Ianali both were an attempt to illustrate the way African Americans "proved" they weren't inferior to whites. The bright colors, glitter, and artifacts chosen were arranged to tell a glamorous story of the Harlem Renaissance and the coming of black artists, authors, poets, musicians, and politicians, among others. The size of the people in proportion to the other artifacts emphasized the impact the people of the Harlem Renaissance had on proving African Americans were equal. The instruments and musical notes further emphasize the role of music during this era.

Collage Connections

To celebrate Dr. Seuss's birthday, we watched a digital version of *Oh, The Places You'll Go!* We then discussed places that the students wanted to go. Some said SeaWorld, and others mentioned visiting family members that live in another state or country. I then asked the students to think about going somewhere where they could make a difference. I gave them a few seconds to consider places, while I thought about my own response. Modeling my expository essay, I wrote about wanting to go to a small village in Africa and study the literacies in practice there so that I could share stories of people engaged in literacies differing from those valued in the US. As I modeled, I made sure to discuss the "skills" of expository compositions that are assessed on standardized assessment, such as central idea, topic sentences, and relevant details. But mostly, I wanted the students to visualize themselves making a difference in the world.

The children wrote down some of the places to which they may want to travel. After thinking about which one they were the most passionate to visit, they created a collage to represent their "central idea." The collage served as their "brainstorming" and helped the students consider their topics they wanted to discuss. From there, they planned, revised, and edited their expository essays. Once a student published a piece, she or he orally presented it to me as I transcribed the essay. The next three to four minutes, I spent conferencing with the student about patterns I noticed in her or his writing. After negotiating the meaning behind the piece, we printed them, and the student created a balloon to hang on our door for Dr. Seuss's birthday. Examples from Katelynn and Stella are provided.

Both Stella and Katelynn want to return to their native land to assist with a critical issue. The girls took a different approach in composing their pieces, however. Katelynn used the images to represent the problems facing Thailand after the Tsunami. The images compiled assisted her in the details of her expository

Student Summary

Going back to Tonga is so important to me because this is where my family is from. My mom and dad's family is from there, so I want to make sure that the people of Tonga are safe and have all the resources they need, like I do here in Texas.

Student Artwork

Helping Thailand is so important to me because my family is from Thailand, and while they were there, they had to face tsunamis. My grandma still cares a lot about Thailand, so that makes me care about it, too. My culture is important to me, and that all started in Thailand.

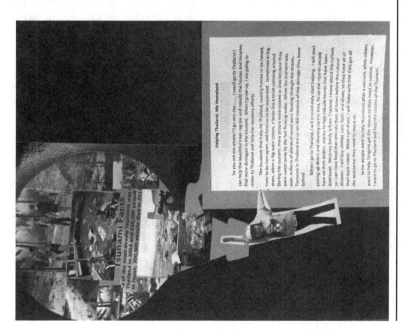

FIGURE 7.3 The Places We'll Go Collage and Essay

essay, and her reference to the water looking "like a toilet bowl spinning around" came from videos she watched online to build background on this topic. Stella, on the other hand, created her collage with photographs of Tonga as a beautiful island. When I asked Stella her intentions behind this, she reiterated that she wanted people to see how beautiful Tonga was and to not think that it was a "bad place." Katelynn chose to use the photographs to highlight the problem, while Stella used the photographs to ensure that readers did not leave with stereotypes about her native home.

These multiphasic approaches to communicating portray the way each girl was able to share a visual narrative text side-by-side with a traditional text to create a larger meaning and share a grander narrative. The amalgamation of these two texts highlight their ability to recognize the way each text carries its own meaning, but when combined a new meaning is communicated. Further, this assessment positioned the children to begin seeing themselves as citizens who can make global changes that have local ties. Most important, Stella's and Katelynn's work uncovers the limitations of solely relying on traditional practices of composition.

Conclusion

Standardized assessments privilege and value traditional literacies in academic settings, resulting in disadvantaged literacies (Purcell-Gates, 2007). We see this in the way standardized assessments misrepresent Gabrielle, Stella, Ianali, and Katelynn. All four of these students make meaning and communicate in diverse forms each day, depending on their contexts. Yet current literacy assessments only afford one form of communication, one that may not align with their out-of-school forms.

As educators, we are responsible for setting conditions that both provide a range of opportunities to demonstrate learning and address local, state, and national standards. The multimodal, art-based assessments afforded to the linguistically diverse students in this chapter opened a space for them to take on critical perspectives, synthesize a wide range of information, communicate new ideas, share their visions and voice, and engage in the practices laid out in the state-mandated standards. These assessments eliminated language, social, and cultural barriers, ones present with assessments that value one literacy form. This afforded students with opportunities to communicate in alternate forms. Multimodal assessments, like those presented in this chapter, value the assets children bring into the classroom, showing an acceptance of their diverse backgrounds and avoiding a deficit perspective (Moll, Amanti, Neff, & Gonzalez, 1992). Moreover, a broadened perspective of the child and more accurate narrative is shared, one that reflects in-school and out-of-school literacies thus providing educators a more accurate understanding of students' abilities, what they know and are able to do.

Most important, these assessments provided insight into the students' abilities to synthesize a wide range of information and create new meaning, share

TABLE 7.1 Students' Standardized Assessment Scores

Student	Reading Score in Third Grade	Math Score in Third Grade
Ianali	Not in country	Not in country
Gabrielle	50%	76%
Stella	63%	76%
Katelynn	0%	46%

narratives of critical events, and see themselves as part of the change in our world, insight not valued on standardized assessments. Therefore, such assessments miss the mark in providing insight into literacy practices and events children are and will be faced with in the real world.

From this analysis, it is apparent that these children are both making meaning of diverse texts and communicating in a variety of forms, utilizing a wide range of modes. However, if we rely solely on standardized scores, this is the story that would be told of the students in this investigation, despite our success in achieving the literacy learning goals outlined previously in this chapter.

It is obvious in the narratives shared in this chapter that these numbers cannot be and are not an accurate representation of these children as meaning makers and communicators. Bringing in alternative systems to communicate and make meaning afforded children from linguistically diverse backgrounds opportunities to demonstrate their understanding of a wide range of topics in multimodal, art-based forms. Students showed they were able to engage in transmediation. Children value their family and culture at home, and these alternate systems of communication are inclusive of ones that students engage in out of school. Therefore, exploration into literacy assessment practices that lead to inclusive spaces for the participation and contribution of students from diverse linguistic and cultural backgrounds is imperative.

Our children come into classrooms with diverse communicative and meaning-making practices. These are reflective of their engagements, interactions, and experiences in their homes, local community, and classroom. In order to make sure our children are prepared to face the complex issues of the world, there is a critical need for deeper exploration into assessment practices that build on, rather than deny, the cultural, social, and historical practices our children bring into the classroom.

Digging Deeply into Art

Surface Level

- What immediately caught your eye?
- What objects are noticed immediately?
- Where are the details located?

- Where is the information located?
- Are warm or cool colors present?
- Are active or passive colors present?
- Are certain objects grouped together?
- If so, is there a pattern to this grouping?
- Is there any unused space?

Digging Deeper

- What is the artist trying to get you to notice?
- What objects are important in this art?
- What is the mood or tone of this art?
- Why did the artist probably create this piece?
- What is the artist's attitude toward the subject?

Thinking Beyond

- Is there a social or political message?
- What history positions this art?
- Is the art intended for someone?
- Would you feel the same about the art if it were produced by someone from a different age, race, or gender?
- What piece of this art stuck with you the most? Why?
- Is there a hidden message? If so, what is it?

Children's Texts

Bearden, R. (1964). *The dove*. New York, NY: Museum of Modern Art.

Hartfield, C., & Lagarrigue, J. (2002). *Me and Uncle Romie*. New York, NY: Penguin.

Lawrence, J. (1993). *The great migration: An American story*. New York, NY: The Museum of Modern Art.

Seuss, Dr. (1990). *Oh, the places you'll go!*. New York, NY: Random House.

Walker, J., & Zunon, E. (2011). *My hands sing the blues: Romare Bearden's childhood journey*. Las Vegas, NV: Two Lions.

References

Albers, P. (2007). *Finding the artist within*. Newark, DE: International Reading Association.

Albers, P., & Harste, J. C. (2007). The arts, new literacies, and multimodality. *English Education, 40*, 6–20.

Greene, M. (1995). *Releasing the imagination: Essays on education, the arts, and social change*. San Francisco, CA: Jossey-Bass Publishers.

Kress, G. (2010). *Multimodality: A social semiotic approach to contemporary communication*. London: Routledge.

Moll, L., Amanti, C., Neff, D., & Gonzalez, N. (1992). Funds of knowledge for teaching: Using a qualitative approach to connect homes and classrooms. *Theory Into Practice, 31,* 132–141.

New London Group. (2000). A pedagogy of multiliteracies. In B. Cope & M. Kalantzis (Eds.), *Multiliteracies: Literacy learning and the design of social futures.* London: Routledge.

Pahl, K., & Rowsell, J. (2010). *Artifactual literacy: Every object tells a story.* New York, NY: Teachers College Press.

Purcell-Gates, V. (2007). *Cultural practices of literacy: Case studies of language, literacy, social practice, and power.* Mahwah, NJ: Lawrence Erlbaum.

Sanders, J. (2010). Relationships between artistic and written composing: A qualitative study of fourth grade students composing experiences. In P. Albers, & J. Sanders (Eds.), *Literacies, the arts, & multimodality* (pp. 110–135). Urbana, IL: NCTE.

Sanders, J., & Albers, P. (2010). Multimodal literacies: An Introduction. In P. Albers, & J. Sanders (Eds.) *Literacies, the arts, & multimodality* (pp. 1–25). Urbana, IL: NCTE.

Siegel, M. (1995). More than words: The generative power of transmediation for learning. *Canadian Journal of Education, 20,* 455–475.

Towndrow, P. A., Nelson, M. E., & Yusuf, W. F. (2013). Squaring literacy assessment with multimodal design: An analytic case for semiotic awareness. *Journal of Literacy Research, 45,* 327–355.

Trilling, B., & Fadel, C. (2009). *21st century skills: Learning for life in our times.* San Francisco, CA: Jossey Bass.

8

PICTUREBOOK ILLUSTRATIONS

Powerful Pathways for Literacy Learning and Language Acquisition

Katherine Egan Cunningham and Grace Enriquez

At an afterschool partnership program between Benjamin Franklin Elementary School[1] and a local college, emergent bilingual learners (EBs) in grades 3–5 met weekly with a literacy professor and literacy specialist candidates. During one session, the following exchange took place as a literacy specialist candidate prepared to read aloud the picturebook *Wings*, written and illustrated by Christopher Myers:

Teacher: *What does bravery look like and sound like?*

Adonis: *Bravery is saying something when you are not sure. Or going first like I just did.*

Teacher: *You're right, Adonis. You were brave by going first. We sometimes think of bravery as something huge, but really we are all brave every day.*

Teacher: *(after first few pages of the story): How do the cut-out illustrations help us better understand what matters most in this story?*

Sophia: *The girl is always in yellow and Ikarus's wings are always white. The yellow girl is like a shadow. And the other kids are other colors. They are like shadows, too.*

Teacher: *Let's look closer. What else do you see that seems important?*

Sophia: *The boy and girl look sad.*

Teacher: *How do you know?*

Sophia: *Well, the faces look down.*

Melany: *We do not see the clothes or faces.*

Teacher: *I wonder why.*

Melany: *Hmmm. . . . I don't know but maybe it's like you and me.*

Teacher: *Ah. . . . so you're saying it's like we could be Ikarus or we could be the girl. Let's keep reading and see what else this story and the illustrations make us think about.*

In this chapter, we present a series of similar vignettes from this afterschool program, each chronicling the transactions of EBs with picturebook illustrations as well as their responses to the picture-making process. Picturebooks, as defined by renowned children's literature scholar Perry Nodelman (1988), are "books intended for young children which communicate information or tell stories through a series of many pictures combined with relatively slight texts or no texts at all" (p. vii). In picturebooks, content is conveyed through illustrations and words or through illustrations alone.

Central to the framework of the afterschool program was that pictures are a powerful tool for thinking and sharing ideas. In this setting, the language of pictures and the language of words served as complementary languages for learning, a paradigm shift for both the students and the teacher candidates (Olshansky, 2008). The emphasis on the power of pictures represented a critical divergence from the literacy specialist candidates' previous thoughts about supporting literacy learning, which reflected popular but rudimentary understandings that literacy is simply the ability to read and write words. Their work with students in a supervised setting was designed to expand the candidates' definitions of literacy to include reading, writing, speaking, listening, viewing, and creating. In particular, the course emphasized multiliteracies as defined by the New London Group (2000) including the "increasing multiplicity and integration of significant modes of meaning-making, where the textual is also related to the visual" (p. 5). The parallel and complementary language of pictures and words through quality picturebooks (Olshansky, 2008) made it possible to teach literacy elements while supporting language acquisition and development, and deepening students' understanding through visual as well as verbal means.

The students in the previous example noticed details about Christopher Myers's use of color to help readers determine significance. All of the elementary school students were native Spanish speakers who had immigrated to the US from mostly Central American countries in the last few years. They all spoke Spanish at home. Melany noticed that the absence of facial features in the cut-out illustrations positions readers to become the character and to empathize with Ikarus's situation. Sophia drew conclusions about the mood of the story because of the downcast faces and slumped shoulders of the figures. Through their interpretation of the illustrations, the students used verbal language to express thoughts that deepen their understanding of the story.

We draw upon reader response theories (Beach, 1993; Rosenblatt, 1978, 1985; Sipe, 2008) to frame children's interactions with picturebooks as transactions in which both the reader and text's meaning are potentially transformed through the encounter. We also consider the use of picturebooks with strong illustrative qualities to provide richer opportunities for meaning-making and literacy learning. Together, these stances form a mosaic that depicts how children's transactions with picturebook illustrations and their own picture making facilitate language exploration and learning, perhaps more readily than the written text within such books.

Using Picturebooks with Emergent Bilingual Learners

The use of picturebooks as tools that facilitate language acquisition and comprehension for bilingual learners is not a new concept. For example, Lado (2012) notes
how picturebooks provide teachers with built-in simplifications of language that
can mirror their learners' abilities, along with scaffolds of text patterns, illustrations,
themes, and formats that can facilitate learners' language acquisition. Montelongo,
Duran, and Hernandez (2013) found that the amount of cognates in picturebooks
is significant enough to promote cognate instruction with bilingual learners. Others
(e.g., Allen, 1989; Hadaway, Vardell, & Young., 2002; Hadaway & Young, 2009) advocate using children's literature with bilingual learners because of their authentic and
natural texts. However, much of the literature on using picturebooks with bilingual
learners focuses on the ways the written text in picturebooks can aid bilingual
learners, with illustrations treated as secondary supports. We align ourselves with
literacy scholars (e.g., Jewett & Kress, 2003; Kist, 2005; Leland, Lewison, & Harste,
2013) who assert that "image, as well as other visual modes, is fast becoming the
source through which many read, experience, and build beliefs about the world"
(Albers, 2008, p. 165). Thus, we believe the illustrations themselves can be the primary pathways for bilingual learners to acquire and develop their language abilities.

Furthermore, we are guided by children's literature scholars who distinguish
between different kinds of picturebooks based primarily on the qualities of the
book's illustrations. Here, we specifically employ the single-word term *picturebook*,
rather than the conventional two-word term *picture book*, to emphasize the union
of text and illustration for meaning-making and to selectively focus on books
that stress such interdependence as opposed to books that are merely illustrated
(Kiefer, 1995; Marantz, 1977; Sipe, 2001). In picturebooks, Arizpe and Styles
(2003) point to the aesthetic intention of not just the author but the illustrator
as well to create the story. In other words, picturebooks (again as opposed to the
two-word term *picture book* that may include any kind of illustrated book) require
readers to attend closely to the illustrations in order to construct understanding
of the text or story as a whole. Not doing so would ignore important layers of
meaning that are relayed through the illustrations. The use of picturebooks draws
specific attention to the interdependence of art and language to convey meaning.

In fact, picturebook illustrations seldom relay the exact same information as
the written text (Wolfenbarger & Sipe, 2007). In contrast with picture books in
which the illustrations merely provide a visual mirror of what the written words
say, picturebook illustrations may indeed provide more information, contradict, or
even subvert the accompanying text. Nikolajeva and Scott (2001) identify several
ways the illustrations and written text in a picturebook relate to one another:

- Symmetry, where the words and illustrations equally tell the story with the
same information;
- Complementary, where words and illustrations each provide important
information;

- Enhancement, where words and illustrations extend the meaning of the other;
- Counterpoint, where the words and illustrations tell different stories;
- Contradiction, where the words and pictures conflict with each other.

Because of the illustrations' significance in picturebooks for conveying meaning, we posit that as EBs transact with those illustrations, they can find much to talk about and in doing so, explore and build their language skills.

In this chapter, we focus on the use of picturebooks that provide opportunities to explore a theme, concept or essential question as well as opportunities to explore multiple perspectives within and beyond the text. We argue that such picturebooks are tremendous tools for developing students' language acquisition, specifically when the illustrations are carefully considered and centered in instruction. Furthermore, we showcase the use of picturebooks in text sets— which are collections of texts around a particular concept, topic, or theme. Text sets provide an opportunity to strengthen thematic networks of meaning for students thereby deepening literacy understandings as well as providing greater opportunities for language development through connections across texts (Cappiello & Dawes, 2012).

Reader Response Theories and Interactive Read-Alouds

Children's transactions with picturebook illustrations create pathways that facilitate language exploration and learning, perhaps more readily than the written text within such books. We draw upon reader response theories (Beach, 1993; Rosenblatt, 1978, 1985; Sipe, 2008) to frame children's interactions with picturebooks as *transactions* in which both the reader and the text's meaning are potentially transformed through the encounter. Rosenblatt (1978), in fact, recognizes that through such transactions, a new text is constructed—a metaphorical text comprised of new meaning and understanding, which she calls a *poem*. She explains that this kind of poem "must be thought of as an event in time" (p. 12) as opposed to conventional understandings of a poem as a written or spoken text.

The pedagogical strategy known as the interactive read-aloud is particularly helpful in facilitating students' transactions with picturebooks. Interactive picturebook read-alouds support language acquisition through increased peer interaction providing opportunities for students to turn and talk about their responses to the text. As opposed to the kind of read-aloud where the teacher reads aloud a text to a silent audience, interactive read-alouds allow the teacher to demonstrate via questions and modeling how one makes sense of the text while reading (Burkins & Croft, 2010). During interactive read-alouds, Fountas and Pinnell (2006) encourage teachers to focus on how one makes meaning "within the text," "about the text," and "beyond the text" (Fountas & Pinnell, 2006, p. 33). Students' language acquisition is further supported as teachers pause periodically from reading aloud the book to ask for student responses. Usually, these discussions aim to develop students' understandings of the word and the world (Freire & Macedo, 1987) as they make intertextual and real-life connections or disconnections to the text, hear the connections and disconnections of others, and are encouraged to manipulate the text demonstrating their own agency and imagination. Since many EBs come from different backgrounds, the visual narratives and content of picturebooks may connect with their backgrounds more than oral or written communication.

Methods

Site, Participants, and Context

Benjamin Franklin Elementary School is 25 miles outside New York City. According to the New York State Education Department (2015), of the school's 439 students, 89% are Latinx, 8% White, 2% African American, and 1% Pacific Islander. At Benjamin Franklin, 30% of the student body receive English as a New Language services and 88% of the students come from economically disadvantaged households as defined by reduced and free lunch figures; 73% of the students are eligible for free lunch and 15% are eligible for reduced-price lunch.

Benjamin Franklin has been a professional development school partnered with a local college for over ten years, giving undergraduate and graduate teacher candidates in the college's School of Education the opportunity to work with K–5 students at Benjamin Franklin. As a full-service community school, the primary focus of the school experience is on meeting the developmental needs of the students. As Ferrara and Santiago (2014) explain, "Community schools garner the resources of the community through partnership with social service agencies or nonprofit organizations to provide a network of easily-accessible programs at the school site" (para. 3). With a focus on the whole child, Benjamin Franklin School provides afterschool enrichment programs, offers English Language classes for parents and community members in the evenings, and has available for students an on-site health center and a full-time social worker. Part of the professional development school partnership includes the literacy specialist practicum course held each Monday from 4:20–7:00 over 14 weeks as part of the afterschool program at Benjamin Franklin.

In the spring of 2016, 13 third, fourth, and fifth graders were partnered individually with a literacy specialist candidate. The students' native language was Spanish. Some students were at the speech emergence stage of language learning where they typically responded with single-sentences; others were at the intermediate fluency stage, responding to texts and teacher questions with multiple sentences, drawing on their inferential thinking, and building a strategic approach to texts (Perie, 2008). Students in the state where this afterschool program took place and who identify as speaking a language other than English at home take a formal English as a Second Language Achievement Test. Information about students' language acquisition was sought out but not always confirmed by the school. As such, the professor and candidates used the WIDA Can Do Descriptors to help identify students' language acquisition levels and support instruction-ally purposeful academic language. In addition, suggested activities from Krashen and Terrell (1995) were used to facilitate language with students, including con-ducting book talks with peers, encouraging predictions with students who had characteristics of the speech emergence stage of second language acquisition, and paraphrasing, outlining, and comparing and contrasting with students at the intermediate fluency stage of second language acquisition.

While the students were Latinx, native Spanish speakers, from working-class homes, the literacy specialist candidates were mostly White, middle-class, native English-speaking women in their early 20s. They prepared reading, writing, and word study lessons each week with an emphasis on literacy as a social prac-tice (Lewis, 2001; Street, 1999) and culturally relevant pedagogy (Moll, Amanti, Neff, & Gonzalez, 1992; Wlodkowski & Ginsberg, 1995). The practicum was not designed to remediate. Rather, the goal of the partnership through the course was to build on students' strengths where their lived experiences were an intellectual resource. Each session began with students and candidates seated on the rug for an interactive read-aloud session with an emphasis on narratives of courage, compas-sion, empathy, and belonging. In particular, texts were selected to support students to see themselves in the stories and to springboard students' own narratives. Can-didates were encouraged to learn from and provide space for students' own rich storytelling traditions (Campano, 2007). The literacy specialist candidates were encouraged to ask questions during interactive read-alouds, particularly follow-up questions such as "why do you think?" and "how do you know?" to support stu-dents to say more about their thinking. In addition, candidates were encouraged to rehearse their lessons with particular emphasis on the clarity of their language choices to best support the students' language development. Candidates worked together in small groups for planning and teaching purposes.

In addition to demonstrating their knowledge and skills with regards to plan-ning and implementing literacy instruction, the literacy specialist candidates were expected to apply their growing knowledge of second language acquisition theory to their planning and teaching and to draw on the full linguistic support of all four language processes—reading, writing, speaking, and listening. This was empha-sized across their literacy specialist program but specifically targeted in a course titled Literacy Teaching with English Language Learners. The full spectrum of linguistic support through multiple language processes enables EBLs to enjoy and make sense of grade-level books they are reading and that are read aloud to them (Gibbons, 2009). In particular, the literacy specialist candidates were expected to make academic language more comprehensible (Cummins, 1981) and to garner students' attention to linguistic input through texts that were compelling and that would catch and sustain student interest (Crawford & Krashen, 2007; Mah, 2014).

With guidance from the professor, candidates were considerate of contextual support through their text selection, instructional language, use of questions, gestures, and body language, and in the feedback they provided students.

Data Collection

Data was collected during interactive read-alouds of picturebooks and during teacher candidates' work with bilingual learners during small-group instruction. Interactive read-alouds involved the professor and teacher candidates modeling their thinking about the books while reading, asking students to respond to the text while it was being read aloud, and periodically asking students to discuss their responses to the book with peers. In this way, both students' and teachers' voices were part of the literacy engagement. Field notes were composed by the professor following the sessions. In addition, student work samples were collected from students and reflections were collected from teacher candidates for analysis.

Data Analysis

Using tenets of grounded theory (Glaser & Strauss, 1967) and a process of analytic induction, we engaged in an iterative process of independently examining data for emerging themes, then discussed findings and emerging hypotheses, revisited the data for additional or contradictory cases, and finally revisited and revised themes accordingly. We examined student language and their own illustrations to better understand their transactions with text, particularly the visual images. We then noted the ways in which the readers were transformed by the texts and the ways in which the texts were transformed by the readers.

Participants

In this chapter, we highlight the transactions of four bilingual learners, two boys and two girls, in the afterschool program. Spanish was the first language of all of the students. Both boys, Andre and Miguel, exhibited characteristics of Emerging language acquisition (WIDA ELP 2), while the girls, Yannelly and Ruth, used English more characteristic of the Developing (WIDA ELP 3) and Expanding (WIDA ELP 4) stage of second language acquisition.

Andre was a fourth-grade boy and the first student to arrive each week and the last one to leave each session. He often arrived at least 20 minutes early and flipped through the pages of a book on the rug while waiting for others to arrive. He played with his own hand-drawn characters from one of his favorite T.V. shows, *Yo-Kai Watch*, and could often be found creating dialogue between these pieces of art. When asked about setting rules for our work together, Andre stated that teachers and students should always start out by asking each other how their days were. Andre was interested in drawing existing characters from the stories he enjoyed but he had also written ten of his own comic books about a brave character, Super Jeff, "a superhero who fights bad guys."

Miguel was also a fourth grader at Benjamin Franklin Elementary School. He had two older sisters and one younger brother. His two sisters lived "back home" in Guatemala and he lived with his parents and younger brother. Miguel began learning English in second grade and he explained that many of his family members have a difficult time speaking English. Miguel also shared, "I normally read at home alone and sometimes my parents will listen to me read but it is hard for them to understand." Miguel explained that he enjoys learning more in a group setting and learns through having conversations with his peers and his teacher.

Ruth was a fifth-grade girl who lived with her parents, two younger siblings, aunt, uncle, and cousins. Ruth preferred books to movies and loved reading when she has the freedom to choose the topic. She explained that she uses reading to "tune out what's around me." She enjoyed fantasy stories and comic strips because "they are different from my life." During read-alouds, Ruth was always attentive with her eyes locked on the reader and the story. She was often the first one to speak whenever asked to "turn and talk" to a partner and she was eager to share with the whole group afterwards.

Melany was also a fifth-grade girl and the oldest of three siblings. She often shared her ideas on the rug during read-alouds. She seemed comfortable with the whole group, in small groups, and in partnerships with a range of students. Melany reported that she enjoyed a variety of genres and liked historical fiction the most. When asked about what she thinks are the qualities she looks for in a book, Melany responded, "something that shows character's reactions."

Picturebook Selection

The picturebooks shared with students were selected by the course professor as well as by the teacher candidates. Picturebooks were chosen based on powerful character development, compelling social issues, and characters and contexts that represent diverse society. Text selections built upon one another to strengthen thematic networks of meaning within and across the texts. In addition, consideration was given to picturebooks that have won prestigious awards for their illustrations. Such awards include the Caldecott Award (best illustrated children's book), the Pura Belpré Award (best illustrated children's book by and/or about Latinx), and the Coretta Scott King Award (best illustrated children's book by and/or about African Americans) each given annually by the American Library Association. The picturebooks selected were *Last Stop on Market Street* (de la Peña, 2015), *Drum Dream Girl* (Engle, 2015), *A Chair for My Mother* (Williams, 1982), *The Table Where Rich People Sit* (Baylor, 1992), *Wings* (Myers, 2000), and *When the Horses Ride By: Children in the Time of War* (Greenfield, 2006).

The following sections reflect the transactions bilingual learners had with picturebooks from the text set that demonstrate the ways the pictures played a key role in students' use of language and in their strategic approach to make meaning within and beyond the texts. In particular, the students used the texts' illustrations to monitor their emerging understandings by using metacognitive strategies to assimilate new information from the picturebooks and to create new meaning. In addition, students were then encouraged to use their own art making process to further transact with the picturebooks and to verbalize their understandings with one another.

Mediating Meaning-Making: Deepening Understanding through Illustrations

Picturebooks, and specifically picturebook illustrations, provide rich resources for powerful transactions between student and text to construct poems of new meaning. Andre and Miguel were particularly engaged during the read aloud of *The Last Stop on Market Street* (de la Peña, 2015), selected for its themes of finding beauty in unexpected places and for the opportunities to take notice of details that are unstated in print but revealed through the illustrations. The book provides space for readers to make inferences and encourages readers to look back to remind themselves who characters are referring to and the relationships between characters.

> *As the teacher came to the end of the book, the illustrations depicted characters that were mentioned earlier in the text by name but had not been illustrated yet.*
>
> Andre: Wait. Who are they? *(referring to faces of characters that have not appeared before in the book)*
>
> Teacher: *Great wondering, Andre. Any thoughts?*
>
> Miguel: *I think it's the people from before (mentioned in the text).*
>
> Teacher: *I wonder if we can look back in the text for some ideas about who they might be. (Andre and Miguel helped the teacher look back in the book to identify the characters whose names come several pages before their illustrations do.)*
>
> Teacher: *Wow, in this book neither the author nor the illustrator give it all away. We have to work hard to go back and forth to notice details in the words and the illustrations and sometimes that means looking back or looking ahead.*

Because the illustrations in this picturebook both complement and enhance—rather than symmetrically support—the story narrated in the written text, a conventional emphasis on the written language for bilingual students' comprehension would most likely achieve limited success. Yet, by suggesting that the unnamed characters could be "the people from before," Miguel astutely discovered a likely answer, using the illustrations as a mediating pathway back to what was stated earlier in the book. Thus, both the meanings of the image and the text on the previous page were transformed for the boys through this transaction.

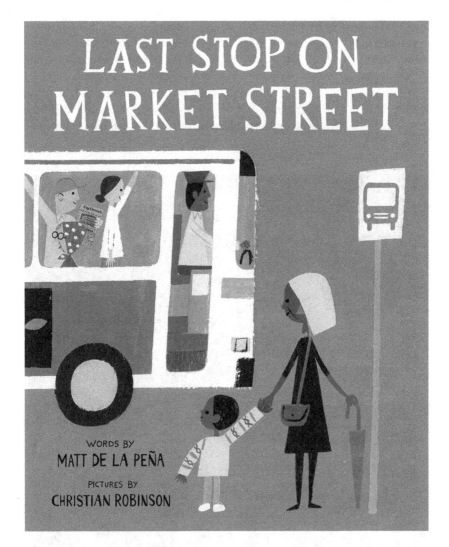

FIGURE 8.1 *Last Stop on Market Street*

Additionally, proficient readers monitor their comprehension of texts and ask questions to confirm their understanding and to voice confusion. The illustration of characters that were introduced much earlier in the text by name only, offered an opportunity for Andre to pause, take note of his (mis)understanding, and to verbalize his confusion since the print on the page did not reveal who the characters were. This, in turn, provided an opportunity for Miguel's voice to emerge and to support Andre's reading process. Transacting first with the illustration and then with the text as a whole fostered discussion and the reinforcement of a reading strategy that all of the students could apply to other texts moving forward.

Meanwhile, both Melany and Ruth were particularly interested in *Drum Dream Girl: How One Girl's Courage Changed Music* (Engle, 2015), which tells the tale of a young girl growing up in Havana during the 1930s, a time when society shunned the idea of female drummers.

FIGURE 8.2 *Drum Dream Girl: How One Girl's Courage Changed Music*

The picturebook was selected for its Latinx-centered storyline to support students to make connections with the characters, setting, and their own funds of knowledge (Moll et al., 1992). It was also used to build on themes of courage and belonging that became central to the literacy engagements each week. The professor selected a page for discussion where a drum with wings is caged. While Ruth emphasized the bravery of the main character to go against societal expectations of girls, Melany explained her own disconnection to that bravery. This was an unanticipated line of discussion.

Teacher:	*Let's look closely at this page.*
Teacher reads aloud:	*"even though everyone kept reminding her that girls on the island of music had never played drums." Let's stop on this page because I noticed that the drums have wings on them and are locked in a cage. Any thoughts about what that might mean?*
Ruth:	*It's like the drum is like a bird. It wants to fly away.*
Melany:	*The drum is a bird trapped in a cage.*
Teacher:	*I notice that the girl is looking up at the drum in the cage. It looks like she is longing for the drum. Like above all things she wants to play the drums but she's not allowed.*
Ruth:	*I think it took a lot of bravery for her to play the drums even when nobody wanted her to.*
Melany:	*I don't think I could do that. I don't think I'm brave like that.*
Teacher:	*What do you mean?*
Melany:	*I mean I couldn't do that if I was told I couldn't.*

In the excerpt above, Melany's disconnection with the drum dream girl's bravery extended Ruth's reflection on the character. Both of their conclusions—Ruth's about the story's protagonist and Melany's about herself—grew from their transaction with the illustrations, rather than the words on the page. Guided by the teacher, both girls were able to extend their understanding of the book's themes by reflecting on the visual image of the drum.

A key reading strategy to aid students with comprehension of text often emphasized by literacy educators and supported through proficient reader research and schema theory (Anderson & Pearson, 1984; Narvaez, 2002) is the notion of making connections with the text. While making connections helps readers be more actively engaged and focused while reading (Keene & Zimmerman, 1997; Tovani, 2000), so too can disconnections with the text. Jones and Clarke (2007) posited that overemphasizing text-to-self connections can have an adverse effect in which students disengage with the text as well as have limited opportunities to build understanding of their own lives. Thus, valuing disconnections alongside connections affords students a more robust literature-based learning experience.

While connections were falsely assumed as the central driver of understanding in *Drum Dream Girl*, disconnections were assumed in the reading of the illustrated poetry collection *When the Horses Ride By: Children in the Time of War* by Eloise Greenfield.

FIGURE 8.3 *When the Horses Ride By: Children in the Time of War*

Cover image from: When the Horses Ride By: Children in the Time of War. Poems © by Eloise Greenfield; Illustration © by Jan Spivey Gilchrist. Permission arranged with Lee & Low Books Inc., New York, NY 10016.

This book was selected by a teacher candidate who wanted to incorporate poetry as well as historical topics students identified in their interest inventories. The teacher candidate was also a history major and was dedicated to including books on social injustice in her small-group instruction. The following transcript is from small-group instruction led by the teacher candidate:

Teacher: *In each of these poems, we are going to see how the words and the illustrations tell us more. We're going to notice what we see, think, and wonder about both the words and the pictures.*

Ruth: *It's like war is about not listening.*

Teacher: *Ah. I see the poet uses the word "listen" to talk to us as the readers but maybe she uses that word to also explain how in war people don't listen to each other. What about the illustrations might also show us that?*

Ruth: *The kids are whispering to each other.*

Melany: *And the boy is staring out and thinking about planes I think.*

Teacher: *Great job zooming in on the illustrations. What else do you see?*

Ruth: *I see smoke and people from different places.*

Teacher: *How do you know?*

Ruth: *That women is dressed differently and that man has a scarf on. Look, that man is helping another.*

Melany: *And those boys are talking. One looks surprised.*

Teacher: *Let's look at the color choices of the illustrator.*

Ruth: *The kids are in black and white. The wars are in yellow and green and blue.*

Melany: *I think the bigger pictures are today.*

Teacher: *How do you know?*

Melany: *They look like kids I know.*

In this exchange, the teacher candidate drew the girls' attention to the illustrations but then offered little of her own insights. Rather, she positioned the girls to actively transact with them by asking "How do you know?" to support them to do more of the thinking and speaking. Ruth interpreted the meaning of the poem by centering the conversation around the complex idea that war is about not listening. Both girls then used the illustrations to say more about this interpretation, noting details about the people and surroundings.

In all three exchanges, the students were not only supported to further their strategic approach to understanding texts, but they used language to express their connections, disconnections, wonderings, and confusion. The illustrations in the picturebooks were not merely mirror supports of the print, rather the illustrations extended the narratives by providing new visual information that led the students to verbalize their understandings.

Employing Illustrations to Create New Texts

While the students' understandings of text and themselves were transformed through their transactions with picturebook illustrations, they in turn employed illustrations to create new texts of meaning. Melany chose to create a watercolor to express what she most wanted to remember about *When the Horses Ride By*. When asked about her choices as an artist she explained, "I wanted to paint this boy's face. I thought I would try and I wanted to remember the poem because of the boy." Melany then came back to the idea that some of the children in the illustrations look like "kids I know." In this sense, she understood the power of an illustration for extending meaning of a text.

Ruth employed art in a similar manner. During a read aloud of *The Table Where Rich People Sit* (Baylor, 1994), students were instructed at stopping points throughout the text to take notes on "thinking squares" (sticky notes) to keep track of plot points to help them determine a central message or theme. Without prompting or modeling, Ruth constructed her thinking squares using the illustrator's technique of swirling lines to represent the major plot points.

This self-directed means of strengthening her understanding demonstrated the ways in which Ruth now felt comfortable recording her thinking through words and pictures. When asked about her choice of jotting in this way, Ruth explained that she knew she would remember the way the illustrations were drawn and it

FIGURE 8.4 Melany's Watercolor in Response to *When the Horses Ride By*

FIGURE 8.5 Ruth's Jottings in Response to *The Table Where Rich People Sit*

would help her make sense of the author's message. She further described that the use of color and the swirling lines made her feel peaceful which helped her connect to the mood of the story and the theme of the book that we are rich in many ways in life.

Drawing from their own reading experience with *The Last Stop on Market Street*, Andre and Miguel chose to write, draw and narrate a collaborative comic book that used the technique of requiring the reader to make inferences across the words and illustrations.

FIGURES 8.6 Comic Book Pages Composed by Andre and Miguel

FIGURES 8.7 Comic Book Pages Composed by Andre and Miguel

Following their writing and illustrating, Miguel and Andre used an iPad to create a movie of their comic by narrating the story for readers going beyond the print they provided in the frames and instead they narrated the actions and characters' feelings that their illustrations portrayed. For the panels above, Miguel and Andre narrated the following:

Super Jeff and Dead Pool are at Playland having a wonderful day. They were so excited to ride the big log flume but when they were going down they screamed. Then,

Deadpool was about to fall off the ride. Then they saw something. I think it's a big balloon. Super Jeff and Dead Pool jump off the ride. They saw their friend Ironman in the sky listening to music.

In each of the three examples, the students used their previous transactions with picturebooks to generate their own texts through watercolor, sketching, and comic book drawing and moviemaking thereby transmediating the texts (Siegel, 1995). This iterative process of reading, speaking, listening, and creating extended the opportunities students had to verbalize their process and to learn from one another.

Conclusion

The primary goal of the interactions with the picturebooks selected was to catch and sustain the interest of the students and to further their literacy understandings alongside their language acquisition. While more explicit instruction on the elements of visual literacy could have been employed to further students' academic language about what they were noticing in the illustrations, the examples provided demonstrate the ways in which students made meaning even with limited explicit instruction. The selection of *picturebooks*, rather than picture books or illustrated books, was intentional and furthered student thinking and talking within and beyond the texts. Central to the text selection were the overarching strengths of hope, courage, and belonging exemplified by the characters that served as entry points for conversation. These texts were found to be particularly supportive of language development for the emerging bilingual students in the afterschool program. The structure of the sessions was critical to both the literacy development and language acquisition of the bilingual learners in the sessions. The use of interactive read-alouds and arts-based opportunities to create new texts allowed for increased interaction among students furthering dialogue about their understandings of the texts.

Picturebook illustrations do not facilitate bilingual learners' language acquisition simply because they support the written text. Indeed, when the relationship between illustrations and text go assuredly beyond the symmetrical, they provide bountiful pathways for students to develop profound insights about both the text they are reading and themselves as people. We argue that the illustrations are rich resources for mediating students' meaning-making of texts and the medium through which students create new texts. In sharing these findings, we hope educators add quality picturebook illustrations to the criteria used to select instructional materials for bilingual learners.

Some Resources for Finding Quality Picturebooks

American Library Association—www.ala.org

- The world's oldest and largest library association, publishes annual "Best of" lists in different genres.

Association for Library Service to Children—www.ala.org/alsc/

- Awards several prestigious honors in children's literature, including the Caldecott Medal, the Newbery Medal, the Pura Belpre Medal, the Geisel Medal, and the Sibert Medal.

Children's Literature Assembly—www.childrensliteratureassembly.org

- An affiliate of the National Council of Teachers of English, publishes annual lists of Notable Children's Books in the English Language Arts.

Cooperative Children's Book Center—https://ccbc.education.wisc.edu/

- A comprehensive resource that compiles theme- and topic-based recommended booklists, publishes "Book of the Week" reviews, and awards the Charlotte Zolotow Award.

School Library Journal—www.slj.com

- The world's largest reviewer of books for children and young adults.

The Classroom Bookshelf—www.theclassroombookshelf.com

- A School Library Journal Blog, co-written by the chapter's authors, dedicated to reviewing recently published children's books and providing ideas and resources for incorporating them into K-8 classrooms.

The Horn Book—www.hbook.com

- The premiere journal for reviews of children's and young adult literature.

We Need Diverse Books—http://weneeddiversebooks.org/where-to-find-diverse-books/

- A grassroots organization that promotes the publishing of children's literature with diverse characters and putting those books in children's hands.

Note

1 The names of the school and students are pseudonyms.

Children's Literature Cited

Baylor, B. (1994). *The table where rich people sit*. New York, NY: Aladdin Paperbacks.

De La Peña, M. (2015). *The last stop on market street*. New York, NY: G.P. Putnam's Sons Books for Young Readers.

Engle, M. (2015). *Drum dream girl: How one girl's courage changed music*. Boston, MA: HMH Books for Young Readers.

Greenfield, E. (2006). *When the horses ride by: Children in times of war*. New York, NY: Lee and Low Books.

Myers, C. (2000). *Wings*. New York, NY: Scholastic Press.

Williams, V. (1982). *A chair for my mother*. New York, NY: Scholastic.

References

Albers, P. (2008). Theorizing visual representation in children's literature. *Journal of Literacy Research, 40,* 163–200.

Allen, P. (1989). Analytic and experiential aspects of second language teaching. *RELC Journal: A Journal of Language Teaching and Research in Southeast Asia, 20*(1), 1–19.

Anderson, R. C., & Pearson, P. D. (1984). A schema-thematic view of basic processes in reading comprehension. In P. D. Pearson, R. Barr, M. L. Kamil, & P. Mosenthal (Eds.), *Handbook of reading research* (pp. 255–291). New York, NY: Longman.

Arizpe, E., & Styles, M. (2004). *Children reading pictures: Interpreting visual texts*. London: Routledge/Falmer.

Beach, R. (1993). *A teacher's introduction to reader-response theories*. Urbana, IL: National Council of Teachers of English.

Burkins, J. M., & Croft, M. M. (2010). *Preventing misguided reading: New strategies for guided reading teachers*. Newark, DE: International Reading Association.

Campano, G. (2007). Honoring students' stories. *Educational Leadership, 65*(2), 48–54.

Cappiello, M.A., & Dawes, E.T. (2012). *Teaching with text sets*. Huntington Beach, CA: Shell Education.

Crawford, J., & Krashen, S. (2007). *English learners in American classrooms: 101 questions * 101 answers*. New York, NY: Scholastic.

Cummins, J. (1981). The role of primary language development in promoting educational success for language minority students. In California Department of Education (Ed.), *Schooling and language minority students: A theoretical framework* (pp. 3–49). Los Andres: Evaluation, Dissemination and Assessment Center, California State University.

Ferrara, J., & Santiago, E. (2014). *Community schools: Whole child education in action. ASCD in service*. Retrieved from http://inservice.ascd.org/community-schools-whole-child-education-in-action/.

Fountas, I. C., & Pinnell, G. S. (2006). *Teaching for comprehending and fluency: Thinking, talking, and writing about reading, K-8*. Portsmouth, NH: Heinemann.

Freire, P., & Macedo, D. (1987). *Literacy: Reading the word and the world*. Westport, CT: Praeger.

Gibbons, P. (2009). *English learners, academic literacy, and thinking: Learning in the challenge zone*. Portsmouth, NH: Heinemann.

Glaser, B. G., & Strauss, A. L. (1967). *The discovery of grounded theory: Strategies for qualitative research*. Chicago, IL: Aldine Publishing Company.

Hadaway, N. L., Vardell, S. M., & Young, T. A. (2002). *Literature-based instruction with English language learners, K-12*. Boston, MA: Allyn & Bacon Longman.

Hadaway, N. L., & Young, T. A. (2009). Dispelling or reinforcing myths? Learning a new language as portrayed in children's picture books. *Language Arts, 86*(3), 165–177.

Jewett, C., & Kress, G. (Eds.) (2005). *Multimodal literacy*. New York, NY: Peter Lang.

Jones, S., & Clarke, L. (2007). Disconnections: Pushing readers beyond connections and toward the critical. *Pedagogies: An International Journal*, 2(2), 95–115.

Keene, E. O., & Zimmerman, S. (2007). *Mosaic of thought: The power of comprehension strategy instruction* (2nd ed.). Portsmouth, NH: Heinemann.

Kiefer, B. (1995). *The potential of picturebooks: From visual literacy to aesthetic understanding*. Englewood Cliffs, NJ: Prentice Hall.

Kist, W. (2005). *New literacies in action: Teaching and learning in multiple media*. New York, NY: Teachers College Press.

Krashen, S., & Terrell, T. (1995). *The natural approach: Language acquisition in the classroom*. New York, NY: Phoenix ELT.

Lado, A. (2012). *Teaching beginner ELLs using picture books*. Thousand Oaks, CA: Corwin.

Leland, C., Lewison, M., & Harste, J. (2013). *Teaching children's literature: It's critical!* New York, NY: Routledge.

Lewis, C. (2001). *Literacy practices as social acts: Power, status, and cultural norms in the classroom*. New York, NY: Routledge.

Mah, G. (2014). Worlds possible beyond English. In L. Bridges (Ed.), *Open a world of possible: Real stories about the joy and power of reading*. New York, NY: Scholastic.

Marantz, K. (1977, October). The picture book as art object: A call for balanced reviewing. *Wilson Library Bulletin*, 148–151.

Moll, L. C., Amanti, C., Neff, D., & Gonzalez, N. (1992). Funds of knowledge for teaching: Using a qualitative approach to connect homes and classrooms. *Theory Into Practice*, *XXX1*(2).

Montelongo, J. A., Duran, R., & Hernandez, A. (2013). English-Spanish cognates in picture books: Toward a vocabulary curriculum for Latino ELLs. *Bilingual Research Journal*, 36(2), 244-259. DOI: 10.1080/15235882.2013.818074

Narvaez, D. (2002). Individual differences that influence reading comprehension. In C. C. Block & M. Pressley (Eds.), *Comprehension instruction: Research-based best practices* (pp. 158–175). New York, NY: Guilford.

New London Group (2000). A pedagogy of multiliteracies: Designing social futures. In B. Cope & M. Kalantzis (Eds.), *Multiliteracies: Literacy learning and the design of social futures*, (pp. 9–38). South Yarra, Australia: MacMillan.

New York State Education Department (2015). *School at a glance: Student enrollment data*. Albany, NY: New York State Education Department. Retrieved from data.nysed.gov.

Nikolajeva, M., & Scott, C. (2001). *How picturebooks work*. New York, NY: Garland Publishing.

Nodelman, P. (1988). *Words about pictures: The narrative art of children's picture books*. Athens, GA: University of Georgia Press.

Olshansky, B. (2008). *The power of pictures: Creating pathways to literacy through art*. San Francisco, CA: Jossey-Bass.

Perie, M. (2008). A guide to understanding and developing performance-level descriptors. *Educational Measurement: Issues and Practice*, 27(4), 15–29.

Player, G. Ngo, L, Campano, G., & Ghiso, M. P. (2016). The community researchers project: The role of care in critical work. In G. Campano, M. P. Ghiso, & L. Rosenblatt (Eds.) (1978). *The reader, the text, the poem: The transactional theory of the literary work*. Carbondale, IL: Southern Illinois Press.

Rosenblatt, L. M. (1978). *The reader, the text, the poem: The transactional theory of the literary work*. Carbondale, IL: Southern Illinois Press.

Rosenblatt, L. M. (1985). Viewpoints: Transaction versus interaction—A terminological rescue operation. *Research in the Teaching of English, 19*(1), 96–107.

Siegel, M. (1995). More than words: The generative power of transmediation for learning. *Canadian Journal of Education, 20*(4), 455–475.

Sipe, L. R. (2001). Picturebooks as aesthetic objects. *Literacy Teaching and Learning: An International Journal of Early Reading and Writing, 6*, 23–42.

Sipe, L. R. (2008). *Storytime: Young children's literary understanding in the classroom.* New York, NY: Teachers College Press.

Street, B. (1999). The meanings of literacy. In D. Wagner et al. (Eds.), *Literacy: An international handbook.* (pp. 34–40). Boulder, CO: Westview Press.

Tovani, C. (2000). *I read it, but I don't get it: Comprehension strategies for adolescent readers.* Portland, ME: Stenhouse.

Wlodkowski, R. J., & M. B. Ginsberg. (1995). *Diversity and motivation: Culturally responsive teaching.* San Francisco, CA: Jossey-Bass.

Wolfenbarger, C. D., & Sipe, L. R. (2007). A unique visual and literary art form: Recent research on picturebooks. *Language Arts, 84*, 273–280.

9

CONSTRUCTING STORIES USING LANGUAGE AND DIGITAL ART

Voices of Multilingual Learners

Sally Brown

A busy hum trickled across the table as students designed digital art and selected the perfect words to tell their stories. Linda and Jade eyeballed one another's pages as they worked. Linda leaned over and said, "Hey Jade, you know writing like this makes me want to write, write, write. I just get so excited thinking about what I am making, like this one [pointing to grandmother image] about my abuela. . . . I keep thinking about it even when I get home. I think about what I will make tomorrow and what to write." Linda responded, "Yeah, I get it. Me too. The pictures we making keep me thinking. I think and think about what faces so [I can] show how I feel in my story. You know, it puts me in my book."

Introduction

In this chapter, I present a pedagogical strategy using arts-based work to develop an understanding of how multilingual learners use oral and written language in concert with digital art to construct stories based in cultural experiences. Included are the details of a year-long qualitative study that investigated the literacy development of 12 multilingual third graders (home languages—Spanish, German, and Vietnamese) as they engaged in collaborative dialogue while constructing their own digital art to create stories through a cloud-based platform called StoryJumper (www.storyjumper.com/). The research was guided by the following question: How did a group of multilingual learners use language and digital art to express their culture in narrative stories? All names of participants are pseudonyms.

Connections to Theory

New Literacies Studies (NLS) provides a sociocultural framework that focuses on the social, cultural, and historical perspectives of communication in the 21st century (Barton & Hamilton, 1998). These new forms of literacy may include "generating, communicating, and negotiating encoded meanings by providing a range of new or more widely accessible resource possibilities for making meaning" (Lankshear & Knobel, 2011, p. 56). In fact, these literacy practices are explicitly linked to culture as people transact with texts to construct knowledge in their world (Zentella, 2005). For example, culture influences the way a book is read, a story is written or told, and how an image is crafted.

In addition, interactions among people adds to our understanding of the ways in which social practices, local literacy patterns influenced by the presence of technologies (Scribner & Cole, 1981), nurture academic growth in children. Language is used as a means to participate in community events. Sharing the cognitive workload with others through dialogue is one way students have to actively construct meaning while producing cultural artifacts like stories (Rogoff, 2003). Students learning a new language frequently manipulate materials during these interactions with others in order to generate original productions (Knobel & Lankshear, 2008).

As multilingual students engage with their English-only peers, they simultaneously cultivate both their written and oral development of English. Telling stories does not occur in isolation. It usually involves oral rehearsal through peer-to-peer interactions (Samway, 2006). As such, composing incorporates talk where students make decisions about details and events that become part of their stories.

Furthermore, when multimodal aspects of meaning-making (such as digital art) are added to the authoring process, learners use oral language to talk about the best ways to represent their points of view. Artistic elements like visual design cause children to move beyond the words of the text (or written language) and push them to consider the ways in which images convey additional layers of meaning. As students engage in this process, they learn to connect various aspects of literacy, art, and language development for communication purposes (Edwards-Groves, 2011). Writing, talk, and art become tools for thinking.

Research Study

The experiences and artifacts in this chapter represent the data from a year-long qualitative study in a Title 1, urban elementary school with a 70% free/reduced lunch rate. The third-grade multilingual participants were 12 of 24 students in the classroom. While the classroom teacher taught whole group literacy lessons, I offered students additional literacy instruction in small groups where students negotiated their text productions through technology, content, and language. Small-group interactions were videotaped, transcribed, and documented through field notes and included student interviews. The digital art stories were collected as work samples.

Digital storytelling software (StoryJumper) afforded students the freedom to create from scratch or locate culturally relevant images from the Internet (using a Google search). The nature of the software gave rise to students creating speech bubbles that allowed characters to talk. Students carefully placed design elements such as character faces (happy, sad, eyes open/closed, skin tone, etc.), clothing, and gender together to produce images or art that matched their ideas. This was followed by the addition of words to the story.

Findings

Over the course of the school year, the multilingual students composed 26 books that incorporated text and digital art. Their books revolved around four themes: friends and family, holidays, popular culture (television shows and video games), and animals. Each student incorporated cultural perspectives that represented their storied life experiences. The stories were intentionally written for specific purposes which the students deemed important such as a birthday present or to teach someone else about a significant life event (Yoon, 2013). Overwhelmingly, agency stood out as the students had control over the story topics and artwork. Upon conclusion of the analyses, two overarching themes emerged from the data: art first and I am an author. Each of these themes is presented in detail below.

Art First

All 12 of the participants began each story by first designing their digital art followed by the construction of a narrative text. Hai's (an English newcomer) book exemplified this process. He began his story, *Robot Man*, (Figure 9.1) by constructing a series of four related images one after the other. Hai worked quietly but methodically as he selected two specific robots from the available clip art. He utilized each of the images on every page, but changed the background and placement of the robots. When asked about his process, Hai responded, "Need them [robots] all page. I make them different place." Here, Hai developed knowledge about the graphic space of the page and saw ways in which images produce or add to meaning (Kenner & Kress, 2003).

After completing the digital images in the four-page sequence, Hai went back to the first page and began "reading" his images and adding text. In other words, he was constructing meaning visually first (Albers, 2007). In this case he said the words aloud as he typed, "Two robots" on page one. Hai knew how to spell the number "two" and the word "robots." As he moved to page two, Hai thought about descriptors that could be added to assign meaning to the changing picture. Then, he consulted Javier to assist with spelling the word "down." Javier also helped with the spelling of "house" on page three. Another peer, Jason, interrupted the two boys and said, "Hey you have to put the apostrophe on there." Hai seemed unsure and stated, "You do it." Jason pulled Hai's computer over and added the punctuation mark. Hai smiled and continued adding text. This talking and listening was a negotiation or collaborative approach to learning (Walsh,

FIGURE 9.1   Sequence of Images From Hai's Book.

2010). The book was simple, yet reflected Hai's interests and development of English (Gordon, 2007). This really broadened the notion of what it meant to be an author and moved away from traditional views that locked students into writing only or writing first (Kuby & Rucker, 2016).

Using a multimodal framework for understanding the nature of the students' work, the visual mode (or digital artwork) assisted in questioning how students represent their experiences when engaged in this work first. In this study, students signified their cultural understandings of objects and people by assigning features to represent the ways they understood the world (Kenner & Kress, 2003). For example, primary characters were built based on family members' traits and actions. Students took advantage of the available digital tools to convey their role as sign makers representing their view of the world.

In Figure 9.2, Valeria created a book, *Paloma and the Trip to Mexico*, for her friend Paloma who had never been to Mexico. Valeria's intent was to teach Paloma about Mexico since she was from the Dominican Republic. In this case, Valeria worked over the course of a month to meticulously create the artwork for her story about Mexico. She wanted the images to communicate her cultural understandings of her country and family. She chose background scenes that depicted both the rural and urban nature of Mexico along with animals that could be found in the surrounding areas like chickens, horses, turtles, geese, and dogs. The careful development of the story's characters resulted in different facial expressions for each one along with clothing and hair appropriate for the character. The objects were designed and placed to form a particular cultural perspective about Mexico. Even though the artwork took much time and effort on Valeria's part, it was crucial for an authentic representation of her culture and country.

The artwork also served as a scaffold for her written language in English. None of the storyline in Valeria's book took the form of narration. Instead, she chose to tell her story through dialogue after all of the artwork was completed. By this time, she knew who her characters were, the multiple settings in her story, the sequence of events, and how the story ended just by reviewing her pictures. The images set the stage for the "writing" part of the process (Albers, 2007). The characters welcomed Paloma to Mexico and indicated where they were located. The speech bubbles allowed Valeria to establish an ongoing conversation that led to Paloma having a house in Mexico.

When asked about the composing process, Valeria said, "I didn't write too, too much because they were talking [characters], telling about Mexico and you could see from, from pictures I made how beautiful it is. Really nice. I wanted Paloma to see how nice it is in Mexico, so she would want to come there with me." Here, Valeria discussed the importance of her images in her story and placed the dialogue as secondary to meeting the needs of her message to Paloma. However, the character dialogue was central to the actions within the story (Dyson, 2013).

Along with art first, student talk was embedded in the process and influenced the construction of images. For these multilingual learners, the experience was not about creating art first independently and quietly. Instead, it was a socially active constructive process where students (focal participants and their English-dominant peers) conversed with one another about ideas, ways to use the available digital tools, appearance of the artwork, and methods for improving one's images to match the intended effect. These interactions were fluid, collaboratively constructed, and rooted in a cultural context (Larson & Peterson, 2013). Students were able to access the English-speaking world through meaning-making as opposed to being objects of standardized instruction.

Paloma and the Trip to Mexico!

Pages 1–3 No text (Series of images of plane ride).

Page 4—Hi, my name is Valeria (Image—city with police officers).

Page 5—Let's go to the city (Images—girls and family walking on the trail).

Page 6—Meet my grandfather. You can sit down. Let's go for a walk (Image—man and family).

Page 7—Who are you? Mam or miss? (Image—girls, grandfather, horses, and trees).

Page 8—I am Paloma, exploring Mexico (Image of the countryside).

Page 9—Is this Mexico? Yes, it is. (See image to left).

Page 10—You can live with us Paloma. Really, you want me to live with you? I do want to live with you (Image—people and animals at the beach).

Page 11—It is cute in here. I love it (Image—inside of house).

Page 12—Goodnight (Image—sleeping in beds).

Page 13—Where are we going? (Image—grandfather, grandmother, and girl eating at table).

Page 14—We are going to a like Miss Paloma. (Image—people riding on the bus)

Page 15—It is a pretty place for a house (Image— paddling in a canoe).

Page 16—Wow, it looks pretty now (Image of tractor building a house).

Page 17—Wow, it is really pretty (Image—house is complete).

FIGURE 9.2 Valeria's Book.

Eduardo's book, *Animals Live at the Zoo*, and transcript (Figure 9.3) was used to illustrate the need for student talk during the composing process. This story was based on Eduardo's experience visiting a zoo in the U.S. with his family. It was his one and only zoo visit, and therefore he needed peer assistance in representing his encounter accurately. In this case Eduardo was interacting with another English learner, Javier, as well as two English-dominant peers, Tom and Caleb.

The language used in this interaction showcased Eduardo's need for the social aspects of creating artwork that as a result supported writing (Edwards-Groves,

2011). This was particularly true for multilingual learners like Eduardo who learned English at school while negotiating the academic language arts curriculum mandated by the state. Here, Eduardo eagerly used English to engage his peers in order to produce a picture that represented a true fact about a giraffe. His request provided an avenue for him to make sense of the type of tree that is needed in his picture. The meaning that Eduardo focused on was situated in a specific context—his one trip to a zoo (Gee, 2014).

As the interaction continued, Caleb was unsure of Eduardo's initial choice of a tree, and Javier quickly jumped in to help by showing other choices. The boys agreed on tree, and Tom interjected about the placement of the giraffe. Each peer took a contingent stance where they were able to pause, listen attentively, and respond appropriately (Boyd & Galda, 2013). Javier offered an additional suggestion for improvement which was relevant to the context. As a result, Eduardo moved the giraffe closer to the tree. The spoken language created a situation where Eduardo was able to build a support system for authoring (Gee, 2014). Later, Eduardo commented, "I know this page is good. I got help on this one. See my tree. Lots of leaves for giraffe." He appeared to be satisfied with the final image. This graphic means of representing his understanding of giraffes in zoos was governed by the social interaction that guided his revised "drawing" (Yoon, 2013). This conversation was followed by Eduardo independently writing the sentence,

Transcript

Eduardo: Hey, I need help this part. I know I see giraffe at zoo, but what they eat? You know?

Caleb: They eat leaves off trees.

Eduardo: Oh, ok. Let me find a tree. (Looks through clip art.) Caleb, what you think about this? Here? See it?

Caleb: (Looks.) Maybe.

Javier: Let me see. (Leans over to see computer screen.) No, get one with lots of leaves. I will show you. (Touches Eduardo's computer). What about this?

Eduardo: Yeah, that one has lot of green. It is good one. (Inserts tree.)

Tom: (Looks at Eduardo's story). Move that giraffe over. He needs to be next to the tree, so it's like he's eating the leaves.

Eduardo: (Moves giraffe.) How this?

Tom: (Nods). Yea. Good.

FIGURE 9.3 Eduardo's Book and Transcript

"The giraffe was eating leaves." The oral rehearsal with the "drawing" provided the context for writing.

This was a clear example of peers sharing the cognitive load of "generating, extending, and connecting ideas" (Boyd & Galda, 2013, p. 3). Progress in the composing process (artwork + text construction) was intermeshed with language-based interactions among all learners in the classroom. Language (both first and second) allowed students to make sense of their ideas. It helped them negotiate ways to edit and revise pictures and text in order to improve their communication. Drawing or digital art is a legitimate cultural activity for meaning-making (Dyson, 2013). The relationship between drawing and symbols should be interwoven as in this example where students like Eduardo make sense of their experiences and represent them in multimodal forms.

I Am an Author

The second theme encompassed all of who the students were as authors in several ways. First, the multilingual students' cultural experiences were validated as content for published books, and they developed a sense of agency through the all of the choices they enacted. The formal literacy curriculum taught by the classroom teacher required students to respond to district-mandated writing prompts. Students were not given a choice of topics or format for writing. Once provided with freedom of choice for topics and format, the multilingual students opted for personal narratives that closely tied to their cultural experiences. The children were "the agents of their own cultural and social making" (Kuby & Rucker, 2016, p. 13). In other words, students manipulated available materials to create a meaningful text (Gordon, 2007). Trying out new ideas or ways to engage with tools opened up paths for new ways of being and being an author was one possibility (Kuby & Rucker, 2016). These experiences were empowering and seemed to be one reason why students saw themselves as authors.

Mateo provided a case for understanding the ways in which agency was fostered through choice. His book, *Iron Man*, was based on a video game (which was a writing taboo at school) blended with a personal adventure. Mateo inserted himself and his personality into the character of Iron Man. The artwork in his book was key to understanding the storyline as he left much to be understood from the images. Figure 9.4 shows one image from Mateo's book while the text in the second column features his talk about the role of choice in the authoring.

In this case Mateo felt free to bypass the scripted progression of writing in the school curriculum, and instead actively engaged as an illustrator and author in a topic he was passionate about and familiar with from his home experiences (Dyson, 2013). In the dialogue below, Mateo recognized that the Iron Man story had a different purpose and he saw this as an opportunity to capitalize upon his interests. This writing helped Mateo reconfigure his world by enacting or creating possibilities through experimenting with multimodal forms of materials (Kuby & Rucker, 2016). In other words, he was becoming an author on his own terms. It seemed that the freedom to choose writing topics and design digital images created a shift in agency for Mateo as a writer. He appeared to develop more capacity to act as a change agent and make independent decisions. Mateo along with many of the other participants are now able to recognize available resources, and use them to communicate (Fisher, 2010).

Second, the participants truly developed a sense of recognizing themselves as authors. They had a legitimate identity as authors in the official realm of school. The entire production process (brainstorming through talk, drafting, revising, editing, image construction, and publishing) solidified students' identities as capable writers. As Paloma stated, "For once, it [digital storytelling tool] helped me think of why I'm, how I'm successful. I am going to be a writer when I grow up. It kinda made me think that I am a great writer. You know I wrote a book called *Dakota's Journey*." Paloma made a connection between her work with the digital storytelling software and her ability to see herself as an author now and in the future. According to Gee (2014), she is doing Discourse work where she is being recognized as a particular kind of person, a Latina author at an English-dominant

---

Mateo's Talk

Well, I made this book about Iron Man. I am Iron Man. I wanted to go on adventure, but I said I was him in book. It's like, you know from the video game on Xbox. . . . So, I got to write this story with you [researcher] but Mr. B [teacher] would never let me write this. You cannot do it. He would be mad. You have to write about other stuff and this book let me tell my story about myself on a adventure. You see here I go to volcano and get key to go in the secret place and unlock the monsters. It is scary. . . . This [using digital software] helped me be a author. I did not know I could write a book. I did not even want to write a book before. Most times I don't want to write, you know the paper stuff where Mr. B says what you have to do. Plus you don't get to do pictures for Mr. B.

FIGURE 9.4 Mateo's Book and Talk

school where she is able to use "discourse" or language in action to talk about the books she has authored.

Additionally, a pedagogy that affords students choice in the learning process is central to student success as designers and writers. Simply providing students with restrictive writing prompts and limiting the use of digital tools will not have the same result. Instead, teachers must adjust their instruction to embrace a multitude of choices in student learning. For example, it is essential that authentic writing experiences include art forms such as digital images. Multimodal products need to be considered equally worthy along with traditional formats (Albers, 2007; Walsh, 2010). In many instances, schools tend to value literacy topics that are limited by district mandates or teachers. This causes students' cultural backgrounds and art to be overlooked and undervalued. It is through choice that students can develop a sense of agency or empowerment to make decisions and impact their own trajectories as learners (Fisher, 2010).

Conclusion

Language, art, and technology are influential aspects of a 21st-century curriculum when integrated in a culturally responsive manner. Creating a classroom environment where literacy learning takes into account diverse social practices involving respectful interactions with others and cultural tools is not a simple process (Rogoff, 2003). Teachers must guide learning in ways where authenticity is valued and students are encouraged to compose creative texts mediated by their sociocultural environments (Gordon, 2007).

In order to meet the cultural, linguistic, and academic needs of multilingual students, I recommend some practical applications. One, teachers need to remain flexible in allowing students to use multimodal forms to represent their learning (Kenner & Kress, 2003). Written text offers students a limited way of expressing themselves. The value of artwork can often be overlooked, and it is a powerful way to set the stage for writing and learning a new language. Texts often require a number of elements to collectively represent the author's intended meaning and the creativity that art affords (whether digital or not) is significant (Albers, 2007).

In addition, since we know the value of collaborative dialogue in the learning process, it would be beneficial for teachers to organize instructional time where students can enhance their learning through rich dialogue with peers (Edwards-Groves, 2011). Peer support and feedback cannot be underestimated and have a deep impact on the revision process. Writing is a social process that is often negotiated with others (Samway, 2006; Walsh, 2010).

The language and actions of teachers contribute to who students are in the classroom and how they see themselves (Gee, 2014). So, it is critical for teachers to evaluate the ways in which they use language with multilingual learners. It has an impact on identity in terms of academic expectations (such as being an author)

TABLE 9.1 Additional Technology Resources for Multilingual Writers

StoryBird	https://storybird.com/
Little Bird Tales	www.littlebirdtales.com/
ZooBurst	http://zooburst.com/
Tikatok	www.tikatok.com/
Picture Book Maker	www.culturestreet.org.uk/activities/picturebookmaker/

TABLE 9.2 Technology Alternative

If your school lacks technology resources or a connection to the Internet, you can still apply this technique through traditional methods. A writer's workshop approach can be implemented where students regularly have time to talk, write, and draw about topics of their choice. Students can use crayons, markers, and paper to illustrate their stories rather than creating digital art on the computer. Stapling together blank pages will allow students the space to visually design and craft their written texts. In addition, as the teacher you will want to meet individually with students to confer about the content of the stories and English conventions.

as well as the ways in which cultural identities are embraced or rejected by the students themselves. We must ask ourselves who do students have the opportunity to be on a daily basis in the classroom. Are we limiting students or are we opening up new avenues for how they see themselves as learners and cultural beings?

References

Albers, P. (2007). *Finding the artist within: Creating and reading visual texts in the English language arts classroom*. Newark, DE: International Reading Association.

Barton, D., & Hamilton, M. (1998). *Local literacies: Reading and writing in one community*. New York, NY: Routledge.

Boyd, M., & Galda, L. (2013). *Real talk in elementary classrooms: Effective oral language practice*. New York, NY: Guilford Press.

Dyson, A. (2013). *Rewriting the basics: Literacy learning in children's cultures*. New York, NY: Teachers College Press.

Edwards-Groves, C. (2011). The multimodal writing process: Changing practices in contemporary classrooms. *Language and Education, 25*(1), 49–64.

Fisher, R. (2010). Young writers' construction of agency. *Journal of Early Childhood Literacy, 10*(4), 410–429.

Gee, J. (2014). *An introduction to discourse analysis: Theory and method* (4th ed.). New York, NY: Routledge.

Gordon, T. (2007). *Teaching young children a second language*. Westport, CT: Praeger.

Kenner, C., & Kress, G. (2003). The multisemiotic resources of biliterate children. *Journal of Early Childhood Literacy, 3*(2), 179–202.

Knobel, M., & Lankshear, C. (2008). Remix: The art and craft of endless hybridization. *Journal of Adolescent and Adult Literacy, 52*(1), 22–33.

Kuby, C., & Rucker, T. (2016). *Go be a writer! Expanding the curricular boundaries of literacy learning with children.* New York, NY: Teachers College Press.

Lankshear, C., & Knobel, M. (2011). *New literacies: Everyday practices and social learning.* (3rd ed.). New York, NY: Open University Press.

Larson, J., & Peterson, S. (2013). Talk and discourse in formal learning settings. In J. Larson & J. Marsh (Eds.), *The Sage handbook of early childhood literacy* (2nd ed., pp. 501–522). Los Angeles, CA: Sage.

Rogoff, B. (2003). *The cultural nature of human development.* New York, NY: Oxford University Press.

Samway, K. (2006). *When English language learners write: Connecting research to practice, K-8.* Portsmouth, NH: Heinemann.

Scribner, S., & Cole, M. (1981). *The psychology of literacy.* Cambridge, MA: Harvard University Press.

Walsh, M. (2010). Multimodal literacy: What does it mean for classroom practice? *Australian Journal of Language and Literacy, 33*(3), 211–239.

Yoon, H. (2013). Rewriting the curricular script: Teachers and children translating writing practices in a kindergarten classroom. *Research in the Teaching of English, 48*(2), 148–174.

Zentella, A. (2005). Perspectives on language and literacy in Latino families and communities. In A. Zentella (Ed.), *Building on strengths: Language and literacy in Latino families and communities* (pp. 13–30). New York, NY: Teachers College Press.

Questions for Reflection and Further Applications for Practice

In the Heights: Lifting Potential, Expanding Possibilities

Vivian Maria Poey

> There is a deep connection between assessment and our understanding of students' potential. Lifting that potential requires that we make that potential visible beyond the narrow confines of standardized tests in math and reading that are made even less adequate by the fact that they are delivered only in English. How then do we discover student talents? How do we begin to understand what students know if they only get to communicate their understanding in a language they are still in the process of learning? And how can we grasp the depth of their cognitive abilities when we only provide standardized questions with a single right answer? What are we missing by not inviting students to bring in their experiences, ideas and imagination?

> In Documenting Communities, Meehan and Nora show how, when schools value the complicated and hybrid cultures of all students, photography can seamlessly address the third-grade social studies standards and show powerful understanding not only of the curriculum but also how it applies in their daily lives. Lawrence and Mathis present collages where students demonstrate in depth understanding and significant connections between their own lives and the Harlem Renaissance. Cunningham and Enriquez provide a framework for students to do close readings of picturebooks for building their literacy in ways that address multiliteracies far beyond simply reading and writing, and Brown shows us how digital books can support students in writing their own books that tell stories that matter to them.

> These chapters present challenging curricula that provide unexpected windows into the depth of student knowledge and understanding. From single photographs to collage, digital books and picturebooks, visual texts tell stories. As students develop visual literacy

they learn to read images. They also learn to tell stories with images and make meaning, to critique, revise, and refine for sharing with their communities beyond the school. This is work that reflects high engagement and high expectations; it is work that expands the possibilities of what is possible.

Questions for reflection

How do I know what I know about my students? How much of what I know is based on assumptions? How much of what I know comes from what students share with me and other students? What do I not know about my students and how can I support them in unearthing their funds of knowledge to make them visible?

What strengths and gifts of my students are easily overlooked in traditional assessments? What opportunities does my curriculum provide for my students to teach us about their lives, their questions, the connections they make and the richness of their ideas? How do we make room for the unexpected?

How does my curriculum build on students' resources, imagination and gifts to prepare them to function in a diverse, creative context beyond the school where communication is primarily multimodal and questions are open-ended? How can the arts support make this complex learning visible?

Review your curriculum, consider your texts, classwork, and homework. Where are there silences? What voices are missing? Where are your students represented and their voices included or not? How can reading, telling, and writing through images, drama, and other art forms expand the curricular framework to include student voices that reveal depth of understanding ?

Further Applications

Images in Two Languages

As Nieto reminds us, language, literacy, and culture are inextricably linked. Language is more than just a communication tool, it reflects our culture, what we care about, how we experience the world and our relationship to others, including relationships of power where some experiences are often valued and others disregarded (2009). In the sociopolitical context of schools, it is vital that we honor students' multiple languages. For those of us who are bilingual or multilingual, each language reminds us of particular places, people, and experiences. When I started making photographs in art class, I began to understand that I was "speaking" English in Spanish, the images I had as reference points reflected values and moods that I associated culturally with English. It wasn't until I found Latin American photographers that I began to see the part of my culture that to me reflected the Spanish language. *Images in Two Languages* is a way to make this fragmentation visible and to provide a space for thinking and speaking in both, to make visible that we live in more than one language.

Invite students to consider the language(s) they speak. What language(s) do they speak with teachers, friends, people in their family, others? Where do they speak which languages?

Then ask them when they think in Spanish, what images come to mind? When I asked a group of emergent bilingual third graders, they said Spanish made them think of the beach, church, and abuela's house. Proceed to ask the same question about English. Building on the photographic literacy developed through work such as Meehan and Nora's *Documenting Communities*, provide students with cameras and have them photograph in and around the school. What do they see? What makes them think of English? Spanish? Can framing create a shift in language? Go through the images individually and collaboratively. Ask: What do you see? What languages do you see in each image? What makes you say that? Some images reflect both. Have students notice where they "see" one language or the other in their daily lives. Have them photograph those moments that stand out and bring back their images. Students can then discuss, select, and curate images to tell a story about the languages in their lives.

Collaborative Storytelling and Storybooks

Using their knowledge of storybooks, teachers can use this strategy with learning in any curricular area. They can focus on quirky fictional topics or they can create a story where they apply knowledge of science such as animals and their ecosystems. Through this strategy students respond to a story prompt, listen to each other, use their imagination, incorporate their knowledge of story and narrative development, and build on each other's ideas.

Sitting in a circle provides the beginning of a story; this could be about anything including a curricular area you want to assess. Begin the story by explaining the setting, at least one character and a problem to be solved. Pass the story to the first student to add one or two sentences. The story develops as each successive student adds their contribution. As the circle nears the end remind students that they need to start finding a resolution and then an ending. Be sure to document every contribution so that by the end you can re-tell the whole story.

Expanding on Cunningham and Enriquez's research with *picturebooks*, work with the students to refine the story, consider what the setting and the characters look like and invite each student to make a picture that describes each student contribution to the story. How much can they communicate without words? Once each student has completed their image, compile the sequence of images into an accordion book. *Read* the whole book together without words; what do the images say? Decide as a group what words you need in what pages and in what language to clarify and complete the story. This book can become part of the classroom library and read to others. Alternately, the collaborative story can also be told via performed gestures such as in drama, as each student acts out each contribution.

Collage: Found Images

We often think of heroes as famous people who have accomplished extraordinary things. Lawrence and Mathis use collage to have students connect to and represent artists, writers, and other heroes from the Harlem Renaissance. Collage also encourages students to make connections to the present as students use bits and pieces of current images and headlines.

Working with diptychs, triptychs, and four-panel accordion books can provide expanded opportunities for students to juxtapose personal heroes with historical ones. Invite students to think about heroes in their own circle of family and friends; who do they look up to? Ask students to ask family members and friends to share a story about someone they admire. Have students create a collage portrait for each hero in their community. Create a series with as many panels as necessary; portraits can hang around the classroom or become small personal accordion books.

Found Poetry: Transforming Meaning

Collage is a remix of fragments of images; in a similar fashion students can create found poems. Found poems are a great way to use and transform words found in a text into a new creative text. There are many kinds of found poems: erasure poems, headline poems, or invented found poems from a particular text or a combination of sources. Have students create found poems out of words pulled from a hat, from an academic text, from conversations they hear at home, or from a school handout. Invite students to reflect, transform, or resist the meaning of a text.

Zine-making

Zines are small, easily reproducible, usually photocopied self-published magazines/booklets. A basic zine template, which can be found through a simple online search, includes eight panels: six inside panels and front and back covers.

Have students compile their found poems about a single subject into a zine. Make copies, submit one to a library, and have students share them with their families and friends. As students work through a unit of study and they create found poems, collages, work word? banks and other artistic representations of their understanding, they can photocopy the various facets of their learning and compile them in a zine that documents their learning process. Students can also make digital zines, which can be easily shared through social media and email.

Documenting Histories: Storytelling

We all have long histories that precede us, with ancestors that moved from one place to another at some point in time. For some of us, personal stories of migration are more recent than others. Our stories and the stories of our ancestors represent a rich source of knowledge about parts of history that are rarely if ever represented in textbooks. And if our students are emergent bilingual students that come from a wide range of places, those stories can provide insight into how our understanding of history is connected to other places both locally and globally. To excavate these stories, have students ask an elder in their lives to tell them a story about an elder they remember from their childhood. Have students record the stories with tape recorders or in writing. When I worked with 4- and 5-year-olds, I asked them to tell us the stories they heard each day and we would write them down in class. You can do this with each successive generation. These stories can be placed on a historical timeline along with historical events from textbooks. Have students create a historical comic book from the perspective of someone from their community.

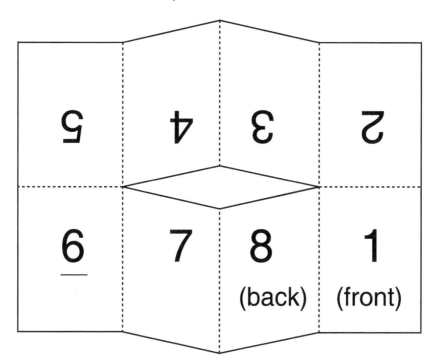

FIGURE 9A.1 Template From Open Source https://en.wikibooks.org/wiki/Zine_Making/Print_version

SECTION III
Lift Every Voice
Democratic Practice Before, During, and After School

Muhammad Walad

Muhammad Walad Ya Muhammad Walad. The sing-song tone replayed in my head like a broken record. Ten years since I've been back to the motherland. Smirks broke out and looks put out, that's how I imagined it to be like when I ride a bike in Sudan.

Light colored jeans, sweat dripping from my soft, brown skin as the dry sun hits my face. I look up with the biggest smile on my face and embrace my theme song. "Muhammad Walad ya Muhammad Walad" embracing the hot air.

Those words in Arabic were music to my American ears, my "fisting pounding, wanting equity" eyes. Muhammad Walad translated to tomboy in English. Meaning the rights that Zol min Ahmira bled for. So I say to my people with my buck teeth, small eyes, and small self personality and yell "ahyo ahyo ahyooooo ena Muhammad wallad ya Muhammad walad" taking those music to my ears chant and stood the hell out because God and my momma didnt create me to fit in.

But to get out of American soil, I smiled. And to touch the floor of bayt abooy with my small brown toes and inhale the smell of moolah and kisra, it was home, and although I didnt speak my native tongue, we all spoke one universal language; love. Because once our hands touched that moolah, we became one. Soon conversations that were once short, became long. Where the sun rose and the laughter never stopped, where cousins I never spoke too, became my best friends. Secrets were spoken and shared, cultures were switched and as soon as this sweet love came to an end, they were too singing my favorite song, "na3na bardo muhammad walad ya muhammad walad"

August Summer of 2016, by Rianne Elsadig

10

¿QUÉ CAJA? WHAT BOX?

Inclusivity, Assessment, and the Political Possibilities of Preschool Drama

Beth Murray and Gustave Weltsek

Introduction

When "political" and "preschool" meet in a widely-read sentence, the topic usually involves access or accountability. Positive correlations between preschool and:

- school readiness;
- improved standardized test performance in primary grades;
- effective school-home connections;
- academic growth among culturally diverse and socioeconomically challenged youth

have catapulted preschool attendance to silver-bullet-solution status for many in the education reform business (Hanushek, 2015; Copple & Bredekamp, 1987/2009). Governmental, educational, and philanthropic bodies rally 'round replication efforts for scale of tried-and-true curricula and best practice with far less deep, systemic inquiry about what and how preschoolers communicate to create meaning in richly diverse contexts (Wohlwend, 2011). Many "rigorous" preschool curricula are driven by politics of exclusion rather than a pedagogy of equity.

As drama and language/literacy community-engaged scholars who work with preschool children and their teachers and families in culturally and/or linguistically diverse urban settings, we argue preschoolers know—and need to know— quite a bit about themselves as active participants in an emergent democracy. In this chapter, we lay out our common foundation and share descriptions of two arts-based inquiry projects that use theatre/drama as a means to foster and interrogate multiliteracies (Schneider, Crumpler, & Rogers, 2006) among preschoolers and their intricate contexts highlighting language acquisition practices and orientations as primary manifestation of agency and/or oppression. Along these lines, we agree with Makoni and Pennycook who explain that "all languages are social constructions, arti-facts analogous to other constructions such as time" (2007, p. 1). In this way we looked at how our students played with language invention (Pennycook, 2007). We positioned these playful utterances as representative of individual students' and teachers' ways of making meaning in and of the world and not as whether they adhered to any notion of standard American English. To share children's "invention" of language, we enliven select scenarios to both capture and question the politics of language in these particular preschool contexts, paying particular attention to how choice, power, inclusivity and identity play out in what counts—and doesn't count—as arts-infused language assessment. In our engaged scholarship we try to: advocate for seriousness about play, inquire how the arts and multimodal literacies mingle and are assessed, and focus a critical lens on the idea of deficit. Each of these priorities contributes to an orientation centering language acquisition as a deeply contextual, politically laden act of childhood witnessed, lived, interpreted, and reinterpreted across lifetimes but deeply rooted in the earliest years where wisdom does not always linger in words.

Advocate for Seriousness About Play

Both theatre and formalized early-childhood learning claim roots in play. Play appears in every culture and reaches across every border. Play links to social, emotional, and academic growth (e.g., Vygotsky, 1967) leading many preschool programs to label their curricula "play based." Many believe playful pedagogies scaffold habits and sensibilities that map readily onto every discipline, igniting, enlivening, and situating literacies learning. Yet beloved play remains marginalized in "serious" educational assessment (Broadhead & Burt, 2012). The insipid impact of this dismissive orientation to assessing play only in the low-stakes confines of "social skills" reinforces limited and limiting views of literacy and language learning.

Inquire How the Arts and Multimodal Literacies Intersect and Are Assessed

Like play, the arts—particularly the embodied arts of theatre/drama and dance— are viewed positively by teachers, administrators, and parents. The arts have long been correlated with increased student achievement in literacy (e.g., Walker, Tabone, & Weltsek, 2011), school engagement (Smithrim & Upitis, 2005), and overall academics (Wilkins et al., 2003) particularly among underserved students for whom the arts show the greatest benefit and the least access (Catterall, 2009).

Progress in the New Literacies (New London Group, 1996; Cope & Kalantzis, 2009) movement with its embodied and contextual sense of multiliteracies—far beyond the traditional, replicable linguistic paradigm—has created opportunities for attention to how the arts in learning operate as a complex multimodal enterprise involving gestural, spatial, visual, and aural modes as well as beyond uniform assessment check boxes and into the situated nature of diversity, identity, and humanity (e.g., Barton, 2013; Albers & Sanders, 2010). This broadening encompasses and echoes multilingual and second-language learning dynamics (Ntelioglou, 2011). Such inclusivity emboldens educational reform efforts challenging the value and ethics of standardized tests as the sole measure of what constitutes "learning." Theatre/arts-based and sociocultural multilingual pedagogies share a habitually marginalized curricular space reflected in assessment practices in which legitimacy stems from compliance with traditional input-output assessment structures prevalent in more privileged subject areas, like reading and writing. However, ties to social context—which can confound standardized assessments—unite the arts and language as complex and complementary communicative processes.

Focus a Critical Lens on the Idea of Deficit

As preschool's collective cachet has grown, one might expect awareness about inherently early-childhood ways of knowing and being—like play and arts-based activity and modal flexibility—to gain legitimacy, shaping and inspiring curriculum beyond. Instead, preschool looks increasingly like its elder school counterparts with standardized, nationally-normed assessments, and model curricula, such as the Individual Growth and Development Indicators (IGDI) system (Missall, Carta, McConnell, Walker, & Greenwood, 2008). As Morrell (2002) explains, "Often, the failure of urban students to develop 'academic' literacy skills stems not from a lack of intelligence but from the inaccessibility of the school curriculum to students who are not in the "dominant" or "mainstream" culture" (p. 72). Morrell reveals the racist, sexist, and classist epistemology at the core of standardized testing as a hegemonic educational paradigm protecting the status quo. He challenges educators to re-envision assessment and evaluation, curricular delivery methods, and ultimately how we understand and articulate what we mean by "learning." Lisa Delpit's (1988) "the silenced dialogue" echoes the broad view's sentiment with calls to examine the local, nuanced cultural layers at play—and sometimes silenced—when teaching across cultural borders, particularly with a power differential fostering white-privileged constructions of norms, baselines, progress, and outcomes.

Here, we each take up Morrell's charge. Using a self-reflective frame for critical action research (McKernan, 1991; McTaggart, 1991; Lewin, 1946) in conversation with each larger study, we report findings and observations in relation to each case in isolation. In the final section we consider connections and intersections between the two cases and within our broader blurred fields of drama, literacy, and language education.

As researchers we work in US urban schools almost 600 miles apart, but operate from similar stances—involving language development within multiple literacies and arts-based learning, while looking to serve students linguistically marginalized by the current system. We use this article to highlight our productive resonances and challenges in the hope that others curious about permeable borders between arts and language learning recognize the nuanced curricular and political possibilities and responsibilities reverberating across mono and multilingual communities and schools alike.

We share our individual research sites as spaces to ask—apart and together—how do participants, collaborators, and stakeholders entrust play, enact multimodal literacies and arts-based assessments, and frame difference in relation to deficit? What are the impacts on the politics surrounding language acquisition for preschoolers manifested in the checked and empty boxes that have come to represent children linguistically and/or socioeconomically sidelined by current structures and systems?

Preschool Pioneers Project Overview (Gustave)

Context

In 2014–2015, a team of arts educators, education students, a host teacher, and 20 preschool students ages 4–5 took a pioneer journey across the US in the classroom, through drama. I served as the team's theatre artist/researcher. Our team coalesced under a grant in hopes of using arts to improve literacy achievement. The grant required a control and sample preschool of 20 students designated at risk, Title I, repeatedly failing, with over 65% student qualification for federal free-or-reduced lunch. Bringing on federal take-over for its challenged status, the school served students who were all monolingual English speakers, with many labeled officially and unofficially with linguistic and developmental deficits and delays without differentiation for those whose home-based "ways with words" (Heath, 1983) and "funds of knowledge" (Moll, Amanti, Neff, & Gonzalez, 2005) varied from standardized conceptions of universal normative development. As a critical bilingual arts educator in a classroom serving English-only students labeled with "low-socioeconomic status" and "linguistic underperformance," I was still called on to foster access to the language of power through art.

What We Wondered (Research Questions):

- How does drama impact student performance on preschool Individual Growth and Development Indicators?
- How does democracy manifest in and among preschoolers engaged in arts-based learning, in spoken and unspoken language?
- In what ways may the process of drama/theatre create an inclusive space?
- How does valuing, assessing and evaluating arts-based learning materialize in practice?

Research Methods and Data Sources

This mixed-methods study relied on qualitative and quantitative data sources, collection, and analysis methods. Using a qualitative exploratory design (Marshall & Rossman, 2014; Saldaña, 2011) data was gathered from all planning meetings between myself and the host teacher, lesson and unit plans and field notes, as well as student-produced artifacts such as drawings and sculptures and video/audio footage of all drama work. Qualitative insights, by design, emerged (Lankshear & Knobel, 2007; Deleuze & Guattari, 1987), as opposed to being constructed within barriers and borders (Leander & Boldt, 2013), then checked as present or absent, true or false, important or not.

Quantitative data was gathered for both control and sample populations through system-mandated academic Individual Growth and Development Indicators (Missall et al., 2008) assessment results for Picture Naming, Rhyming, and Alliteration. The lead teachers of both the control and sample population used Picture Naming, Rhyming, and Alliteration test segments. In these tests students identify the item depicted, or tell a word that rhymes or starts with the same sound. Analysis details appear elsewhere (Carney, Gustave, Weltsek, Hall, & Brinn, 2016), but are beyond the scope of this chapter.

Activity with Children

Process drama framed the westward expansion exploration. We employed different strategies focused on helping students improvise, problem solve, negotiate complex social choices, and communicate in multiple modes, as opposed to rehearsing for a performance. Mantle of the Expert (Bolton & Heathcote, 1995) accompanied by Teacher in Role were central strategies. The teacher takes on a role who needs assistance from the "expert" students in role. The reversal of expertise dynamic (where kids know and teachers do not) fosters student talk, encouraging voice and varied perspectives.

In our drama, the students were farmers challenged by drought. A wealthy banker (teacher) heard of the troubles, and that the family members (students) were expert wagon builders. The banker offered the family the opportunity to leave the failing farm for the West. He would pay all their expenses. In return the family would design and redesign—depicting, sharing, explaining, and defending—ever-improving wagon plans for the banker as they traveled. The redesign emerged from what students learned about traveling across the US, in and out of role, over the course of the unit. Figures 10.1–10.4 show the design evolution.

The "pioneer family" would also establish a settlement in the west once they arrived. As the drama unfolded, obstacles appeared—wild animals, tornadoes, shortages, and malfunctions were recorded/depicted in their field journals through maps, blueprints, 3D designs, songs, dances, and improvisations. In keeping with process drama tenets, roles shifted to foster exploration of varied perspectives

FIGURE 10.1 Using basic shapes for a first attempt at wagon design, Marcella age 5.

FIGURE 10.2 Second attempt at wagon design freehand crayon and pen, Marcella age 5

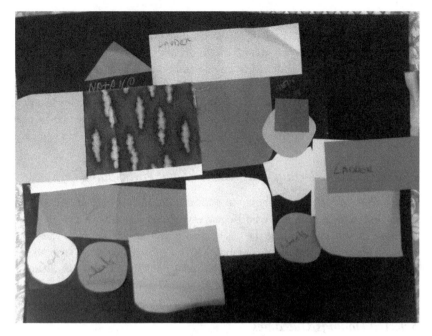

FIGURE 10.3   First attempt at wagon design basic shapes, Micah age 4

FIGURE 10.4   Second attempt at wagon design using free hand crayon and pen, Micah now age 5

through the arts. The ever-present negotiation of who was in charge, and the huge issue of what it meant to come into a place where other people already lived with the intention of "moving in" and maybe "moving them out," was particularly fertile ground for examining democracy in an embodied way through drama. These theatrically-framed spaces for voice and action honed on communication and problem negotiation—rather than performing for an audience—helped students explore and express themselves as multiliterate contributors to the not-so-neat-and-tidy continual construction of a society aspiring toward justice and equity.

Planning and Reflecting with Teacher/Adult Participants

I planned the dramas in collaboration with the treatment group teacher, and we implemented them together, reflecting, assessing, and planning in the debriefing sessions that followed. Because the teacher was new to drama, her roles were often vital, but discrete, to assuage uncertainty about vacillation between facilitation as teacher and interaction in role. I, however, modeled this. I looked to the teacher for curricular guidance and literacy routines; she looked to me for leadership in drama.

Selected Findings/Outcomes

In order to satisfy the granting agency's interest in student literacy achievement, quasi-experimental quantitative data was gathered from the students involved in the Pioneer journey and a control group of like demographics. Growth in three target areas was measured through the district's mandated standardized test, the Individual Growth and Development Indicators. This test measured for growth in vocabulary, alliteration, and rhyming. The statistical analysis showed a clear and consistent correlation between students in the treatment group (who received arts-infused lessons) as opposed to those in the control groups (whose instruction was not arts-infused). In particular, results from the pre- and post-test showed that there was a 135% increase in Vocabulary (oral language), a 271% increase in Alliteration (phonological awareness), and a 466% increase in Rhyming (phonological awareness) for the students involved in the drama. The control group however, made significantly smaller gains in all areas: 78% Vocabulary, 177% Alliteration, and 180% in Rhyming. This quasi-experimental study cannot causally connect arts-based learning to the increase; it also cannot discount a possible correlation. For administrative and funding bodies, quantifiable growth outcome was primary—even singular—for reporting and dissemination. It reinforced evidence that drama aids academic achievement by mainstream literacy standards (e.g., Inoa et al., 2014; Walker et al., 2011). It answered Research Question #1. What about Research Questions 2, 3 and 4, inquiring into the politics of arts-based literacy spaces using arts-based criteria for language learners along school's margins?

The sequence of images in Figures 10.5–10.7 documents such an emergent story. It features Sonya, a preschooler challenged to communicate effectively in her classroom. Figure 10.5 shows the "Sharing Circle," a daily teacher-led group in

FIGURE 10.5   Sonya reluctantly engages in routine "Sharing Circle" discussion.

FIGURE 10.6   Sonya, in-role, telling pioneers to leave.

FIGURE 10.7   Sonya recedes back to "Sharing Circle" mode.

discussion. In this moment, Sonya reflects on their pioneer frontier adventure. In the audio, barely perceptible, she whispers that "We've gone away in the wagon . . . and we've done something . . . and vegetables." She looks down, fidgets uncomfortably, and looks at the teacher to see if what she is doing is okay. Figure 10.6 Sonya—in role as the leader of an indigenous people—emphatically tells the pioneers to leave.

Among the students playing the pioneers is the teacher. In the audio Sonya loudly proclaims "No you can't live here! No you be quiet! I am the boss of the all these people! You can't stay! No!" In the visual (Figure 10.6) she sits upright, hands assertively on the table, leaning forward. She holds direct, stern, and steady eye contact with the pioneer teacher in role whose gaze, moments ago, she could barely engage. Seconds later, in Figure 10.7, Sonya returns to institutionalized Sharing Circle behavior—quiet, submissive, uncertain.

The Mamá Goose Project Overview (Beth)

Context

In 2013, Irania Macias Patterson and I adapted a collection of traditional Latinx nursery stories, games, and rhymes (see Ada et al, 2004), into a performance for children entitled *Mamá Goose*. Irania (a Bilingual Services Specialist for the Public Library and a freelance teaching artist and author) and I (a theatre-education professor and playwright) chose this anthology as an anchor because Ada and Campoy's curation framed Latinx heritage as a global one, and the book's contents were playful evidence. Additionally, the anthologized pieces were collected in Spanish first then translated to English, whereas the reverse is more common in commercial children's books in the United States.

The play used English, Spanish, and American Sign Language as well as theatre, music, dance, movement, games, storytelling, and visual art among its many embodied vocabularies (Murray, Patterson, & Salas, 2015). It told the story of four cousins/primos, their grandmother/abuela and a gigantic magical egg each child found, claimed, and hid as his/her own. The children—one speaking Spanish only, one speaking English only, one bilingual, and the fourth communicating in American Sign Language—play and sing and dance in full understanding of one another. The cast consisted of three university-student and two community actors, with varying bilingual profiles themselves. The cousins' struggle to each keep the egg gives way to games, songs, giant egg hiding—and arguments. In their dreams, Abuela opens the egg and, with the help of a magical spider, gifts each child with what appears to be junk. However, when taken together the trash assembles into a small guitar and a book of bilingual songs called *Mamá Goose*. The children realize that when "We share"/ "Compartimos" things are better for all.

The five-actor production toured to diverse monolingual and multilingual sites in schools and communities up and down the urban socioeconomic scale in an urban region of the southeastern US experiencing exponential growth in Latinx immigration over the last decade. Following the tour, Irania and I have been returning to work with teachers and librarians to develop arts-based strategies.

What We Wondered (Research Questions)

During and since that tour time, we have set about answering the questions:

Which dynamics of intermingling arts, literacies, and cultures developed, rehearsed, and performed in the *Mamá Goose* play, translate readily to everyday classroom pedagogy by non-arts specialists? How? Which don't translate? Why?

Research Methods and Data Sources

The *Mamá Goose* project was a decidedly a/r/tographic (Springgay, Irwin, & Leggo, 2007) undertaking as it blended our artist(A), researcher(R) and teacher(T) roles, as opposed to keeping them distinct. For instance, the linguistic profile of characters sprang from field-based research and teaching, thus teaching and research shaped play construction. We sought to create a play with authentically multimodal meaning-making mechanisms, diversely scaffolded, and accessible through varied semiotic entryways. However, as co-playwrights and with Irania overseeing the musical creation and me directing the show, the "A" of a/r/tography was prominent in the initial phase. Our way of working sprung from a collaborative history as well as our individual identities in which language figured prominently. Irania is a tri-lingual Venezuelan native and I am a US-born emergent bilingual. Neither of us were fluent in sign language, but we both "spoke" music, dance, theatre—and play. Though data emerged through participant observation, surveys, interviews, student-created artifacts, and video/audio recordings of classroom, performance, and professional development events, our primary focus remained the art of the performance and responses to it.

Once the tour ended, we picked up the "R" (for research) and "T" (for teaching) threads woven initially, with particular attention to the idea of multimodal, multilingual literacies in action. What might that look and sound like in the beautifully messy realities of early childhood classrooms? Play emerged as a central pillar.

Activity with Children

Audience age composition included large early-childhood groups chaperoned by a few teachers as well as multigenerational family groups with few members in the "target" age range. The selected school and community sites included both those serving predominantly emergent bilinguals as well as those serving few, or none. In the classroom phase, our target audience is teachers. We continue to work with teachers to help design responsive pedagogy they can implement. This puts us in the role of observers, mentors, co-planners, and facilitators. Each site includes some form of model teaching or demonstration.

Planning and Reflecting with Teachers/Adult Participants

As Irania and I reflected on *Mamá Goose*, searching for ways the production's vibe could pervade everyday classroom pedagogy, we realized our complicity in denying play—as a language—its due. This is most evident in descriptions. Every tag line referenced language (bi- or multilingual), yet its more pervasive, universal vocabulary was play. Whenever the word "play" appeared, it referred to the stage representation of a story rather than spontaneous recreational activity. This is as clear in media coverage as it is in our own descriptions (see Table 10.1).

TABLE 10.1 Adult Descriptors of *Mamá Goose*.

Adult Play Descriptors / Tag Lines for Mamá Goose	
Venue	*Primary Descriptor*
Title page	"A bilingual play with music and dance in one act for young audiences"
Poster and promotional materials	"new Spanish/English bilingual play with music and movement for 3-to-7 year olds"
Press release	"a delightful bilingual play for children and their families"
Local city newspaper article (English)	"a children's play for all cultures"
Regional newspaper (Spanish)	"teatro bilingüe para los niños/bilingual theatre for children"
Public library website	"free bilingual play for children"
University website	"bilingual play (with music and dance)"

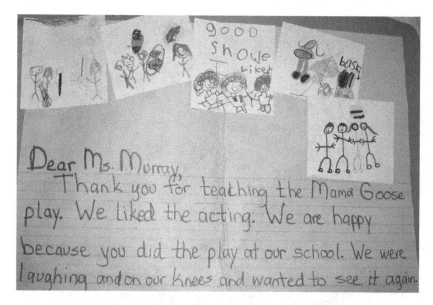

FIGURE 10.8 Shared writing letter with student patchwork art

Playfulness transgressed the many multis: multilingual, multicultural, multigenerational, multimodal. However, language became a—or *the*—defining feature.

Parent and teacher survey responses pointed to a primary awareness of language though ideas about access varied. One parent who identified as a monolingual English speaker noted that "The majority of it was in Spanish, so he couldn't follow." Yet another monolingual English-speaking parent of English-only children said: "They loved it." In post-show interviews and focus groups, most children, regardless of first language, could recount the major dramatic action of the play, identify and describe a favorite character, and identify a memorable moment or image. Post-show chatter and response created a small power-laden stage of its own, articulating adult positions through their respective child proxies.

In the linguistic realm (see Figure 10.8), the choice to thank us for "teaching" the play was interesting. Similarly, the complimentary phrase "we were laughing and on our knees" points to the nonverbal peer assessments of engagement students employed (which were also behaviors corrected by adults in the room). In the visual realm, characters identified by costume color (and sometimes hairstyle) rather than name appeared in formations that echoed stated "favorite parts" including "playing," "hiding," "fighting," "sharing," and "singing." Spiders, spider webs, guitars, baskets, and giant eggs further expressed what was vivid and memorable.

While linguistic elements remained a defining feature for adults and media, the prominence of play as a key "language" for children was undeniable. This was abundantly clear in the idea of hiding. The children in the play hid from each

FIGURE 10.9 "Estelita hides. Westin seeks."

other in two different games, El escondite/Hide and Seek and Juguemos en el bosque/Let's Play in the Woods (see Figure 10.9).

Each child cousin in the play also hid the egg. Audience children were active agents in the finding process, challenging the actors to respond and frame the audience's genuine, unsolicited vocal and physical support. Hiding play transgressed linguistic barriers, whether the hidden was gigantic egg, living person, or baby guitar.

Selected Findings/Outcomes

In moving to help teachers consider the place of the arts in multiple modes and languages, Irania and I tried to construct an approach that honored where teachers were in their zones of proximal development with respect to artistic and multimodal risk. A simple survey guided our initial conversation with teacher teams. The broad categories included:

- Language comforts and proficiencies
- Arts and arts-based experiences
- Literacy pedagogy
- Student demographics and assets
- Arts integration successes and challenges
- Diversity and social context.

The conversations catalyzed the work. Exchanges like the following happened with faculty at a bilingual preschool, lending insight to the way these teachers saw their classrooms.

IRANIA: Tell us about how you use language over the school year.
TEACHER 1:   At the beginning of the year, it's all Spanish.
TEACHER 2:   Especially for the younger class.
TEACHER 1:   Yes.
TEACHER 2:   Then, by the end of the year, mostly English.
IRANIA: Just naturally.
TEACHER 2:   Mmm-hmm.
TEACHER 1:   Yes.

While helpful, the focus interviews evoked conversations about activities; about what teacher do or do not do. This was emblematic of the initial conversations Irania and I would have with teachers, trying to slow down and unpack the how of our linguistic and artistic choices. Our school-based sessions span several months and include information gathering meetings, classroom observations, then model lesson planning and implementation. The imagined trajectory is modeling, then co-teaching, then supported independent work, at first within co-planned lessons, with eventual responsibility for the entire process. A full recounting of this activity is beyond the scope of this chapter, but four findings from early sites have shaped next steps:

- Activity that looks and sounds like something teachers already do creates a safe starting point, but can also create a stalling point without criteria about depth, risk and quality;
- Approaches where the end is known—or contained—usually resonate with mainstream comfort and views of curriculum (e.g., visual art, songs and poems with motions, games, re-enacted stories, call and response);
- Approaches where the end is unknown or emergent (interpreted by several as "potentially chaotic") engender less familiarity with and more uncertainty/reluctance from teachers (e.g., process drama—including teacher in role, improvisation, exploratory movement, open-ended inquiry);
- Mandated assessments shape the way teachers envision possibility, evaluate potential activity, and communicate about what and how children learn.

Table 10.2 captures recurring teacher responses to potential artistic innovations with unknown ends from planning sessions. In our growing group of research participants it is clear that the teachers' views of what is important and possible is deeply shaped by standardized assessments and mandated standards.

No teachers (yet) expressed a will to shape these established frames and expectations through questioning, suggested revision, or boycott—not that we sought such things. This could mean teachers truly endorse and support the existing

TABLE 10.2 "Let's Try" Teacher Response Chart. Range of teacher responses when a play or arts-based orientation challenges established curriculum-based assessment approaches and priorities during planning.

"Let's Try" Teacher Response Chart

Comments in planning	Orientation to current curriculum and assessments reflected (subtextual)	Resulting action in classroom
"But we need to cover" or "That might confuse"	Endorse	Potential innovation does not happen.
"There isn't time for" or "I am not an artist"	Accept	Potential innovation does not happen.
"I suppose we could" or "Is there a way to include?" or "That could help teach"	Adapt	A compromised version of the innovation happens, (usually) assessed with existing instruments and criteria.
"The students will really enjoy"	Overlook	Potential innovation happens, but is not rigorously assessed.
"Why do we have to?" (*hypothetical*)	Question	Has not happened yet.
"We need to change" (*hypothetical*)	Revise	Has not happened yet.
"I refuse to" (*hypothetical*)	Boycott	Has not happened yet.

structure, or it could have other interpretations. However, when potential innovation is introduced, it is filtered in ways that preserve rather than augment or challenge current practice. In a conversation about where the student growth in a process drama session might be expressed to a parent on a report card, all preschool teachers pointed to the "Character and Social Development" section at the end of the assessment form. Thus all the play-based complex layers of multimodality, multiliteracies, and multiple art forms was reduced to "Shares with others"—or not.

A practical example of this habit of mind occurred during center time when a dramatic play opportunity emerged. A young girl danced a newly dressed paper doll in front of her teacher, then awaited comment.

TEACHER: How nice. What color is her dress?
STUDENT: Green.
TEACHER: Yes. Good. Beautiful. What color is her hair?
STUDENT: Yellow.
TEACHER: Yes. Very nice.
STUDENT: Her shoe is brown.

The opportunities—to improvise, to speak as another rather than about another, to express and receive information verbally and non-verbally, to collaboratively storytell, to scaffold imagining, to risk—were all short-circuited when the focus became color quiz rather than playful arts adventure. Progress occurred but work also remains in nurturing and encouraging artful bilingual educators to strengthen access for bilingual and monolingual students alike, in their own playful ways.

Conclusion

In considering our cases in light of one another and the field, we return to assessment, with particular attention to the politically charged role of language. We used the following broad categories to begin wondering between and beyond our individual inquiries: What counts? How do choice and power function? How are efforts for inclusivity and identity tracked? How do assessment boxes and boundaries mingle across disciplines and orientations, or not? And how does language—in all its modes—play a part?

What counts?

What counts really depends on who is counting. In both locations, the value of drama-based literacies fell into two categories: those that helped preschoolers grow in mainstream literacy assessment measures and those that helped preschoolers grow as people. For classroom-based teachers, the affordances (Jewitt, 2008) of particular drama modes that correlated with discrete competencies appeared both more valuable and more comfortable. In both settings, what counted as literacy was measured in discrete sets or patterns of practice, articulated and prioritized by mandated assessment tools. Track-able and report-able language growth in preschool needed to fit into an existing box. For arts-based researcher/practitioners, there appeared a clear need to articulate arts-based assessment spaces as well as advocate for their legitimacy in order to have teachers realize the full potential of arts-based pedagogy.

How do choice and power function?

Choice and power emerged in both studies in two ways—one as multimodal liberation, the other as censorship. First, liberation. For the Pioneer Drama and the *Mamá Goose* project, instances where preschool children experienced immersion in an arts-based event (in-role work, experiencing the play, etc.) the traditional communication power dynamic of school was suspended. Kids communicated bravely across sign systems with grown-ups and peers alike, sharing ideas and challenging planned structures to insert themselves as co-creators. Spoken student voices and embodied student postures, like Sonya's, found verve and reinforcement in the dramatic context, moving past traditional expressive hesitations, inherent in orderly classrooms. Some adults saw these as moments of art. Some saw these as moments of chaotic danger. Some saw these as a combination, varying by degree and perspectives. Few described these as "assess-able" moments, rather as emotional ones with terms of "enjoyment," "engagement," "confidence," or "confusion," over-generalizing the affective as less than and/or extracurricular.

Censorship appeared in every planning moment in both programs. It was not always clear whether censorship grew from the teachers' interpretation of standardized expectations, teachers' personal comforts, or a cocktail of the two. Standardized assessments wielded tremendous un-interrogated power over the content, scale, and depth of arts-based literacies pursuits. In the absence of spelled-out standards, teachers would reference and categorize possible activity by comparing it to other activities done. How can we stretch the borders of such a living and site-specific compendium, so risk may follow?

How are efforts for inclusivity and identity tracked?

In both studies, intentions for inclusivity are clearly stated, but scantily articulated and tracked. Both studies looked to voiced, drawn, and written responses from participants as key evidence, with observed embodied para-lingual communication as a supplementary source. Are we really seeing and hearing and observing well enough to say: "Yes. This is inclusive. Multiple identities have been honored"? Is it true that when students feel included and their identity is honored, they will express themselves—vocally, spatially, bodily—thus taking a stand in the politics of their schools and futures? Or might we still have work to do?

How do boxes and boundaries of assessment mingle across disciplines and orientations, or not?

It is clear in both cases that the arts—drama in particular—push the bounds of what counts. Arts-based literacies work provides a vehicle to carry knowledge of letter sounds, position words, rhyming, and sequence of events as well as more complex and abstract competencies. Explicit teaching of discrete skills is a necessary part of helping those without access to dominant forms of English at home (Delpit, 1988). However, we cannot stop there, just because existing, endorsed assessment tools do. The arts also help children rehearse social capacities and apply abstract and possibility thinking in a truly situated context. Teachers, laudably, remain open to artistic possibilities. Yet, the layers of communication at play when a child inhabits a role or responds in an improvised drama explode the tiny box for "follows directions" and "shares with others." How do we put words to those outcomes, beyond a critique of their oppressive absence?

In their 1995 book, *Tinkering Toward Utopia: A Century of School Reform*, David Tyack and Larry Cuban chronicle school reform in the United States, capturing the patterns and pull between micro and macro efforts that foster, but more frequently stunt, real school change. Their apt title keying on "tinkering" and "utopia" touches the riddled conversation between specialized local attention to minute detail and global expectations for schooling as the site for fixing society's gravest challenges. Throughout the text, they argue for attention to both but reiterate the importance of teacher agency:

> Reform, then, must emerge from the inside out rather than be imposed from the top down, as has been the twentieth century pattern. That will require greater community involvement and a redirection of resources but, more fundamentally, it will require a new image of teachers.
>
> *(p. 136–37)*

Over a decade later, Julie Cullen and Randall Reback (2006) penned an article called "Tinkering Toward Accolades: School Gaming Under a Performance Accountability System" which curates a sad tale of teacher and administrator behavior in an environment prioritizing standardized assessments.

Now, yet another decade has passed. We find ourselves in a place where the dynamic preschool has gained educational and political legitimacy but is being systematically disentangled from its naturally playful, multimodal and arts-based roots to maintain its status. Language and communication capacities are fast becoming capacities tested in isolated bits so as to—admirably—scaffold a manageable step-by-step. Yet, there are multiple language milestones and missed opportunities beside the singular, falsely universal, path. We ask—what are we tinkering toward now? And how do we help each other get there?

Pennycook (2007) explains the obsession with teaching English viewed "in terms of new forms of power, control and destruction—and in its complexity—in terms of new forms of resistance, change, appropriation and identity" (p. 5). Teaching ANY language necessarily engages sign systems replete with political agendas running the continuum from foreign to familiar, invisible to boldly blatant. When the language learners are preschoolers just beginning to play with language as a means to explore themselves and the world, the act of "teaching" English becomes particularly—in some cases insidiously—political. With this chapter, we seek to join others turning strength and attention to the fruitful ways playful, arts-based approaches fracture entrenched culturally segmented linguistic domains, like "first language" and "second language" learning. We aspire to plural pedagogies that honor the multiple, multimodal and multiliterate learning spaces and more accurately represent the mosaic democracies under construction as preschoolers invent and re-invent language pathways, individually, collectively, artistically—across expansive linguistic systems.

References

Ada, A. F., Campoy, F. I., Suárez, M., & Hefferman, T. (2004). *Mamá Goose: A Latino nursery treasury/un tesoro de rimas infantiles*. New York, NY: Hyperion Books for Children.

Albers, P., & Sanders, J. (Eds.). (2010). *Literacies, the arts, and multimodality*. Urbana, IL: National Council of Teachers of English.

Barton, G. (2013). The Arts and Literacy: What Does it Mean to be Arts Literate? *International Journal of Education & the Arts, 14*(18).

Bolton, G., & Heathcote, D. (1995). *Drama for learning: Dorothy Heathcote's mantle of the expert approach to education*. Portsmouth, NH: Heinemarm.

Broadhead, P., & Burt, A. (2012). *Understanding young children's learning through play: Building playful pedagogies*. London: Routledge.

Carney, Charles L., Gustave, J., Weltsek, M., Hall, Lynne & Brinn, Ginger. (2016). "Arts infusion and literacy achievement within underserved communities: A matter of equity." *Arts Education Policy Review, 117*(4), 230–243.

Catterall, J. S. (2009). Doing well and doing good by doing art: A 12-year longitudinal study of arts education—Effects on the achievements and values of young adults. *CA: I-Group Books*. Charleston, SC: CreateSpace Publishers.

Cope, B., & Kalantzis, M. (2009). "Multiliteracies": New literacies, new learning. *Pedagogies: An International Journal, 4*(3), 164–195.

Copple, C., & Bredekamp, S. (1987/2009). *Developmentally appropriate practice in early childhood programs serving children from birth through age 8*. Washington, DC: National Association for the Education of Young Children.

Cullen, J. B., & Reback, R. (2006). *Tinkering toward accolades: School gaming under a performance accountability system* (No. w12286). National Bureau of Economic Research.

Deleuze, G., & Guattari, F. (1987). *A thousand plateaus*. Minneapolis, MN: University of Minnesota.

Delpit, L. (1988). The silenced dialogue: Power and pedagogy in educating other people's children. *Harvard Educational Review, 58*(3), 280–299.

Gonzalez, N., Moll, L. & Amanti, C. (2005). Funds of knowledge for teaching: Using a qualitative approach to connect homes and classrooms. In *Funds of knowledge: Theorizing practices in households, communities, and classrooms* (pp. 71–87). Mahwah, NJ: Lawrence Erlbaum Associates.

Hanushek, E. A. (2015). The preschool debate: Translating research into policy. *How Public-Policy Innovation and Evaluation Can Improve Life in America's Cities, 25*.

Heath, S. B. (1983). *Ways with words: Language, life and work in communities and classrooms*. Cambridge: Cambridge University Press.

Inoa, R., Weltsek, G. and Tabone, C. (2014). A study on the relationship between theater arts and student literacy and mathematics achievement. *Journal of Learning Through the Arts, 10*(1). http://www.escholarship.org/uc/class_lta

Jewitt, C. (2008). Multimodality and literacy in school classrooms. *Review of Research in Education, 32*(1), 241–267.

Leander, K., & Boldt, G. (2013). Rereading "A pedagogy of multiliteracies" bodies, texts, and emergence. *Journal of Literacy Research, 45*(1), 22–46.

Lewin, K. (1946). Action research and minority problems. *Journal of Social Issues, 2*, 34–46.

Marshall, C., & Rossman, G. B. (2014). *Designing qualitative research*. Los Angeles, CA: Sage Publications.

Makoni, S., & Pennycook, A. (2007). Disinventing and reconstituting languages. In S. Makoni and A. Pennycook (Eds.), *Disinventing and reconstituting languages: Bilingual education and bilingualism* (pp. 1–41). New York, NY: Multilingual Matters/Channel View.

McKernan, J. (1991). *Curriculum action research: a handbook of methods and measures for the reflective practitioner.* London: Kogan Page.

McTaggart, Robin (1991). *Action research: A short modern history.* Geelong, Vic: Deakin University.

Missall, K. N., Carta, J. J., McConnell, S. R., Walker, D., & Greenwood, C. R. (2008). Using individual growth and development indicators to measure early language and literacy. *Infants & Young Children, 21*(3), 241–253.

Morrell, E. (2002). Toward a critical pedagogy of popular culture: Literacy development among urban youth. *Journal of Adolescent and Adult Literacy, 46*(1), 72–77.

Murray, B., Patterson, I. M., & Salas, S. (2015). TYA playwriting in the New Latino South: Multilingual, multimodal cultural improvisation in the I-85 corridor. In *Theatre Symposium* (Vol. 23, No. 1, pp. 106–116). The University of Alabama Press.

The New London Group. (1996). A pedagogy of multiliteracies: Designing social futures. *Harvard Educational Review, 66*(1), 60–93.

Ntelioglou, B. Y. (2011). 'But why do I have to take this class?' The mandatory drama-ESL class and multiliteracies pedagogy. *Research in Drama Education: The Journal of Applied Theatre and Performance, 16*(4), 595–615.

Pennycook, A. (2007). *Global Englishes and transcultural flows.* Oxon, UK: Routledge.

Saldaña, J. (2011). *Fundamentals of qualitative research.* Oxford: Oxford University Press.

Schneider, J., Crumpler, T., & Rogers, T. (Eds.) (2006). *Process drama and multiple literacies: Addressing social, cultural, and ethical issues.* Portsmouth, NH: Heinemann.

Smithrim, K., & Upitis, R. (2005). Learning through the arts: Lessons of engagement. *Canadian Journal of Education/Revue canadienne de l'education,* 109–127.

Springgay, S., Irwin, R. L., & Leggo, C. (Eds.). (2007). *Being with a/r/tography.* Boston, MA: Sense Publications.

Tyack, D. B., & Cuban, L. (1995). *Tinkering toward Utopia: A century of school reform.* Cambridge, MA: Harvard University Press.

Vygotsky, L. S. (1967). Play and its role in the mental development of the child. *Soviet Psychology, 5*(3), 6–18.

Walker, E., Tabone, C., & Weltsek, G. (2011). When achievement data meet drama and arts integration. *Language Arts, 88*(5), 365.

Wilkins, J., Graham, G., Parker, S., Westfall, S., Fraser, R., & Tembo, M. (2003). Time in the arts and physical education and school achievement. *Journal of Curriculum Studies, 35*(6), 721–734.

Wohlwend, K. E. (2011). *Playing their way into literacies: Reading, writing, and belonging in the early childhood classroom.* New York, NY: Teachers College Press.

11

TELLING STORIES OF CHALLENGE AND TRIUMPH

Emergent Bilinguals Claim the Curriculum through Spoken-Word Poetry, Hip Hop, and Video

Debi Khasnabis, Catherine H. Reischl, Coert Ambrosino, Jamall Bufford, and Alysha Mae Schlundt-Bodien

Ninety students sit elbow to elbow with 200 family members and teachers at the Neutral Zone, a community-based teen center in Ann Arbor, Michigan. Music pounds, heads bob, feet tap, and voices ring out as the crowd chants in chorus:

> "*A challenge—standing in the way of who I want to be!*
> *I faced it! I triumphed! And it made me, me!*"

These fourth-eighth grade emergent bilingual learners have spent the last three weeks telling their personal stories of challenge and triumph through the mediums of spoken-word poetry, hip hop, and video. A teen from Mali performs her poem about meeting her father for the first time in the US, where he had immigrated to secure a safe home for the family. A pair of young sisters, recently arrived from Iraq, rap about their challenge of facing stage fright. And a group of elementary-aged students present their video that portrays their challenge of taking standardized tests.

The Summer ESL Academy (SESLA), involved a partnership between Ann Arbor Public Schools, the School of Education at the University of Michigan, the Neutral Zone, a community-based organization serving youth, and the Community Television Network. In the 2015 program, the 95 SESLA students were emergent bilingual learners, a majority of whom are Spanish-fluent Latino students as well as speakers of Arabic, French, German, Korean, Vietnamese, Chinese, Bengali, Hindi, and Bambara. Many students were recent immigrants or refugees; 80% or more qualified for free or reduced lunch. The program was staffed by seven ESL teachers, who worked in partnership with 18 ESL teaching interns from the University of Michigan School of Education and two faculty coordinators (the first and second authors). Three mentor artists (the third, fourth, and fifth authors), partnered with this group of educators to teach workshops on poetry, hip hop, and digital video.

Unlike the curriculum students have encountered during the regular school year, where they infrequently found their own experiences or histories represented, students' lived experiences became the curriculum in the summer program. Given the multilingual and multicultural lives of our students, their stories ranged widely in content and form; thus they created and shared artifacts that reflected the pluralistic society in which we live, but that is rarely evident in school curricula.

Educational anthropologist Marilyn Eisenhart (1995) describes how new participants in a setting work to "construct" culture as they become part of the setting. Telling "stories of self" as a mediational device is key in this process:

> telling stories about self is not only a way to demonstrate membership in a group or to claim an identity within it. Telling stories about self is also a means of becoming; a means by which an individual helps to shape and project identities in social and cultural spaces; and a way of thinking about learning that requires the individual to be active as well as socially and culturally responsive.
>
> *(p. 19)*

Thus, when emergent bilingual learners create video, poems, and hip hop music that vividly depicts their lived experiences—and when the curriculum has been cracked open to provide space for this expression—the potential for contextualized language learning that is meaningful and motivating increases (Spindler & Spindler, 1993). Such curricula align with the notion of culturally sustaining pedagogy (Paris, 2012; Paris & Alim, 2014), where linguistic and cultural pluralism is central to the content and process. Not incidentally, curricula that draw on the contexts and experiences of children's lives, also engage students in meeting Common Core State Standards as they strive to hone their language (ccss.ela-literacy.ccra.l.5), depict and interpret key stories from their lives (ccss.ela-literacy.ccra.w.3), and tell these stories persuasively to a range of audiences (ccss.ela-literacy.ccra.sl.1).

In this chapter, we wrestle with these concepts of pluralism, language learning, and academic growth as they intersect with the work of curriculum design. Specifically, we consider the following two questions:

> "How do we use the arts to create opportunities for emergent bilingual learners to expand their uses of language and grow in their academic skills as they claim their spaces within the school curriculum?"

> "What pedagogies and structural elements of the curriculum support this kind of engagement?"

Our work draws on the work of other teacher-researchers who enact and study the pedagogy of hip hop based education (Decoteau, Hall, & Hill, 2013; Emdin, 2013), use poetry with emergent bilingual learners, and explore multimodal literacy pedagogies (Dalton, 2012). We describe the structure and content of the curriculum below, including key examples of mentors' and teachers' explicit teaching moves and students' evolving work. Several key features of the work surface in this description:

- Teachers and students gathered around one central theme, "Stories of Challenge and Triumph" that centered the work yet opened up many possibilities;
- Students chose stories of personal significance as their content and chose from a range of multi-genre opportunities;
- Students learned process and content language through purposeful interactions and explicit instruction;
- Teachers and students recursively engaged in processes of writing, rehearsal, and performance.

Considering these features of the work in both the design and enactment stages of instruction may inform the practice of others who are undertaking similar culturally sustaining pedagogies in arts-based instruction with emergent bilingual learners.

Structure of the Instruction

The structure of the unit included three stages of language learning. In the first week, which we refer to as "The Launch," students engaged in background building activities to generate ideas about times in their lives when they'd experienced challenges and triumphs. A mentor artist for each of the genres of poetry, hip hop, and video came to the school to give a performance and lead an initial workshop in which students "dipped their toes" in the genre. After reading and viewing a variety of mentor texts, and exploring each art form in scaffolded lessons, students chose which medium they wanted to use to go public with their story. In the second week, which we refer to as "Design Work," students took three field trips to the Neutral Zone, where they created pieces and developed technical skills within their genre while working alongside their mentor artist and teachers. In the third week, which we refer to as "The Culmination," students made final revisions to their projects and prepared a final celebration performance to mark the culmination of the program for their families. Using examples of practice from the work across the three genres, in the following sections we describe the three phases of the *Challenge and Triumph* unit of study and explain how this curriculum created academic access for our emerging bilingual students.

The Launch

Mentor Artist: Jamall

Jamall's visit had been much anticipated by the students. Since morning, they had been asking with enthusiasm when "the rapper" was coming. Finally, the performance time arrived. Jamall had approached the mic ready to entertain countless times before; but this time was different. The sea of wide-eyed faces he gazed upon sat in the very same space he had once sat as a 12-year-old. To a round of applause, he announced to the children that he was from their community and that he had lived in the complex adjacent to the school itself.

Jamall continued by engaging the students in his art form. As novice rappers, they started with the known—the alphabet! Jamall coached the large group of 95 students to rap the alphabet to different four-count bar structures. He sang for them, sharing music that told of the challenges he had faced; and he shared a writing tool that a rapper could use—a heart map. Projected on the auditorium stage, he shared his own heart map, adorned with symbols of what he loved—his mother, his faith, music. "How many of you have something that you love? It could be your mom, your dog? It could be chicken nuggets!" He went on to explain that sometimes his music was not just about what he loved, but about things that were important to him. He explained, "There's a lot of injustice in the world . . . that is important to me. Making sure at least through my music I try to do something positive. Something that can help this country. Something that can help you guys. Something that can help me."

Before sending the students off to practice writing their own raps with their teachers, Jamall coached them in rapping the challenge and triumph chorus, a refrain we had written to frame the program's theme that ultimately became an anthem for our students.

Across the Genres

In the *Challenge and Triumph* unit, we started with the heart (Wood-Ray, 1999) and wrote with the culminating event in mind. We were purposeful in the ways that we supported students to dig deep wells of ideas to draw from: wells filled with important family stories and topics that truly mattered to students. This work began in the first family meeting, which took place before the start of the program, when we asked students to work with their parents and siblings to create a "bubble map" of family memories. As families buzzed throughout the room, they began to fill their pages with sketches, names of people and places, and words and phrases in both English and their home languages. These initial brainstorming sessions served as starting points for students' topics for writing, and this activity also sent the message that the knowledge and experiences that our students brought with them to school were important resources to be drawn upon in our program.

Equally important to the meaningful topics that students chose was the way in which we framed the genre projects toward a concrete purpose. From the beginning, students were aware of the culminating performance three weeks down the road in which they were to share their work with peers, family, and community members. We kept this venue and its audience at the forefront of our work with students, familiarizing them with the performance space and involving them in decisions about how their work would be shared that night.

Not only did the final performance prove to be a great source of excitement that pushed students to do their best work, but having a specific audience in mind also helped to frame the language work that teachers did with students around content, organization, word choice, and expression. Students received explicit vocabulary instruction that targeted language specific to our "challenge" and "triumph" theme. They read and analyzed leveled mentor texts in small-group guided reading instruction, and they listened and responded to story after story from their peers, their teachers, and their mentor artists as they worked together at school and at the Neutral Zone. As they learned about the three genres, they also were supported by their teachers to use language in principled ways to tell their stories. Coert's advice to the students, "to play the memory like a movie in your head" enabled students to recall their stories in detail. They wrote 6-Room poems to add texture and detail to each memory of a story (Heard, 1999). On Alysha's video launch day, students drafted story boards and used sequential language (i.e., "first, second, third") to describe the "scenes" from their memories. She also introduced the language of production, coaching students to use "close up," "wide shot," or "medium shot" so that they planned both sequence of scenes as well as digital techniques. On Jamall's Hip Hop launch day, teachers and interns worked with students to write a rhyming verse and practice reciting it to a beat.

The work of developing meaningful topics continued throughout the first week of the program, when students brought in personal "artifacts" to share, created "Heart Maps" representing important parts of their lives, and read and viewed a wide variety of mentor texts in guided reading instruction and live performances from mentor artists. We took special care to expose students to a broad range of examples to honor the diverse range of experiences and interests that students brought to our classrooms. Our intention was to give students great freedom to choose what they wrote about, and later how they represented their stories, as they selected poetry, hip hop, or video. In addition to authentically demonstrating how artists use their mediums to express ideas, the initial mentor artist performances and workshops engaged students in developing some of the basic technical skills specific to each art form and in learning about the thinking processes that a writer engages—whether writing a rap, a poem, or a story to be produced on video. Each mentor artist made efforts to make their medium feel accessible to the students. Jamall began with the alphabet. Alysha noted and built upon the students' interest and knowledge about television and film; and Coert introduced the genre of poetry with a performance about the most ordinary and relatable of events—losing a first tooth! The mentor artists, in this way, shared content that intrigued students and also gave them a point of entry into what might otherwise have been daunting terrain. These launch lessons and activities around brainstorming, planning, and drafting provided students with structured opportunities to practice the initial stages of an artistic project.

Design Work

Mentor Artist: Alysha

> *"Miss Alysha, Miss Alysha," says eighth grader, Carlos,*★ *as he runs into the art room at Neutral Zone. "We want to add color to our video and don't know how, can you please show us?" Alysha follows Carlos to the room his team is working in. She walks them through the color correction steps in iMovie, explaining, "First you select the clip and open up the color correction filter window. Next you select your changes." The boys follow along, chiming in when they see the color effect they each prefer. Excitedly they notice how the color effect will add just the right feeling of horror to the scene that they were aiming for, leading them to wonder how audio can also contribute to this tone. Farhad*★ *asks, "Can we add audio effects too? How do we do that?" Alysha engages the boys in considering the composition of the shot and the audio editing effect that would contribute to the tone they are going for. She shows them another series of steps, navigating the application in order to split clips and add audio effects. When she leaves the room, the boys are engaged in animated debate about the right audio effect that will add the feel of dread to the scene when the "bully" transforms into a zombie.*
>
> *The boys continue to work on their video for the next day. Their film ultimately portrays an intense battle depicting a bully as a zombie approaching a new student to the school, played by Carlos. An array of high-contrast reds and greens and hollow roars and screeches depict the fear that the students once felt when they attended a new school. The viewer soon realizes that the zombie scene is an intensely bad dream, as a captioned bilingual transition slide reading "In the real world . . . En el mundo real. . . . " and an upbeat rock beat transforms the scene back to reality, a normal day at a new school for Carlos. Alysha recalls that she had never shown the boys several of these effects—but that they had themselves added these elements to convey dramatic shifts in tone to the video. She notices the bilingual English and Spanish captions the students have also added throughout the video, making the story engaging and accessible for different audience members.*

Across the genres

Across the genre groups, students worked together to solve problems during the design work phase of the unit. They frequently gave each other feedback, with teachers providing sentence frames to the students, such as "I like how you _____, because _____. I think you could also _____." They could also often be heard giving each other words of encouragement. We recall one incident where a student was shocked to hear how strange his voice sounded on the video. His peers quickly reassured him, "You sound sooo good! You're doing great!"

As they practiced the interpersonal communication skills necessary for effective group work, they also gained the technical skills they needed within their genre that would allow them to address those problems. As we've shown, Alysha's students developed facility with a wide range of editing tools—audio, visual, and textual. In the hip hop workshops, Jamall's students worked in small groups with peers who were focused on similar themes, such as family challenges, school challenges, or social challenges. Each group produced different stanzas, and students helped each other brainstorm rhyming words to use at the end of each line, often adding to rhyming dictionaries that they had begun making in class. Jamall made every effort to ease students' entry into rap, for example by describing slant rhyme and explaining, "Rapping doesn't have strict rules. You can be loose with it! Blur the lines of proper English." He drew on examples from his own rap music, sharing a song he had written about advice he gave to a young man: "You keep úp with that *attitude*. I'm goin'a see your face on the *tube*, live action *news*." This freedom was unusual and welcome to our students. Jamall also taught them to have a good time while learning about rhythm and cadence, a new area of focus for many students. "Nod your head to the beat. Feel the rhythm, tap your feet!"

In the poetry group, students began by working together in a large group "we do" structure, and experimented with transforming "ordinary language" to poetic language. Coert began each session by having students listen to and read a mentor text, through which he scaffolded the students' identification of a bank of literary devices that were recorded on anchor charts. These included both "sound tools" such as onomatopoeia, rhyme, repetition, and alliteration; and "meaning tools" such as metaphor, simile, personification, and imagery (Heard, 1999). Through these discussions, students negotiated the author's message to the reader and built on one another's ideas. They took ordinary language and made it poetic, working first as a whole group, in pairs, and then independently. They explored metaphor, discussing how comparisons that are unlikely or exaggerated in some way can make a stronger impact on readers. They moved on to do this with a gradual release of responsibility—working next with only a partner, and then independently—applying the poetic devices they had learned to poems they had drafted throughout the week.

During the Design phase, all of this contextualized genre work provided rich opportunities for students to communicate with peers, teachers, and mentor artists around academic content. Their use of both English and their home languages took them into complex language use that combined vocabulary and structures of both interpersonal language and academic language use. This was a week where the language and content learning was all part of the process. Students tried, tried, and tried again; and their teachers and peers encouraged them, pointing out their successes and providing gentle suggestions for improvement. Each day students got closer and closer to their goals.

The Culmination

Mentor Artist: Coert

An eighth-grade boy steps back from the mic and grins shyly as he makes his way to sit down with his family, carefully weaving through the crowd sprawled out on cushions and pillows. A wave of applause rolls through the sea of supporters filling the colorfully painted room, punctuated by piercing whistles from boisterous fathers and calls of "Bravo" and "Bien hecho!" As the buzz recedes, Coert looks around for the next poet to step on stage.

"Fatoumata, would you like to read next?" Coert asks, eyebrows raised in expectation, his smile stretched as invitingly as he can possibly make it. She smiles back, lips closed, eyes pleading. Her head shakes silently back and forth, the soft cloth of her hijab creasing beneath her chin. "You sure?" Coert whispers gently, feeling the heavy tide of stares piling up around her. The tension breaks when another student comes to her rescue, walks to the mic, and dives in.

After the show, Fatoumata is standing in front of her father and brothers at the back of the room, who had quietly slipped in during the final performance. A small crowd gathers around, and Coert realizes that she is reading her poem aloud, looking up at her father every few lines. She had crafted that poem with a specific audience in mind, and that audience had arrived just in time for her debut reading. While many students were eager to step on stage in front of the 200+ people that gathered for the culminating event, as Fatoumata's story demonstrates, some students had more specific audiences in mind.

Across the Genres

Across the genres, week 3 was dedicated to revision, editing, and rehearsal in preparation for publishing and performing. With so much student choice and a relevant purpose, students took great ownership over their projects. In fact, in the case of Fatoumata, she felt so strongly about her "Leaving Home" poem that she (politely) refused to revise it after she'd finished her first draft. It may be that her poem felt so near and dear to her heart that the thought of making changes to her poem was frightening. In the end, Fatoumata was brave enough to engage in the process of revising and publishing her piece, while maintaining the lines and images from her first draft that were most special to her heart. In her final draft, this eighth-grade poet incorporated "sound tools" that she had practiced, such as alliteration ("sadness spilling") and repetition (the "I remember" refrain). She also utilized "meaning tools" like simile ("tears dripping out of my eyes like a waterfall") and idiom ("thousands of butterflies in my stomach"). Fatoumata even chose to include a phrase in her home language, Bambara, in her final draft, something we'd seen Gary Soto do in his "Ode to Los Raspados."

> **Leaving Home**
>
> I remember getting my hair done.
> I remember people saying "ei yanafe be gane" I'll
> miss you too.
> I remember feeling heartbroken and a bucket of
> sadness spilling all over me.
> I remember tears dripping out of my eyes like a
> waterfall.
> I remember wondering when are we leaving?
> I remember being caught by surprise when I
> found out we were leaving that exact same night!
> I remember thinking about my dad, wondering
> what he's like and looks like.
> I remember my heart beating fast as ever, I felt
> thousands of butterflies in my stomach.
> I remember saying good-bye to my family.
> I remember my uncle smiling at me, which lifted
> my spirit a little.
> I remember saying that this was one of the saddest
> and the happiest moment of life, when I saw my dad
> for the first time ever!

FIGURE 11.1   Poem by Fatoumata Bathily, Eighth-Grade Student.

Across the groups, students also prepared to go public with their work. In hip hop for example, students wrung their hands as they practiced, practiced, practiced—right up until the moment they entered the sound booth. They concentrated—focusing on staying with the beat and enunciating their words clearly. In the video group, students added final editing effects to their videos and prepared promotional movie posters to introduce their films to the audience. In poetry, students prepared a printed anthology of their pieces and practiced their performances out loud, focusing on volume, pace, and body language.

In the Culmination, students collaborated with each other, their teachers, and mentor artists on editing, feedback, and rehearsal. In preparation for the culminating event, students applied their learning by publishing their final drafts and preparing to teach their families about their artistic process. Adults and kids collaborated to prepare multilingual programs, anthologies, multilingual scripts that were performed live, recorded audio (a song about making a song!), video, and visual elements to tell the story of the program to the families and audience. In this way, the family night became not only a celebration of students' final products but also of their process—a demonstration of what they'd learned about their particular artistic genre and carrying out an academic project in general.

Telling Stories Through the Arts

Dozens of families mingled together before the culminating event began—chatting with their children's teachers, nibbling on petite sandwiches, observing the brightly colored murals painted on the Neutral Zone's walls and the bubble letter "tags" created by the hip hop group. It was obvious that this was no ordinary school event when students gathered at the stage and began chanting with their teachers:

> *Welcome students, friends, and kin!*
> *Let's come together! Let's begin!*
> *Hola, hola, hola (x2)*
> *Mar-ha-ba, Mar-ha-ba (x2)*
> *When I say Ahn, you say Young (x2)*
> *When I say Nín, you say Hao (x2)*
> *When I say Neutral, You say Zone (x2)*
> *When I say Challenge, You say Triumph (x2)*
> *Welcome to our celebration*
> *Coming together for this special occasion*
> *We made projects with three types of art*
> *And we'll share them with you, straight from the heart! (x2)*

The final event was a night where students' voices, languages, and stories were applauded, and families were recognized. While small programmatic moves like providing free bussing to the event and translating parent communications certainly helped boost attendance, the large turn out and effusive positive energy at the Neutral Zone final event was rooted in the fact that students' own stories made up the program's core curriculum. It was a moment of firsts for many of the stakeholders involved: the first time many families had utilized the downtown community teen center, the first time many of our emergent bilingual learners were front and center on stage rather than relegated to the side in non-speaking roles, the first time many of the educators in the room had seen students so proud and excited to share their learning.

It's certainly true that our high-ratio of adults to students is a unique circumstance that affords us the opportunity to introduce more complexity into our curricula, such as incorporating multiple genres. Still, our core principles for designing each summer's programming could be applied to a range of settings (see Reischl & Khasnabis, 2016). We believe that most critical to our curriculum was the recognition and honoring of our students' knowledge, experience, and stories.

So, we seek out opportunities to draw on the knowledge in our students' communities, and to create academic learning opportunities that are meaningful in the lives of students. We encourage readers to do the same, and also to think flexibly about the products that emerge from your programming. Student products that traverse different genres and mediums open up a world of possibilities.

Our students had stories to tell and wisdom to share; they generated ideas, chose a medium, and carefully edited their work—culminating in moments of going public with their stories of self. By observing mentors perform and discuss their art forms and through interactions with peers and through explicit teaching, they learned to craft their oral and written English to communicate messages that linked them to their peers and community. Through recursive, iterative process that included relationship building with peers and adults, they built language fluency, practiced composing and editing processes, and expressed confidence as they voiced their stories—skills that will serve them well as they advance to academically challenging work in the next grade in the fall.

Note

* Starred names indicate pseudonyms

References

Dalton, B. (2012). Multimodal composition and the common core state standards. *The Reading Teacher, 66*(4), 333–339.

Decoteau, J. I., Hall, H. B., & Hill, M. (2013). Schooling teachers, schooling ourselves: Insights and reflections from teaching K-12 teachers how to use hip-hop to educate students. *International Journal of Multicultural Education, 15*(1), 1–18.

Eisenhart, M. (1995). The fax, the jazz player, and the self-story teller: How do people organize culture? *Anthropology and Education Quarterly, 26*(1), 3–26.

Emdin, C. (2013). Pursuing the pedagogical potential of the pillars of hip-hop through science mindedness. *International Journal of Critical Pedagogy, 4*(3), 83–99.

Heard, G. (1999). *Awakening the heart: Exploring poetry in elementary and middle school.* Portsmouth, NH: Heinemann.

Paris, D. (2012). Culturally sustaining pedagogy: A needed change in stance, terminology, and practice. *Educational Researcher, 41*(3), 93–97.

Paris, D., & Alim, H. S. (2014). What are we seeking to sustain through culturally sustaining pedagogy? A loving critique forward. *Harvard Educational Review. 84*(1), 85–100.

Ray, K. W. (1999). *Wondrous words: Writers and writing in the elementary classroom.* Urbana, IL: National Council of Teachers of English.

Reischl, C., & Khasnabis, D. (2016). Affirming the identities of English learners through purposeful project-based literacy instruction. In Lakia M. Scott, & Barbara Purdum Cassidy (Eds.), *Culturally affirming literacy practices for urban elementary students.* Rowman and Littlefield.

Spindler, G., & Spindler, L. (1993). The processes of culture and person: Cultural therapy and culturally diverse schools. In P. Phelan & A. L. Davidson (Eds.), *Renegotiating cultural diversity in American schools* (pp. 27–51). New York, NY: Teachers College Press.

12

STORIER WARRIORS

New Waves of Indigenous Survivance and Language Revitalization

Laura Cranmer, Jocelyn Difiore and Jeffrey Paul Ansloos with Ryan L'Hirondelle and Paul Arthur

Notes from the Professor: Introduction by Dr. Laura Cranmer

> Confronting linguistic and cultural racism in Canada involves understanding Indigenous languages and worldviews as protected Indigenous rights. They are constitutionally protected zones of linguistic and philosophical integrity (Turpel 1989–90). Indigenous languages and worldviews are protected by sections 2(b), 21, 22, 25, 27 of the Canadian Charter of Rights and Freedoms and section 35 of the Constitution Act, 1982.
>
> (Battiste & Youngblood Henderson, 2000, p. 84)

Gilakasda'xwla naℏnamwayut. Nugwa'am K̲'ixtlala. Gayuλan laxida 'Yalis. Gayuλamxa'an laxida Haida laxan abaskutamɛ. Gayuλan laxida 'Namgis laxan 'oskutamɛ. Hɛman gagampwała G̲wanti'lakw 'i'axsila gaxan. Ax'ɛsdan kan mumałkagałɛxoxda Routledge ka'ans gaxanayans kwała laxux 'awinagwisas. Gilakasla

Welcome to those with whom I am one. My feast name K̲'ixtlala roughly translates to a large fire, or many sparks on top, with which to feed many. I am from the Namgis[1] River through my father David Cranmer, and I am from Haida Gwaii through my mother Pearl Weir. My paternal grandmother Agnes Cranmer cared for me during my childhood years. I would like to thank Routledge for the reasons we are sitting on this land (here land is a metaphor for the discursive space provided by Routledge Publishing).

St. Michael's Residential School in Alert Bay, British Columbia, became the confluence of the great lineages of my paternal and maternal ancestors. Not ordinarily given to expressions of prideful exclamations of origin, here I honor the struggles of my ancestors without whose love, patience, and strength I would not have transcended the early childhood experiences suffered by so many in my community. From the court convictions of my ancestors for practicing our potlatch traditions (hosted by my paternal grandfather Dan Cranmer) in 1922, to the disruption of my maternal line in 1953, my colonial history runs as an undercurrent that at times surfaces as an unwelcome smell and at other times surfaces as a geyser of anger and resentment. This undercurrent has been the impelling force in my attempt to make meaning of my familial history through my various post-secondary choices, which was guided by my undergraduate professors' affirmations of my aptitude for literary expression. Studying and writing poetry and analytical essays of poems and plays, along with researching for term papers, all contributed to my love of the literary arts such that I chose to write my MA in Curriculum Studies thesis as a full-length play that creatively symbolized a dialogue between the colonial and contemporary eras. Although there is no Kwak'wala word for art, artistic expression is infused in the daily material and ceremonial life of the Kwakwa̱ka̱'wakw. On reflection, beyond the western conception of art, I here acknowledge the legacy of my resiliency through creativity, which is connected to the spiritual fire inherited by my ancestors. My personal journey of transformation that honors the lived experience of my community and me, connects to how contemporary Indigenous hip hop artists create and honor their own lived experiences in the next section of this chapter.

Concurrent with my post-secondary programs I also engaged in concerted, ongoing personal therapy such that my writing became my therapy and my therapy became my writing. Literary artistic expression, in English and Kwak'wala, became my fuel for transforming my life and my reality. Therefore, I contend that art for the marginalized and the silenced, as has been my lived experience, can be used as a tool to build a platform by which to discover one's voice and creatively express one's truth so necessary in remaking one's reality. This chapter's focus on hip hop promises to extend the connection between art and Indigenous language revitalization.

To begin with, I discuss the interdisciplinary approach to Indigenous language revitalization, with Indigenous Studies as a key frame of the authors and theories that guided my dissertation work. My introduction is followed by the essay, *Storier Warriors* by Jocelyn Difiore along with the supportive input of Ryan L'Hirondelle and Paul Arthur, that inspired the creation of this chapter. Their essay stems from an assignment in the undergraduate third-year First Nations Studies course on Indigenous languages and identities, in which they wrote about how Indigenous hip hop artists are contributing to their community language revitalization efforts. Dr. Jeffrey Ansloos then concludes this chapter with his reflection on how *Storier Warriors* provides a forum for healing and resistance, as well as an expression of identity for Indigenous hip hop artists.

In 2011 and 2015 I designed and offered a Special Topics course in First Nations Studies, also known as FNAT 380: Indigenous Languages and Identities. In creating this course, I drew from my doctoral work, an autoethnographic artistic account of my Kwak'wala[2] language learning process, which was inspired by theorists within the fields of Second Language Acquisition (SLA) (Gass & Selinker, 2008), Language Socialization (Duff, 2010), and Identity Theory (Norton & Toohey, 2011; Pavlenko & Lantolf, 2000). I found that branching out into these fields yielded valuable lessons which helped me make sense of perplexing social dynamics in my Kwak'wala learning, and hoped that my students would find similar resonances. From class discussions and student journals, a consensus emerged that these theories helped make sense of their own lived ancestral language experiences, whether as an Indigenous or non-Indigenous individual.

Emergent from the broad field of SLA research is a growing body of scholarly production by Indigenous scholars who report on their own language reclamation processes and outcomes, as can be found in Daniels-Fiss (2008), McIvor (2010), Rosborough (2012), Cranmer (2016), and Nicholson (2005). By no means exhaustive, this list of authors indexes the internal and external challenges in the urgent work of Indigenous language revitalization. These works also provide valuable insights into the sociocultural conditions and pedagogical strategies for re-awakening and re-learning Indigenous languages. They contribute to a critical mass of scholarship by, for, and about scholars working in the area of Indigenous language revitalization.

In his plenary address to the 1997 Fourth Annual Stabilizing Indigenous Languages conference, Littlebear (1999) observes that young people in his community are not hard-wired to learn Cheyenne:

> They must learn to speak the Cheyenne language in just the same way they would have to go about acquiring Greek or German or Swahili, especially since for almost all of them English is now their first language. Everybody who works with languages should learn about second language acquisition and the theories buttressing it and be able to apply those theories in whatever subject area they are teaching.
>
> (p. 5)

Turning to SLA and identity theories to apply to Indigenous language revitalization efforts has been helpful in identifying a segment of the population of Indigenous language speech communities categorized as latent or semi-speakers. These terms (latent or semi-speakers) grow out of the collective experience of our colonial history of the forced separation of children from their families to attend residential schools, where children were shamed and punished for using their languages. In turn, my generation only understand a minimal amount of our Indigenous languages. And the following generation after mine, belonging to some of those hip hop artists described in this chapter, are in a sense approaching their Indigenous language as second language learners, as explained by Littlebear's observation of the young people in his community earlier.

As Basham and Fathman (2008) explain, "One common factor affecting all groups, as well as most Native American communities, is the educational policy which forcibly excluded use of the indigenous languages in schools" (p. 582). In their 2-year study of speakers from the Alaskan Yupik speech community, Basham and Fathman assert that latent speakers, by and large, demonstrate the following characteristics: an understanding of basic vocabulary and expressions, familiarity with pronunciations, intonation and rhythm, tendency to minimize speaking ability and language knowledge, and implicit awareness of language as well as language shyness (p. 592). Littlebear's exhortation to educators working in Indigenous language revitalization stems from a deep concern for his beloved Cheyenne language and Basham and Fathman's latent speaker research would be quite instructive and enlightening for any language community (Indigenous or otherwise) attempting to support the transformation of semi-speakers to fluent speakers.

In her chapter, "Language and Identity" Norton (2010) offers a summation of ten years of teaching her course "Language, Discourse, and Identity" in which she critiques theories that do not account for "struggles over the social meanings that can be attributed to signs in a given language" and argues, "Every time we speak, we are negotiating and renegotiating our sense of self in relation to the larger social world, and reorganizing that relationship across time and space" (p. 349). Given Norton's argument, how might the art of young Indigenous hip hop artists resist not only state oppression, but also resist institutional racism attempt to "reorganize" the relationship between the Canadian state and Indigenous communities? Norton continues:

> As Weedon (1997) notes, it is through language that a person negotiates a sense of self within and across a range of sites at different points in time, and it is through language that a person gains access to—or is denied access to—powerful social networks that give learners the opportunity to speak. These ideas speak directly to language teachers and learners.
>
> (Norton, p. 349)

The devices, implements, and tools of the arts, whether in the visual arts, in theatre, in song, in poem, in dance, equips the artist—in this instance the Indigenous hip hop artist—with the specialized tools with which to wield and cut space from the air to creatively mediate or negotiate the self in relationship to oppressive living conditions in which to paint, act, sing, write, and move one's truth.

The student essay that follows opens up yet another promising avenue for pedagogical application, scholarship, and indeed for revitalization itself. The work of Indigenous language reclamation ultimately proceeds from a positive and life affirming framework that values and validates Indigenous epistemologies and diverse worldviews as revealed through our language studies in the discipline of Indigenous Studies. That this chapter centers on music, produced by Indigenous hip hop artists who incorporate words and phrases from their heritage languages, speaks to the resiliency afforded by creativity to resist forms of oppression and domination that confront Indigenous peoples in many facets of routine dailyness of life whether on or off reserve.

To accommodate the linguistic diversity represented by my FNAT 380 students, the assignments were designed to elicit and promote the language research interests of individual students. While inquiring into fields such as Narrative Studies, Second Language Acquisition, and Heritage Language Acquisition, Indigenous Studies theories and methods provide our central theoretical framework. This framework centers on Indigenous epistemologies that proceed from Indigenous languages, life experiences, and identities.

The course assignments were closely linked and built on each other beginning with a ten-page autobiography on students' earliest memories of language, followed by a 15-page research paper co-authored with a classmate, and a subsequent poster design based on the findings of their research paper. For their research papers students were asked to choose a topic or an aspect of Indigenous language revitalization from a list of suggested topics. For the poster design segment of the syllabus, the class viewed an hour-long lecture (on video) on the elements of poster design provided by Williams (2015), professor in Digital Media and posted on VIU's Scholarship, Research, and Creative Activity website to assist students learning how to apply elements of graphic design to create what Williams (2015) refers to as "high impact posters." The co-authored research paper assignment was a modified version of an assignment I had been given by Dr. Patricia Duff for my Language and Literacy in Education course (LLED 573), which I found to be such a rewarding collaborative experience that I wanted to replicate this assignment for my students.

We concluded the semester with a poster display and a guest panel consisting of three Indigenous language activists (belonging to different language families on Vancouver Island), one of the Elders-in-Residence (from our department), and a linguist specializing in Hul'q'umin'um. Hul'q'umin'um is one of the dialects of the Coast Salish and specifically our host First Nation, the Snuneymuxw. With special guests, friends, and relatives of students in attendance, the student teams presented their research conveyed through their poster designs which provided a snapshot of current concerns in the scholarship of Indigenous language revitalization.

The 2011 Canadian Census reports that almost half the total of Indigenous populations lives off reserve in Canada in large urban centers (Aboriginal peoples: Fact sheet for Canada, 2011). Beyond the Native Friendship Centers (found in major Canadian city centers that function as welcoming social spaces and providing social referral services) the artistic communities, such as hip hop, create the conditions by which Indigenous peoples can coalesce, collaborate, and co-create from a shared sense of belonging, shared sense of history, and historical memory—even while living far from home territories. The hip hop music genre is particularly important for the messages of colonial resistance and solidarity conveyed to young urban Indigenous folks searching for role models who might positively mirror back their own realities.

At the time of writing the following chapter, lead author Jocelyn Difiore, along with the supportive input of Ryan L'Hirondelle and Paul Arthur, were undergraduate students completing a BA in First Nations Studies. Our BA in First Nations Studies is a program that promotes intellectual, social, and spiritual development through responsive cross-cultural involvement. In addition to acquiring critical academic knowledge and skills, students in First Nations Studies develop strong social bonds, demonstrate a keen sense of social justice, and routinely engage in wider community activities as leaders and volunteers. Their work in this chapter stands as testimony to their ongoing accomplishments in these areas.

Gilakasdạxwla.
Thank you all.
Dr. Laura Cranmer

Storier Warriors: Indigenous Hip Hop and Language Survivance by Jocelyn Difiore with Ryan L'Hirondelle and Paul Arthur

> "language is less a human possession than it is a property of the animate earth itself, an expressive, telluric power in which we, along with the coyotes and the crickets, all participate."
>
> —(Abram, 2011, p. 171)

Studies show that in Canada, Indigenous languages and their speakers are in decline; consequently, these communities are witnessing the greatest language shift of their time (Norris, 2000, 2011). In their chapter "Indigenous, Minority and Heritage Language Education in Canada: Policies, Contexts and Issues," Duff and Li (2009) describe the current context, challenges, and issues connected to heritage language education in an ever-changing cultural and multilingual country such as Canada. They suggest that less than 30% of the Indigenous population in Canada can speak or understand an Indigenous language, and even less report it as their parent language (p. 1). Jessica Ball's (2009) research into the language needs of young Indigenous language learners found that there are "enormous gaps in knowledge about what Indigenous children and families need in order to ensure optimal language development and effective approaches to meeting their needs" (p. 40). In this essay we respond to Ball's call by sharing creative forums for linguistic expression by Indigenous young people.

Gerald Vizenor, an Anishnaabe scholar (re)claimed and (re)coined the word survivance to describe the complex systems of survival and resistance among Indigenous peoples. He argues that "Native survivance is an act of presence over absence, deracination and oblivion; survivance is the continuance of stories that renounce dominance, tragedy and victimry" (Vizenor, 2008, p. 1). Indigenous languages mirror Vizenor's theory of survivance in that they are in a state of constant flux. Growing interest in *linguistic survivance* (Wyman, 2012), among scholars, educators, community, and youth suggest that not all heritage languages will be lost; instead they will continue to evolve and adapt to ongoing change.

Sociolinguist Leisy Thornton Wyman (2012) adopted Vizenor's survivance theory to devise the term *linguistic survivance*, meaning, to "sidestep the pitfall of imposing binary interpretations upon Indigenous people as simply 'speakers' or 'non-speakers' of the endangered languages" (p. 14). Instead, she illuminates ways that individuals and communities use heritage languages, second languages, and the act of translanguaging—the moving across or intermixing of languages and language varieties (García, 2009), to "shape collective identities, practices and knowledge systems in challenging or hostile circumstances" (p. 14). Wyman suggests that Indigenous youth act as language brokers who use modern technologies and systems to "mediate the erosion of their heritage languages" (Wyman as found in Enomoto, 2014, p. 123). In doing so they participate in "one of the most dramatic sociolinguistic phenomena of our times" (Wyman, 2012, p. 1). Emergent from the previously mentioned theories of survivance are Canada's hip hop Storier Warriors[3]—young Indigenous art crusaders, rhyming and rapping and street mapping the future of their cultural identity and mother tongue(s). We will use hip hop culture to explore the roles of Indigenous youth in individual and collective creative expression involving heritage language survivance in Canada. We draw on the discoveries of scholars in the field of hip hop, literature and linguistics, as well as the works of Indigenous hip hop artists to demonstrate how Indigenous languages are being carried forward in their speech communities.

Unveilin' the Hist'ry and Myst'ry of Hip Hop

Hip hop music and culture was born out of the Bronx in the 1970s as a response to the "decline of both civil rights and the Black Power movement" (MacDonald, 2012, p. 95). Primarily used a tool of resistance, hip hop gave voice to marginalized groups in need of a medium to express opposition to the prevailing dominant culture. Over time, news of hip hop went viral, spread globally, and eventually became a new generation of people who expressed themselves through what is known as the four elements of hip hop: DJ-ing, Emceeing, breakdancing, and street art. Harvard professor, Marcyliena Morgan, claims "hip-hoppers literally mapped onto the consciousness of the world a place and an identity for themselves as the originators of an exciting new art form. They created value out of races and places that had seemed to offer only devastation" (Laurence, 2014, October). Many styles emerged from the original hip hop scene, ranging from old school, to gangsta rap, to reggaeton, to "keepin' it real"—a style that is central to hip hop aesthetics in that it highlights urban authenticity through a connection to neighborhood and community solidarity (MacDonald, 2012, p. 95).

Indigenous Storier Warriors: Survivance Stories

In the early 1990s hip hop was adopted in Canada by Indigenous youth who (re)claimed, (re)named, and Indigenized hip hop to fit their own life experiences. See that's the thing about hip hop . . . it's adoptable . . . adaptable . . . always changing . . . never stayin' the same. Here we see the elasticity of Vizenor's theory of survivance applied to the dynamic social phenomenon of the growth of Indigenous hip hop in response to oppressive living conditions. Hip hop became a language with a common thread as an act of resistance and a way to tell one's story.

Indigenous hip hop rapper, Miss Christie Lee (a.k.a. Christie Lee Charles), is a Musqueam First Nations woman with ancestry in both Tsleil-Wauhtuth and Squamish First Nations. She was taught to speak the hənq̓əminəm̓ dialect from an early age by her great-uncle and continued her study of the language at the University of British Columbia. Her music is a fusion of hənq̓əminəm̓ and English dialect that tells stories of hope and renewal. "This music is about my teachings and my culture . . . before creating this type of music I approached Elders and received permissions to use our teachings in this modern way and follow the proper protocols. . . . I use this tool as an outreach for Indigenous youth" (retrieved from www.beatnation.org/music.html). Miss Christie Lee's song, "*Experience*" (2011), is written/rapped in both hənq̓əminəm̓ and English dialect.

> These words I have to say
> ain't like anything you ever heard in
> your day, straight spittin' my ways
> this is how I play. . . .
> you and me be living in a time that they was living for. . . .
> believe it or not we the future of history
> so stop living your life like it was a mystery. . . .
> [See reference list for Miss Christie Lee's recording "Experience" (2011) www.
> youtube.com/watch?v=T17GyBgCYFM]

In a 2011 interview, Miss Christie Lee stated that translanguaging—the intermixing of Indigenous and English languages, "makes me feel a lot more connected to who I am and where I come from. It makes me feel stronger inside. . . . There's a hunger in youth to learn more about their culture" (Dobbins & Walters, 2011). She uses Indigenous hip hop not only to instill pride in her family and community but also to reach marginalized youth nationwide. Her use of the spoken word provides practical examples of linguistic survivance. Parallel to Miss Christie's sentiment, Cranmer and Smith (2008) observe,

> [t]he challenges faced by many Indigenous communities today center on and are interwoven among issues of social ill health, affecting mental, physical, emotional, and spiritual well-being. Identity (and therefore language) are part and parcel of these issues, signifying the extent to which Indigenous languages contribute to and shape one's sense of belonging.

(p. 1)

If Miss Christie Lee's experience of her art contributing to a strengthened sense of identity is any indication, then hip hop as an Indigenous art form has a strong message for young Indigenous audiences.

Indigenous Storier Warriors: Hip hop Aesthetics and Survivance Stories

Indigenous cultures are deeply rooted in stories, many of which are passed down generationally. Nuu Chah Nulth hereditary chief Umeek (a.k.a. Richard Atleo) claims that origin stories are the foundation of knowledge about the state of existence (Atleo, 2004, p. xi); they provide insight into lived experiences that help make sense of the world. As Glancy is cited by Vizenor, "The old stories carry all the voices of those who have told them. When the story is spoken, all of those voices are in the voice of the narrator" (*Designs of the Night Sky* by Diane Glancy found in Vizenor, 2009, p. 1). Glancy's words reflect what Vizenor calls a "Native Storier." According to Vizenor, "Native Storiers create the tropes of oral stories in the silence of narratives and in the imaginic scenes of eternal motion, totemic transmutation, pronoun waves, gender obversion, animal presence, protean voices, and a sense of survivance" (p. 4). Indigenous hip hop artists are present-day Storier Warriors, whose poetry, dance, and art—when pieced together—create "a collective memory of space and time through contextualizing Indigenous lived experiences (both positive and negative) that have been passed down generationally" (Recollect, 2010, p. ii).

Anishinaabe hip hop artist, Wab Kinew, comes from the Onigaming First Nation in Ontario. In his earlier years, Kinew oscillated between two worlds: life as an aspiring hip hop artist in Winnipeg and life within an academic and somewhat affluent home.

Kinew (Everett-Green, 2014) suggests that life behind the scenes reflected transmission of intergenerational trauma from residential school, as indicated in interview discussion about his father, "I think that's the way the residential school legacy impacted me. He wasn't exposed to the loving, nurturing side of parenthood, so I didn't get that from him either (van Paassen, 2014)." Subsequently, Kinew took refuge in the streets where he became a founding member of the hip hop collective called the "Dead Indians" (an action representative of Vizenor's theory of survivance). "We were the first group of Aboriginal kids in Winnipeg to start hitting up hip hop shows consistently, and were a part of the first major wave of Native hip hop in Canada." In 2009, Wab Kinew released his first album, *Live by the Drum*, with lyrics in English, Anishinaabemowin, and French. His song, "A Good Boy" (www.youtube.com/watch?v=ghVHNrNbpII), about the 2005 shooting death of 18-year-old Matthew Dumas by a law enforcement officer, confronts ongoing racism in Canada while echoing the voice of survivance. Recalling Wyman's theory of linguistic survivance that "shape[s] collective identities in hostile circumstances," Kinew's song provide a stark example of the life and death situations for Indigenous youth persecuted by hostile forces informed by racist policies and resulting in discriminatory practices by the justice system in Canada. With this one song, Kinew has memorialized the death of a young Indigenous man—emblematic of ongoing relationships between law enforcement and Indigenous peoples in Canada. Kinew has since moved on to become an acclaimed author, scholar, educator, broadcaster, and political party leader in Canada.

Aligned with Wab Kinew, Muskoday First Nation hip hop artist, Eekwol (Lindsay Knight) was one of the first female emcees to emerge onto the Indigenous hip hop scene in Canada. She uses rhymin' and beats to create unique and complex narratives that echo the realities of Indigenous peoples in Canada. Her music interweaves past traditions with the social, political, and cultural experiences of contemporary Indigenous women, men, and youth. Eekwol sees hip hop as an effective way to relate to young people in that "they love the genre, and because ancestral history runs through our blood and our spirits, and youth can relate to that kind of storytelling" (Marsh, 2009, p. 13). Cultural anthropologist, Julie Cruikshank suggests, "Stories allow listeners to embellish events, to reinterpret them, to mull over what they hear and to learn something new each time, providing raw material for developing philosophy" (as cited in Marsh, 2012, p. 366).

Eekwol's use of translanguaging in songs such as "*Kisay's Song Iskwewak Iskotew Tapwewin*" and "*Ohtaw Nanepanees*," demonstrates her ongoing connection and contribution to Indigenous language survivance. She uses her music and her stories of resistance and renewal as a way to keep her culture, land, and identity alive for future generations. Eekwol is now a mother and a graduate student with a Master's Degree from the University of Saskatchewan. An authentic Storier Warrior, Eekwol continues to deploy her musical curiosities through examining the connections between past and present Indigenous music.

Indigenous hip hop Storier Warriors are not limited to rap music. Artists such as Enpaauk (Andrew Mark Dexel), from the Nlaka'pamux Nation, uses paint as a medium to express his worldview. Enpaauk began his career as a graffiti artist, bringing energy from the streets to his wall paintings. In 2012 he made the move from urban city walls to canvas. His art fuses graffiti style with Coast Salish design, using bold, unconventional colors to "create unique transcultural works that compose modern day interpretations of traditional forms, stories and teachings to inspire future generations" (Enpaauk, 2009).

Enpaauk explains:

> My work relates to my spiritual path; my journey. I express the inspiration lovingly given to me through teachings and stories from my elders and mentors. My work embodies the powerful visions that I have been given through these teachings. I am grateful. My work is a modern expression embodying the abstract inspired by my home: Coast Salish Territory.

In alignment with Vizenor's theory of survivance (2008), Indigenous Storier Warriors are social and political activists who use their music and art to create narratives that demonstrate their ongoing presence over absence, in resistance to tragedy and victimry, one story at a time.

Identity and Community

> "To listen to hip hop is to enter a world of contradiction."
>
> (Perry, 2004, p. 1)

Indigenous youth are often subjected to multiple tensions resulting from the ongoing impact of colonial history on contemporary relationships. Forced diaspora, racism, neglect, and intergenerational transmission of trauma generate feelings of shame, low self-esteem, and a lack of belonging (to name a few) which leads to a constant search for ways to negotiate identity, culture, and worldviews. Feminist writer bell hooks observes:

> Again and again as I travel around I am stunned by how many citizens in our nation feel lost, feel bereft of a sense of direction, feel as though they cannot see where the journeys lead, that they cannot know where they are going. Many folks feel no sense of place.
>
> (hooks, 2009, p. 1)

Indigenous hip hop provides a place and a space for young people to engage in critical discussions that address hard topics. It can be seen as a "culture of belonging" (hooks, 2009, p. 216), a community that emerges from intimate relationships with others, built on mutual respect, acknowledgement, and appreciation; a community that celebrates diversity over adversity. Similar to hooks's observation of her fellow citizens, Richard Littlebear in a plenary speech for a conference on revitalizing Indigenous languages in 1999, had these thoughts to share:

> Teachers of American Indian languages must remember that everybody has to go through some definite stages of acquiring a language. Right now we have children who are mute in our languages, who are migrants to our languages, who are like extra-terrestrials to our cultures. We have youth who are aliens to us because they do not have the vital linguistic link that identifies them as Cheyenne or whatever tribal group they belong to.
>
> (Littlebear, p. 5)

If anything, the art of Indigenous hip hop may very well serve to bridge the divide between generations of speakers that Littlebear laments in his speech. Just as the youth, mute in their heritage languages feel alienated from their elders, so too do their elders feel alienated from their young people. Recognizing the unique dynamics at play in intergenerational language transmission for his community,

Littlebear also encourages his elder community members to exercise more patience, openness, and generosity of spirit toward their young people in order to draw out their language from the youth. There must be creative ways to allow space not only for Indigenous heritage languages to grow as important identity markers for modern youth, but also ways for youth to incorporate their new language learning into contemporary art forms such as hip hop.

The four elements of hip hop play a crucial role in (re)discovering and (re)defining identity among Indigenous youth: DJ's sound and construct narratives out of scratchin' and beats. Emcees are what Karyn Recollect calls the "contemporary manifestations of orality" (2010, p. 1); they interweave languages and complex narratives, metaphors, and rhymes to tell stories of survivance that relate to Indigenous lived experiences. Breakdancers are like a culture within a culture; they dance out their stories to the scratchin and beats of their fellow DJs and emcees. Graffiti artists are the masters of visual stories. Their work in an "in yo' face" act of resistance and renewal that reflects their individual worldview. The four elements of Indigenous hip hop make up a unique youth movement that celebrates empowerment and self-expression through art, music, and community.

Rappin' It Up

This chapter is our interwoven voices which demonstrate how Indigenous youth and the aesthetics of hip hop culture act as language brokers that contribute to Indigenous language survivance in Canada. By engaging in music, storytelling, dance, and street art, Indigenous youth join forces to create communities that address the social, political, economic, and cultural occurrences that mirror the realities of their people. Their complex narratives of resistance and renewal help to make sense of the world and facilitate the ongoing pursuit of identity and belonging. As we have learned, identity is not static, but dynamic and revisiting Norton's observation/theory "is negotiated, renegotiated and reorganized through language across time and place" (p. 350). Languages are in constant negotiations with change. We raise our hands in gratitude to all the Storier Warriors across the globe, for their ongoing contribution to heritage language survivance in an ever-changing world. In closing, the words of famed Cree hip hop artist, Feenix (Shawn Bernard).

> I'm strong
> I'm strong like two people
> Cause I live in two worlds I choose equal
> One world has to do with the past—the other world is a world that's moving too fast
> I'm strong. . .
> We gotta rise up and try to put down
> To live in two worlds with pride that's intact
> I'm Strong
> (Bernard, 2011).

Reflections on Storier Warriors *by Dr. Jeffrey Paul Ansloos: Survivance and Spirit*

> tansi awow, jeffrey ansloos nitisi yih kâson, ochekwi sipi ohci niya kayahtê, win-nipi nikî-nihtâwîkin, W̱SÁNEĆ mêkwâc niwîkin, êkota okiskinwa-hamâkêw niya. sherry, nikâwiy. paul, nôhtâwiy.

> Hello everyone, my name is Jeffrey Ansloos. I am from Fisher River Cree Nation, and I grew up in Winnipeg. I currently live on the territory of the W̱SÁNEĆ, where I work as a Professor at the University of Victoria. My mother is Sherry Ansloos, my father Paul Ansloos.

As a nehiyaw scholar and nehiyawewin language learner, my foundational beliefs about identity and culture are rooted in a relational understanding of being *through*, *of*, and *with* spirit. In a nehiyawin perspective of being, all things are spiritually related. These relationships are the normative ethical context for all the actions we take in the world, and this is why we seek to walk in a good way. This is why, when Simpson in *Under Your Always Light* (www.youtube.com/watch?v=0yLR5g9gUB4) speaks of kwezens and gwiiwizens, she makes clear that Indigenous relations span time, space, human and nonhuman, ancestors and future generations to come, and because of this, we carry responsibility to one another. Simpson reminds us that our ancestors have given us stories in our language, which are the creative force of decolonial love that can guide our actions to give life to future generations. She calls us to "use scar-weapons to hold the land around them," to "infect tiny bodies with the precious things they beat out of you," and "remember: they are everything we could have been." She reminds us that our work today in education, in the creative survivance of Indigenous languages, is to recognize that we are threaded and embedded in dynamic and spirited ecologies which make us all inextricable related to one another. This kinship is inglorious, painful, and beautiful. Recognition of our profound relationality is what Indigenous hip hop and forms of Indigenous New Wave music is teaching us. Rejecting the oppressions of colonialism is about creative acts of love, overcoming the oppression of cultural shame, and holding spirit within us.

In her article *Land As Pedagogy: Nishnaabeg intelligence and rebellious transformation*, Indigenous New Wave artist and scholar, Leanne Betasamosake Simpson (2014) highlights how the knowledge, ethics, and traditions of Nishnaabeg people are relational and co-creative processes which begin and continue through manidoo (manidoo in anishinaabemowin, or manitou as it is said in nehiyaw, means *spirit*). What these reflections on Storier Warriors illuminate for me is what it means to be an Indigenous person surviving in the face of colonial oppression. It reminds me of the boldness and resilience of Indigenous youth fighting for the survival and vitalization of our culture. Reflecting on these pages, it is all the more clear that this work is rooted in manidoo. Our languages have creative life, and our creative actions through our languages, makes manifest a new way of living in a world of settler-colonial oppression. Hip hop is not simply an art form or creative genre, it is a spiritual movement, and the spirit of Indigenous People is nourished through these creative actions. The survivance of our languages is about more than words, it is about the survival of our spirit.

Hip hop, as an extension of a broader genre of Indigenous New Wave is foremost a spiritual movement of Indigenous youth. It represents an innovative nexus of creative actions, art, new media, and social movements. These expressions of Indigenous youth are generating new knowledge and ways of being which are helping us to reclaim aspects of our identity, community, and culture, oppressed by colonialism. Hip hop, in the context of the survivance of Indigenous Peoples' languages, is an evolving constellation of Indigenous tradition, culture, and creative reclamations, inclusive of a wide range of visual and creative traditions (i.e., visual and performing arts), youth generated curation (i.e., hacktivism, street art), dynamic networked communities (i.e., #IndigenousTwitter, #IndigenousNewWave), and sites, materials, and practices of decolonial resistance (i.e., Colonialism 150, #ReOccupy). These are all expressions of survival in the face of colonial violence (Martineau, 2015, 2017).

Hip hop coalesces around the spiritual process of creation, and when that creation comes to include language other than English or French in a context where such languages were imposed violently, these aesthetic actions "within and beyond" dominant representations of Indigenous identities (Robinson & Martin, 2016) demonstrate the power and strength of Indigenous youth. To utter a word like manidoo, in a country where in my grandmother's generation, these words were illegal and would result in abuse, represents power. This power, a hybridity of decolonial and indigenizing praxis (Ansloos, 2013a, 2013b), is embodied by contributors to Indigenous New Wave. Hip hop artists, rappers, poets, and creators are celebrating, reclaiming, and generating new evolutions in Indigenous language, traditions, cultures, languages, and spirit, and in the process actively resisting the complex violence of colonialism (Dixon, 2012; Martineau, 2015, 2017; Wente in Bergstrom, 2015; Northway-Frank in Bergstrom, 2015).

Emerging waves of creative Indigenous pop culture, be it hip hop or otherwise, are nourishing the spirit of language through "stories of re-creation, resurgence and a new emergence (Simpson, 2014, p. 14). Through hip hop Indigenous youth are being awakened in their hearts and minds. Indigenous artists are not simply creating, but also participating within manidoo, "an embodied knowledge animated, collectively, and lived out in a way in which our reality, nationhood and existence is continually reborn through both time and space" (p. 14).

In my own traditions, we call this creative way, living in ceremony. Ceremony is the culturally creative and socially sustaining practices which bring healing, enabling survival in the face of violence (Ansloos, 2017). Put another way, what I see in this chapter are the ways in which Indigenous youth are nourishing manidoo and making manifest new life. Such actions are never one thing. The survival of

Indigenous language through hip hop is not simply a method for language revitalization; further, Indigenous New Wave is not simply an expression of Indigenous culture through art. Hip hop is a politically strategic and culturally grounded set of actions that promote resilience in ecologies of settler-colonialism, and awakens public consciousness of colonial oppression, "creating community connections for decolonial action" (Ansloos, 2017, pp. 104–105).

Indigenous New Wave provides us a way of seeing and speaking truth about the world. Storier Warriors remind us that how we use our languages gives us power to resist colonial oppression, first and foremost by bearing witness to the horrific violence of colonialism. In the song "How I Feel" by A Tribe Called Red (2016) we are reminded that there are indeed sociopolitical dimensions of the loss of language. The fact that I do not speak nehiyawin fluently is because of colonial violence. Colonial violence in Canada is not an abstract idea, it is aggressive, material, and it has robbed generations, including my mother, grandmother, and me of our own culture. How do we reclaim, heal, and survive?

For me, survival is first about listening to the truth. Indigenous hip hop often invites us into creative actions which speak to settler-colonialism, racism, economic apartheid, and other painful dimensions of the experience of Indigenous Peoples. But if we listen closely, we can hear that in the midst of endless iterations of violence against Indigenous Peoples, our spirit has survived. When we utter our language, be it in songs or poems, street art, or in tattoos on our bodies, we are remembering that our people have never stopped climbing. We are:

> the tribe running, rocking, reaching new peaks, so that them young'uns can finally summit, climbing high above and then fly from it, up to the skies, over standing the corruption and then deconstructing the lies.
> (How I Feel" by A Tribe Called Red, 2016).

For me, the survival of our languages is about our own material survival. And Storier Warriors are giving life and nourishing the spirit of our people through their creative decolonial actions.

Notes

1 The 'Namgis people originate from the 'Namgis River located within the traditional territory of the Kwakwaka'wakw at the north end of Vancouver Island and adjacent to mainland British Columbia. Haida Gwaii is the traditional territory of the Haida people and is also located on an archipelago of islands off the north coast of British Columbia.

2 British Columbia is home to a rich diversity of First Nations languages and home to an estimated 60% of the total of such languages across Canada. In 2014 BC Status of First Nations Languages cited 165 fluent speakers. That there are so few fluent Kwak'wala speakers out of a total population of 5,500 reflects the current precarious state of First Nations languages within British Columbia. However, the same report sounded a note

of optimism in that there had been a 9.32% increase in semi-speakers over their 2010 report (p. 19).
3 Jocelyn Difiore, lead author of this chapter, builds on Vizenor's term "storier" with the additional term "warrior" to create the phrase contained in the title.

References

Aboriginal peoples: Fact sheet for Canada. (2011). Retrieved from www.statcan.gc.ca/pub/89-656-x/89-656-x2015001-eng.htm.

Abram, David (2011). *Becoming animal: An earthly cosmology*. New York, NY: Vintage Books.

Ansloos, J. P. (2013a, January). Decolonization, overview. In T. Teo (Ed.), *Encyclopedia of critical psychology*. New York, NY: Springer Press.

Ansloos, J. P. (2013b, January). Indigenization, overview. In T. Teo (Ed.), *Encyclopedia of critical psychology*. New York, NY: Springer Press.

Ansloos, J. P. (2017). *The medicine of peace: Indigenous youth resisting violence and decolonizing healing*. Halifax, NS: Fernwood Publishing, Ltd.

Atleo, R. (2004). *Tsawalk: A Nuu-Chah-Nulth worldview*. Vancouver, BC: UBC Press.

Ball, Jessica. (2009). Supporting young indigenous children's language development in Canada: A review of research on needs and promising practices. *Canadian Modern Language Review, 66*(1), 19–47.

Basham, C. & Fathman, A. (2008). The latent speaker: Attaining adult fluency in an endangered language. *International Journal of Bilingual Education and Bilingualism,* 11(5), 577–597.

Battiste, M., & Youngblood Henderson, J. (2000). The importance of language for Indigenous knowledge. In M. Battiste & J. Youngblood Henderson (Eds.), *Protecting indigenous knowledge and heritage* (pp. 73–85). Saskatoon, Sask.: Purich Publishing Ltd.

Bernard, S. (2011). *Strong*. Retrieved from www.ssdec.nt.ca/ablang/strong/intro.pdf.

Bergstrom, A. (2015, November 1). *The indigenous new wave: A populist stage of indigenous cinema*. Retrieved October 05, 2017, from http://thetfs.ca/article/the-indigenous-new-wave-apopulist-stage-of-indigenous-cinema/.

Cranmer, L. (2016). *Reclaiming Kwak'wala through Co-constructing Gwanti'lakw's Vision* Unpublished Dissertation. Vancouver, BC: University of British Columbia.

Cranmer, L., & Smith, J. (2008). *Reformation and reclamation in indigenous heritage language learning: A review of literature*, Unpublished manuscript.

Daniels-Fiss, B. (2008). Learning to be a Nehiyaw (Cree) through language. *Diaspora, Indigenous, and Minority Education, 2*, 233–245.

Dixon, G. (2012, June 24). Toronto's First Peoples festival spotlights an indigenous new wave that's 'starting to crest'. *The Globe and Mail*. Retrieved from https://beta.theglobeandmail.com/arts/film/torontos-first-peoples-festival-spotlights-anindigenous-new-wave-thats-starting-tocrest/article4364964/?ref=www.theglobeandmail.com&

Dobbins, N., & Walters, K. (2011, April 5). Retrieved from https://thethunderbird.ca/2011/04/05/ancient-musqueam-language-revived-through-hip-hop/.

Duff, P. A., & Li, D. (2009). Indigenous, minority, and heritage language education in Canada: Policies, contexts, and issues. *Canadian Modern Language Review, 66*(1), 1–8.

Duff, P. (2010). Language socialization. In S. McKay & N. H. Hornberger (Eds.), *Sociolinguistics and language education* (pp. 427–452). Clevedon, UK: Multilingual Matters.

Enomoto, N. A. (2014, February 20). [Review of the book Youth culture, language endangerment and linguistic survivance]. *Anthropology & Education Quarterly*. Retrieved from http://onlinelibrary.wiley.com/doi/10.1111/aeq.12051/abstract.

Enpauuk (2009). *CV/Bio*. Retrieved from http//www.visualmedicine.ca/.

Everett-Green, R. (2014). www.theglobeandmail.com/arts/books-and-media/the-accidental-journalist-wab-kinew-emerges-as-contender-for-q-host/article22162473/

Garcia, O. (2009). *Bilingual education in the 21st century: A global perspective.* West Sussex, UK: Wiley Blackwell Press.

Gass, S. & Selinker, L. (2008). *Second language acquisition: An introductory course.* New York, NY: Routledge.

hooks, b. (2009). *Belonging: A culture of place.* New York, NY: Routledge/Taylor and Francis Group.

Laurence, R., (2014). *40 years on from the party where hip hop was born.* Retrieved from www.bbc.com/culture/story/20130809-the-party-where-hip-hop-was-born.

Lee, C. *Bio*. Retrieved from www.beatnation.org/music.html.

Lee, C. (2011). *Experience.* Retrieved from www.youtube.com/watch?v=T17GyBgCYFM.

Littlebear, R. (1999). Some rare and radical ideas for keeping Indigenous languages alive. In J. Reyhner, G. Cantoni, R. N. St. Clair, & E. Parsons Yazzie (Eds.), *Revitalizing indigenous languages* (pp. 1–5). Flagstaff, AZ: Northern Arizona University.

MacDonald, M. B. (2012). Hip-hop citizens: Local hip-hop and the production of democratic grassroots change in Alberta. In B. Porfilio & M. J. Biola (Eds.), *HipHop(e): The cultural practice and critical pedagogy of international hip-hop* (pp. 95–109). New York, NY: Peter Lang Publishing.

Marsh, C. (2009). Interview with Saskatchewan artist Eekwol (a.k.a Lindsay Knight). *Canadian Folk Music, 43*(1), 11–14. Retrieved from www.canfolkmusic.ca/index.php/cfmb/article/view/5/4.

Marsh, C. (2012). Bits and pieces of truth: Storytelling, identity and hip hop in Saskatchewan. In A. Hoefnagels & B. Diamond (Eds.), *Aboriginal music in contemporary Canada: Echoes and exchanges* (pp. 346–372). Ottawa, ON: McGill-Queen's University Press.

Martineau, J. (2015). Creative combat: Indigenous art, resurgence and decolonization. [Doctoral Dissertation] Victoria, BC: University of Victoria.

Martineau, J. (2017, July 4). *Listen to the 1st episode of Reclaimed, a brand new show of contemporary indigenous music.* Retrieved October 05, 2017, from www.cbcmusic.ca/posts/18794/reclaimed-july-4-2017.

McIvor, O. (2010). I am my subject: Blending Indigenous research methodology and autoethnography through integrity-based, spirit-based research. *Canadian Journal of Native Education, 33*(1), 137–151.

Nicholson, M. (2005). Moving forward while looking back: A Kwakwaka'wakw concept of time as expressed in language and culture (Unpublished master's thesis). University of Victoria, Victoria, BC.

Norris, M. J. (2000). Aboriginal peoples in Canada: Demographic and linguistic perspectives. In D. Long & O. P. Dickason (Eds.), *Visions of the heart: Canadian Aboriginal issues* (2nd ed.) (pp. 167–236). Toronto, ON: Harcourt Canada.

Norris, M. J. (2011). Aboriginal languages in Canada: Generational perspectives on language maintenance, loss, and revitalization. In D. Long & O. P. Dickason (Eds.), *Visions of the heart: Canadian Aboriginal issues* (3rd ed.) (pp. 113–148). Don Mills, ON: Oxford University Press.

Norton, B. (2010). Language and identity. In N. H. Hornberger & S. L. McKay (Eds.), *Sociolinguistics and language education* (pp. 349–369). Toronto: Multilingual Matters.

Norton, B., & Toohey, K. (2011). Identity, language learning, and social change. *Language Teaching, 44*(4), 412–446. DOI:10.1017/S0261444811000309.

Pavlenko, A. & Lantolf, J. P. (2000). Second language learning as participation and the (re)construction of selves. In J. P. Lantolf (Ed.), *Sociocultural theory and second language learning* (pp.155–177). New York, NY: Oxford University Press.

Perry, I. (2004). *Prophets in the hood: Politics and poetics in hip hop.* Durham, NC: Duke University Press.

Recollect, K. (2010). *Aural traditions: Indigenous youth and the hip-hop movement in Canada.* (Doctoral Dissertation). Retrieved from ProQuest Dissertation's and Theses. ISBN: 9780494640883, 049464088X. Robinson, D., & Martin, K. (Eds.). (2016). *Arts of engagement: Taking aesthetic action in and beyond the truth and reconciliation commission of Canada.* Waterloo, ON: Wilfrid Laurier University Press.

Rosborough, P. (2012). *k'angextola Sewn-on-Top: Kwak'wala revitalization and being Indigenous* (Unpublished doctoral dissertation). University of British Columbia, Vancouver, BC.

Simpson, L. B. (2014). Land as pedagogy: Nishnaabeg intelligence and rebellious transformation. *Decolonization: Indigeneity, Education & Society, 3*(3), 1–25.

van Paassen, K. (2014, December 19). The accidental journalist: Wab Kinew emerges as contender to host Q. The Globe and Mail. Retrieved from https://www.theglobe andmail.com/arts/books-and-media/the-accidental-journalist-wab-kinew-emerges-as-contender-for-q-host/article22162473/

Umeek (a.k.a. Richard Atleo) (2004). *Tsawalk: A Nuu Chah Nulth worldview.* Vancouver, BC: UBC Press.

Vizenor, G. (2008). *Survivance: Narratives of native presence.* Lincoln, NE: University of Nebraska Press.

Vizenor, G. (2009). *Native liberty.* Lincoln, NE: University of Nebraska Press.

Weedon, C. (1997). Feminist practice and poststructuralist theory (2nd Edition). Oxford: Blackwell.

Williams, A. (2015). Retrieved September 30, 2017 from https://www2.viu.ca/research/create/Workshops.asp.

Wyman, Leisy Thornton. (2012). *Youth culture, language endangerment and linguistic survivance.* Bristol, UK: Multilingual Matters.

13

YOUTH VOICES FROM IN AND OUT OF THE CLASSROOM

Emergent Bilingual Learners, Graphic Novels, and Critical Multiliteracies

Jie Park and Lori Simpson

> *"Graphic novel, with the drawing, explain to you what is going on. You can imagine the people, the characters, you can imagine how sometimes they face look like. Sometime the picture, you get emotion about the picture and sometime, I don't know how to say it, you challenge the picture."*
>
> *(Cleo)*

> *My thinking about graphic novels changed 'cause I used to think it was a cartoon. I learned that it could actually send information in different ways."*
>
> *(Monique)*

At the heart of this chapter are *youth voices* from in and out of the classroom, as they engaged with graphic novels and wrestled with different sign systems in the texts (e.g., writing and visual images), interrogated the beliefs conveyed in and through visual images, and came to see (through) texts as representational and ideological.

This chapter is co-authored by a university-based researcher and a teacher researcher. Lori, a White woman, teaches ESL and English language arts in a grade 7–12 urban school in the Northeast. For 72% of the 497 students at her school, English is not their first language; 90% of students receive free and reduced-priced lunch. Jie, an Asian American woman, teaches adolescent language and literacy at a private university near Lori's school. For four years, we have been documenting the affordances of graphic novels on the literacies of high-school aged emergent bilingual learners, many who are recent arrivals to the country. Drawing on data collected from an afterschool literacy program and Lori's English class, we describe how the visual art in graphic novels supported emergent bilinguals in developing their critical multiliteracies—by which we mean an analytic and critical approach to written and visual language, which includes wrestling with multiple interpretations; and questioning a creator's motivations and worldviews. Our work is situated in a critical multiliteracies framework, and our shared commitment to language and literacy education as a humanizing democratic practice with social justice ends. That is, in addition to language acquisition, we believe that the goals of language and literacy education should include the development of students' insurgent voices (Valdés, 1998), and their capacities to represent, question, and reshape their worlds (Luke & Dooley, 2009; Stein, 2007).

Critical Multiliteracies: Reframing of Texts, Literacy Education, and Learners

Multiliteracies (New London Group, 1996; Jewitt, 2008) and critical literacy (Freire, 1987; Janks, 2014; Luke & Dooley, 2009) have informed our understanding of what counts as a text and what it means to participate in meaning-construction. When reading multimodally, a reader knows and comes to know the text differently from traditional print-based literacies (Lotherington & Jenson, 2011). When reading critically, a reader understands where the text came from, what issues the text speaks to/against, and what the text means to her. Taken together, the two theories have helped us to see that reading powerfully means interrogating not only the text's meaning, but also the discursive and semiotic resources through which meanings get authored. In other words, when we read critically, we are engaging with the codes and discourses that represent possible worlds.

As a corrective to the autonomous model of literacy (Street, 1984), which sees literacy as a set of reading and writing skills removed from context or ideology, critical multiliteracies recognizes that literacy education involves engaging with students' identities, which are implicated in power relations and social structures. We also see critical multiliteracies as culturally relevant, validating youths' cultural funds of knowledge (Moll & Gonzalez, 2001) without denying them access to the dominant discourse or codes of power (Delpit, 1995). We align with critical multiliteracies' emphasis, not on the "problems" of emergent bilingual learners, but on their diverse histories, identities, knowledge, and capacities (e.g., bilingualism, awareness of different cultural norms and perspectives, etc.).

We are aware of the challenges of enacting critical multiliteracies in the classroom. Luke and Dooley (2009) posit that the framework lacks "specificity in terms of how teachers and students can engage with the specialized and complex structures of text" (p. 7). We have learned from our ongoing work with youth in afterschool and classroom settings about how graphic novels, especially their visual art, can support students in becoming text analysts who attend not only to the written language and signs, but also to the values and worldviews within the text. It is our hope that readers of this chapter can begin to imagine the possibilities for leveraging visual texts in critical language and literacy education for emergent bilingual learners.

A Collaborative Inquiry into Graphic Novels

Our collaborative inquiry happened in two sites. The first site was an afterschool program for six girls who were recent arrivals to the US. The afterschool program met every Friday for two hours to discuss graphic novels. Members' home languages included Spanish, French, Mandarin, Amharic, Yoruba, and Krahn. The second site was Lori's senior English class. Seventeen of the 21 students were emergent bilingual learners with varied English proficiency levels (EPLs). In deciding to include data from an afterschool program and English class, we are not setting up a comparative argument. Instead, we hope to achieve theoretical generalizability (Fine, 2006) by illustrating how our findings resonate across groups of youth in different contexts.

Given the scope of the chapter, we limit our discussion to how youth in both settings engaged with *The League of Extraordinary Gentlemen*, a graphic novel written by Alan Moore and illustrated by Kevin O'Neill. Hoping to build on the resources of her emergent bilingual learners—who are adept at navigating multimodal texts—Lori decided to begin the academic year with *The League of Extraordinary Gentlemen*, which draws on characters from *Dracula* (Mina Murray), and *The Strange Case of Dr. Jekyll and Mr. Hyde* (Dr. Jekyll/Mr. Hyde). Over the summer, her students had been asked to read *Dracula* and *The Strange Case of Dr. Jekyll and Mr. Hyde*—titles on the district's required summer reading list.

Documenting her students' engagement with *The League of Extraordinary Gentlemen*, we noticed how they created connections to the text. For example, reading how Mina Murray recruited operatives for the British government, a student compared Murray to the Black Widow from the movie, *The Avengers*. Although we were struck by the relevance students created for themselves and each other, we did not intend to use *The League of Extraordinary Gentlemen* in the afterschool program. With fewer curricular constraints in the afterschool program, we have explored a range of multicultural graphic stories, including *The Pride of Baghdad*, *Abina and the Important Men*, and *Barefoot Gen*. However, after seeing copies of *The League of Extraordinary Gentlemen* in Lori's classroom, two young women in the afterschool program asked to read it. They were drawn to parts of the book with dialogue written in Arabic and Chinese, and to Alan Moore's representations of *their* culture—Muslim women in Egypt and Chinese men in London.

Our Approach to Sense-Making and Learning from Youth

Our collaboration as researchers provided an opportunity to collect a wide range of data sources and perspectives, providing a more complete (and complex) picture of literacy engagement. As part of our collaboration, Jie has supported Lori to conduct systematic and intentional inquires into her students' learning. Lori has supported Jie to understand the institutional history of the school and community, and the biographies of her students. Together we have explored practitioner inquiry epistemologies and tools (e.g., promoting inquiry as stance; using a descriptive review protocol to examine transcripts of student talk).

In our work, we have also found ourselves in contact zones (Pratt, 1991), where our knowledge, commitments, and identities collide, and understandings have to be forged across our differences. While acknowledging our different positionalities, we share an interest in documenting the voices of language learners who are often silenced in schools (Valenzuela, 2010). Hence, our primary data come from audio recordings of what youth said in response to texts and to one another, in Lori's classroom and afterschool program. This paper is based on analysis of 14 tapes and transcripts from the afterschool program, and 25 tapes and transcripts from the English class. In transcribing the tapes, we recruited the linguistic capacities of Lori's students. All data in Spanish—the dominant language of many of her students—were transcribed, then translated by her bilingual students. We also relied on bilingual youth to translate, in real time, what newly-arrived students said during class discussions.

Individually, we read and annotated every transcript. We met weekly to engage in an active and relational process focused on making meaning from transcripts of student talk. From these conversations, we noticed students' varied engagement with graphic novels. As a way to understand this variation, Jie introduced the Four Resources model (Luke & Freebody, 1997). According to this model, readers assume a range of roles as they engage with texts: code breaker, text participant, text user, and text analyzer. Although "text" means written texts in the Four Resources model, we saw how the roles applied to reading multimodal texts. The model holds in focus the idea that reading, whether words and/or images, involves not just decoding, but also experiencing the text; using the text for social and personal purposes; and interrogating the writer/creator's ideologies. Using the Four Resources model, we identified sections where students assumed the roles of code breaker, text participant, text user, or text analyst. This analytical process revealed that students-as-readers focused on not only decoding the written words, but also interrogating the creator's intentions and worldviews. Lastly, we interviewed five youth from the English class, and five from the afterschool program about their background, reading practices, and familiarity with graphic novels.

Art as a Way of Naming and Contesting the World: Youth Voices In and Out of the Classroom

We found that students, even while working to "break" the written code, were engaged in text analysis, and that when assuming the stance of a text analyst, they drew on and referred to the visual images. That is, youth in both settings struggled with the written language (e.g., menagerie, eccentricities, etc.), and background knowledge assumed by the text (e.g., all characters are from Victorian literature). However, when working with the art, they were able to challenge the *representations* of, and discourses around, gender and ethnicity; and question the creator's worldviews. In the rest of the chapter, we will paint rich images of youth, many of whom were labeled as less-than-proficient, as serious and sophisticated text analysts and critics.

In the first example, the young women in the afterschool program were discussing the pages where Mina Murray travels to Cairo to find Alan Quartermain, who is in an opium den. Danielle asked, "Is he sick? Why is he so tired and skinny?" which prompted the conversation as follows:

Cleo: Because he's old.
Danielle: He's ill.
Cleo: He didn't eating.
Carla: It's kind of weird. The image. Maybe he's trapped on cage. Kind of.
Lori: Why do you think he's in a cage?
Carla: Um. Because the windows are closed, and it's, it's very like dirty. I think he's dying.
Jie: Hmmm.
Maryam: Is it like a. . . . Ohhhhh. I know what's that. It's a coffee shop.
Lori: It's a coffee shop?
Maryam: Yeah. Kind of. Cause they drink shisha here. See this?

There was a range of responses to explain Quartermain's appearance, including illness and starvation. Lori was puzzled by Maryam's comment that Quartermain is inside a coffee shop. Maryam, who grew up in Jordan, explained that she meant a place where men "drink shisha (water-pipe)," pointing to an image of Egyptian men with pipes in their mouths. Before we could guide the girls to break down the written language about Quartermain's opium addiction, Maryam took up the pictures on the page, and assumed the role of a text analyst.

Maryam: They make the Arabic look so ugly. And dirty.
Lori: We didn't go there yet.
Maryam: I know. I know. Here. This page. Just look at the page. I don't like the way they represent Arabic people here. Especially this page. This page. Here. This page. Just look at the page.
Lori: Mmm hmmm
Maryam: And I think, yeah, they make them look so clean and beautiful for England, even if they're devil in the story. But still. Even the, the old guy? He's England and he still looks good. But the Arabic people here. They look so ugly and also the covered women. They didn't even show her eyes.
Lori: You think he [Quartermain] looks good?
Maryam: Better than Arabic.
Lori: You think that he [Quartermain] looks better than him [Egyptian]?
Jillian: No.

Maryam:	Not in this picture. In this picture.
Jie:	Which one?
Maryam:	This picture. This picture. This picture. And even there's like, there's knives everywhere. That is not how it looks.
Jillian:	It's so cruel. I was looking for the Chinese part. It's very cruel.

Although Lori attempted to redirect the conversation to the written language (i.e., "We didn't go there yet"), Maryam focused the group's attention to representations of Arab men. She pointed to a series of images: "Just *look* at the page. . . . Especially this page. This page here." Lori decided to follow Maryam, who argued that the images of violence in Egypt were not only false, but in contrast to the images of clean and beautiful England. To support her argument, she reasoned that Quartermain, an opium addict, was represented more favorably than Egyptian men because he rescued Ms. Murray from two rapists. Maryam also challenged the image of a heavily veiled woman on the streets of Cairo. Unless one was paying careful attention, a reader would have missed this image. In fact, Lori admitted, "Oh, I didn't even see her." Maryam added, "Even the woman here, they covered all her face and didn't show even her eyes. Like, that doesn't mean she represent all people in Muslim." Understanding the diversity that characterizes Muslim women, Maryam criticized how the artist represented the woman in a way that renders her invisible. In this discussion Jillian also began to assume the role of the text analyst, aware of how the Chinese were represented as "very cruel."

In addition to interrogating representations of women, the girls wondered what Alan Moore thought about women since many were shown as sexual objects.

Maryam:	And I also, I was talking to Danielle about what she said last time, how is the book using women as like a toy or using them for sexual reasons. And at first, I was like, "No, the range was like normal," but I think now I understand what she's talking about because in this picture, not just in this picture, the picture before, um, this part. This part, and in the pictures before, they do it too much. . . . They're like a lot of not good pictures showing women, like, naked.
Danielle:	Does he [Moore] think of this as natural? You know, like, it's a natural thing?

From talking to Danielle and encountering more images in the text, Maryam began to take seriously, and wrestled with, Danielle's comment about Moore's objectification of women. Danielle took up Maryam's judgment and formed it into a question about the creator's beliefs. She wondered whether the author thought it was "natural" for women to exist for the pleasure of men. Danielle knew that the text had been created by a man, and predicted that he was probably *not* married based on how he represented women.

Similarly, in Lori's English class, youth grappled with not only the discourse about women in the text, but also Moore's *personal* relationship to the discourse.

In the classroom setting we documented students offering questions and comments like the ones below:

> "The way Alan Moore writes things and describes things are perverted and somewhat stereotypical, like the way he wrote the guys from Cairo."
> "He [Moore] thinks of women, he thinks of all women as they not important. They're not great."
> "He thinks that other women are like flirty kinds of women."
> "She [Ms. Murray] uses her body to attract men and she is trying to catch somebody so they used her body to catch the man they were looking for."
> "Is he [Alan Moore] married?"
> "That picture is representing how women should act or what?"

These questions and comments were collected throughout the unit, while students were in whole-class and small-group discussions. In their questions and comments, we saw how youth were sharing different views on what the images might reveal about Moore's stance toward women. Some believed that Moore regarded women as less important than men, whereas others believed that he was portraying, and thereby calling attention to, a male-dominated society.

As stated in an earlier section, Lori's English class was made up of 21 youth, 17 of whom were designated by the district as English language learners. They came from nine countries; had been in the US for anywhere between two and 13 years; and spoke six languages (e.g., Spanish, Swahili, Albanian, Yoruba, French). Regardless of their perceived English language proficiency, Lori's commitment was to foster their critical academic literacies, which she understood to mean analytical and discipline-specific ways of meaning-making (Schoenbach & Greenleaf, 2009).

To cultivate youths' critical academic literacies and leverage their insights about Alan Moore's worldviews, we designed a jury trial as the culminating assessment, with the intention of determining whether students could assume the perspective of another, and use textual evidence to engage with—defend or challenge—the discourses presented in the text. The students voted to charge Alan Moore with sexism, and volunteered to play the role of (1) attorney (prosecution or defense); (2) character witness; or (3) member of the jury. In addition to reviewing the timeline for the project and expectations for each role, Lori assigned daily assignments to help students with their preparation for the trial and conferenced with them daily. Lori made sure students had access to different kinds of important background knowledge, as well as access to tools such as iPads for students to conduct research for the trial.

- Background on jury trials (handouts and TV clips);
- Background on each of the characters (Captain Nemo, Mina Murray, Invisible Man), who would be called up as witnesses in the context of the trial (handouts, which Lori adapted to her students' English proficiency);
- Background on Alan Moore (interview transcripts with Alan Moore; YouTube videos of Alan Moore);

- Background knowledge on the time period in which the story is set, focusing on gender roles (handouts, adapted to students' English proficiency).

When selecting a role for each student, we made sure that emergent bilingual learners would play roles in which they would be challenged and supported to go public with their ideas and thoughts. Lori created access to background knowledge through multimodal texts (e.g., YouTube videos, websites, interview transcripts, television shows). She also encouraged emergent bilingual learners to use their home language (e.g., writing a draft of the opening statement in Spanish before writing it in English), and technology such as Google translate. Observing students, we noticed them rereading parts of the graphic novel through the lens of what they could infer about Moore's stance towards women. During the trial, students took on the perspective of another (e.g., prosecutor, character from the book). Josie, a young woman who moved from Puerto Rico two years ago, played a prosecutor. Below is her opening statement:

> Josie [as prosecuting attorney]: Hi, good morning ladies and gentlemen of the jury. I have come here today to prove to you that Alan Moore is sexist. I have many witnesses that will testify and support this. You will see evidence that Alan Moore is sexist. On October 26, 2000, Alan Moore published *The League of Extraordinary Gentlemen* . . . . He showed women as prostitute and sex objects. With this, he shows that men are more superior than women. . . . He [Alan Moore] will say that one reason he start writing this book is because he wants to prove to the people that violation of women exists in society. He will also argument that he did not draw the picture, he just say the words the characters say.

We saw Josie using academic vocabulary (evidence, testify, support, violation), putting forward a position and anticipating a counterclaim, and differentiating the illustrator and writer.

She continued to demonstrate and hone her analytic capacities throughout the trial, questioning her witnesses, formulating and reformulating her questions to the defense's witnesses, and raising objections to the defense attorney's questions.

The youth who were character witnesses drew upon textual evidence and relevant background knowledge in order to enact their role, and take a stance toward Alan Moore. Barry, a bilingual youth from the Dominican Republic, played Alan Moore during the trial. While on the stand, he argued that he was trying to represent an issue that is often underrepresented: sexual violence against women.

> Barry [as Alan Moore]: I think sexual abuse is a really bad thing in society. It's something we are facing right now. That's why I wrote the book. I noticed that in novels and like pieces of work, authors were not talking

about sexual abuse.... It is something that needs to be talked about. It needs to be represented.

In his statement, Barry argued the distinction between the ideologies in the text and ideologies of the author. Also, in assuming the perspective of Moore, Barry had to wrestle with why authors create what they do. In an interview with Lori, he described what he learned from the jury trial: "I learned it's not only about what you think and what you have learned, but understanding why some people do what they do or, even if you don't agree with it, just trying to understand why they do it and how."

From in and out of the classroom, we learned that while emergent bilingual learners need support in accessing the written English language of graphic novels, they are perceptive and sophisticated text analysts who question images-as-representations. In other words, emergent bilingual learners' struggles to decode written language do not hinder them in analyzing and "speaking back" to the text, its creator(s), and their worldviews. In an interview, Maryam from the afterschool program described her experiences reading *The League of Extraordinary Gentlemen*:

> The language part was really hard for me. Really hard. Sometimes I feel like, Oh I'm done with this. I don't want to read it anymore 'cause I'm breaking it. I'm breaking the word and then breaking each, the sentence, to words. Yeah. I get confused and sometimes don't understand it. . . . I like the pictures. I like how it's different. How it makes us think, all why he's doing that. Why there is different. Like making me see different books and see how people think.

Maryam commented on how she wrestled with "breaking the word" at one moment, then interrogated Moore's representations of Muslims and women in the next.

In addition to learning how the art in graphic novels supported students' critical and analytic engagement, we have also developed through our collaboration several ideas and applications for practice.

- Introduce and focus on the grammar, structure, and vocabulary of visual texts (i.e., following a sequence of panels, differentiating a speech or thought from narration).
- Use academically productive talk moves (Michaels & O'Connor, 2015) such as revoicing ("What I hear you say is) and pressing for elaboration ("Say more") ("What made you say that?") during whole-class discussions about graphic novels.
- Provide multiple opportunities for students to create their *own* representations of discourses, texts, and worlds (e.g., students recreate parts of a graphic novel, create their own graphic novels based on moments in their lives).

- Continue to foster the academic literacy skills that emergent bilingual learners already have by encouraging them to think and work in their primary language and English.
- Create a culture of risk-taking and safety where students can go public with their voices. This involves first and foremost establishing relationships with students where their identities and ideas are valued.

Reading Differently With and Through Art

When assuming the role of text analyst, the youth more often referred to the images(s) than to the writing. When they were trying to "break the code," they focused primarily on the meaning of words and sentences. This was not entirely surprising since the youth are emergent bilingual learners. However, we now believe that there is another explanation to account for the fact that youth engaged critically with the art in graphic novels. The youth understood that art is representational, and that the images were created by a human being with a particular point of view and set of beliefs. Wells explains that the idea that writing is also representational is more difficult to take hold of because the "conventions in terms of which [written texts] are created are much less explicit" (1990, p. 378).

For emergent bilingual learners the art in graphic novels provided an entry point into the text. That is, youth took clues from the art in order to make sense of the written word, and made connections between what they were seeing/ reading and what they have experienced. More importantly, the art in graphic texts promoted a *different* kind of reading—a kind of reading in which language-learning youth became active inquirers and critical analysts, questioning who created the text, with what intentions, and with what beliefs and worldviews. They used art to grapple with how people see, write, and draw the world. Therefore, art in graphic novels served as an equalizing force in Lori's classrooms, creating a more "democratic space" (Stein, 2007, p. 1) where emergent bilingual youths' experiences, interpretive frameworks, and languages became a source of knowledge and power. Finally, art in graphic texts has supported us in "reading" the youth differently. Rather than see emergent bilinguals as disadvantaged, we saw what resources they brought to the act of meaning-making.

References

Delpit, L. (1995). The silenced dialogue: Power and pedagogy in educating other people's children. In *Other people's children: Cultural conflict in the classroom* (pp. 21–47). New York, NY: The New Press.

Fine, M. (2006). Bearing witness: Methods for researching oppression and resistance—A textbook for critical research. *Social Justice Research, 19*(1), 83–108.

Freire, P. (1987). The importance of the act of reading. In P. Freire & D. Macedo (Eds.), *Literacy: Reading the word and the world* (pp. 5–11). South Hadley, MA: Bergin and Garvey.

Janks, H. (2014). Critical literacy's ongoing importance for education. *Journal of Adolescent & Adult Literacy, 57*(5), 349–356.

Jewitt, C. (2008). Multimodality and literacy in school classrooms. *Review of Research in Education, 32*(1), 241–267.

Lotherington, H., & Jenson, J. (2011). Teaching multimodal and digital literacy in L2 settings: New literacies, new basics, new pedagogies. *Annual Review of Applied Linguistics, 31*, 226–246.

Luke, A., & Dooley, K. (2009). Critical literacy and second language learning. In E. Hinkel (Ed.), *Handbook of research in second language teaching and learning: Volume II* (pp. 856–868). London: Routledge.

Luke, A., & Freebody, P. (1997). The social practices of reading. In S. Muspratt, A. Luke, & P. Freebody (Eds.), *Constructing critical literacies: Teaching and learning textual practice* (pp. 188–226). Cresskill, NJ: Hampton.

Michaels, S., & O'Connor, C. (2015). Conceptualizing talk moves as tools: Leveraging professional development work with teachers to advance empirical studies of academically productive talk. In L. B. Resnick, C. Asterhan, & S. N. Clarke (Eds.), *Socializing intelligence through talk and dialogue* (pp. 333–347). Washington, DC: American Educational Research Association Press.

Moll, L. C., & Gonzalez, N. (2001). Lessons from research with language-minority children. In E. Cushman, E. R. Kintgen, B. M. Kroll, & M. Rose (Eds.), *Literacy: A critical sourcebook* (pp. 156–171). Boston, MA: Bedford/St. Martin's.

New London Group. (1996). A pedagogy of multiliteracies: Designing social futures. *Harvard Educational Review, 66*(1), 60–92.

Pratt, M. L. (1991). Arts of the contact zone. *Profession, 91*, 33–40.

Schoenbach, R., & Greenleaf, C. (2009). Fostering adolescents' academic literacy. In L. Christenbury, R. Boomer, & P. Smagorinsky (Eds.), *Handbook of adolescent literacy research* (pp. 98–112). New York, NY: The Guilford Press.

Stein, P. (2007). *Multimodal pedagogies in diverse classrooms: Representation, rights and resources.* London: Routledge.

Street, B. (1984). *Literacy in theory and practice.* Cambridge, UK: Cambridge University Press.

Valdés, G. (1998). The world outside and inside schools: Language and immigrant children. *Educational Researcher, 27*(6), 4–18.

Valenzuela, A. (2010). *Subtractive schooling: US-Mexican youth and the politics of caring.* Albany, NY: SUNY Press.

Wells, G. (1990). Talk about text: Where literacy is learned and taught. *Curriculum Inquiry, 20*(4), 369–405.

SECTION III

Questions for Reflection and Further Applications for Practice

Lift Every Voice: Democratic Practice Before, During, and After School

Amanda Claudia Wager

> *How can we, as teachers, lift every voice in and outside of our classrooms? How can we create a democratic space where every student's perspective can be heard in whatever medium or language they choose to express themselves in? What can we do for our students to see themselves represented in the curriculum, in their teachers, and in their communities? These last four chapters confirm, through multiple examples, how children are active participants in the democracy of the educational spaces within our communities. They tell stories of how emergent bilingual students—beginning in preschool and spanning young adulthood—engage in social and political issues through the power of the arts and multilingualism, furthering their critical thinking and civic engagement. Balancing student individual agency and collectivity, students demonstrate how learning is social and contextual. Perceiving the classroom and curricula as shaped by larger political, racial, socio-historical, economic, and geographic contexts, students of all ages in these chapters critically question the relationship between power and knowledge in order to further the possibility of a more just society. This reiterates how literacy, in its multiple forms, is deeply connected to language, culture, and the social practices of everyday life.*

In this final section, authors offer several inspiring stories of political agency through the arts with different generations of emergent bilingual students. Beth Murray and Gustave Weltsek's work with preschoolers uses drama, both as a process and a production, to advocate for the importance of play as a means for language acquisition and political agency. Debi Khasnabis, Catherine H. Reischl, along with other artists and educators, describe a summer program that engages fourth to eighth grade students in spoken word poetry, hip hop, and digital video with mentor texts and artists. These multimodal strategies affirm the student's culture and agency, defining success on their own terms, individually and collectively. Laura Cranmer, Jocelyn Difiore, and Jeffrey Paul Ansloos illuminate ways that Indigenous youth use the translanguaging of their Indigenous languages and English to explore their generational identities, further resiliency through creativity, and awaken the public's consciousness to colonial oppression through public art. Jie Park and Lori Simpson collaborate, in an urban school setting, to document and describe how graphic novels support seventh-to twelfth-grade emergent bilingual learners in critically unearthing the cultural and political aspects represented in the texts they are reading. Each of the four chapters describe aspects of academic literacy and language acquisition gained through student's creative expression and analysis (e.g., alliteration, repetition, rhyming, simile, idioms, targeted academic vocabulary, digital editing tools, personification, imagery, and oral language fluency, to name but a few).

Questions for Reflection

How can I collaboratively build a space for my students to question symbols and patterns of power within the curriculum? How can emergent bilingual students, families, and communities further civic engagement in their communities?

How do I explain to my administration and teaching colleagues the necessity of art and creativity throughout the curriculum as a culturally responsive pedagogy, in a way that they can understand and support? How do I navigate and work with the requirements, curricula, and assessments that are already in place? Who are supported, included, helped most, and who are discouraged, excluded, and hurt most by the curriculum?

How can I become an advocate for a more equitable and diverse teaching force? How can we recruit bi/multilingual teachers to create a more just teaching force, where students see themselves and their communities represented in their mentors (i.e. teachers, administrators)?

How can I become well informed with the laws that surround emergent bilingual education in my community? I need to know them so that I can repeat them and advocate for my students and their families in our school, local community, and beyond.

Further Applications

Indigenous Land and People's Acknowledgment: As explained in Cranmer, Difiore, and Ansloos' chapter, street art, hip hop music, and breakdancing are forms of advocacy where youth can collaboratively express themselves in multiple languages while speaking to the public. Paul Arthur further suggests,

Educators can take away from this how to bring Indigenous issues to curriculum. Since there is very little mentioned about Indigenous issues, the non-Indigenous students can learn something about history and the reality that many First Nations people live with. The Indigenous students will feel acknowledged and themselves have a better understanding of what survivance is all about for Indigenous cultures. . . . Messages I have for teachers is to bring more Indigenous curriculum to the schools. Acknowledge the Indigenous territory that the school is on through public school announcements in the morning, have Elders in the classrooms since Elders are an amazing and huge part of learning in the classroom atmosphere. Have talking circles in the morning to check in with all kids to see how they are doing.

(personal communication, 2016)

Spoken Word/Poetry/Hip Hop: In order for students to connect to the curriculum, they have to start with their own stories, they have to start with themselves. Reflecting on Rianne Elsadig's spoken word poem in the opening page of this section, she brings her audience on a journey to her "homeland" through her written word translanguaging from Arabic to English. Various youth have created bi/multilingual spoken word poetry to express who they are and the dreams they have (see *Mother Tongue* by Sarah O'Neal). Khasnabis and Reischl explain how students wrote poems and hip hop music lyrics in multiple languages. These forms of expression link closely to youth culture and every day student discourses. In supporting students in the process of writing their own poems and lyrics, provide a model spoken word poem or hip hop song, create sentence frames, supply poetry templates, and have a beat going to jam to. As well, begin to think about why many of these examples of spoken word poetry and hip hop happen outside of traditional school hours and why students gain so much agency from doing them. *What can we learn from afterschool programs about youth-led democrative practices, motivation, and learning?*

Murals/Graffiti/Street Art: Our cities are colored in vibrant public art. Children and youth can voice their stories—their spirits—through public art. And all you need is a wall and some paint! Find a wall—possibly one well-exposed on the outside or inside of your school—where a group of students can create a collaborative mural. Get permission to paint a mural on the wall. Students then decide what image they want to paint. *What message do they have for their school? For their community? What languages will be represented within the mural?* You can begin by having your students "pitch" their ideas by doing a drawing and writing a narrative about what they think the mural should be. The students can then create a collaborative visual and textual design. Using a large gridded piece of paper, have the students draw/paint a miniature example of their final mural. Draw a magnified grid on the wall and begin sketching the larger image to begin paint-ing. This process is intermixed with oral language fluency because students have ongoing discussions while doing the project.

Drama in Education

Drama throughout the curriculum involves many different activities, engaging students through an embodied literacy rather than solely depending on oral or written language. There are multiple forms of drama that can be used within the classroom, such as warm-up activities, role-play, hot-seating, reader's theatre, writing-in-role, and process drama. All of these are fun and engaging for children and youth, using the language of the body for comprehension. When drama is used as a primary tool to frame inquiry (rather than an extra tool), students inhabit marginal characters (like Goldilocks's babysitter) or still-forming perspectives (like the pioneer travelers in Gus's drama) and use drama strategies to flesh out their worlds and ideas. Multimodal literacies emerge naturally and imagination-fueled language propels action.

> **Process Drama**: A process drama, as discussed by Weltsek and Murray, is a series of drama activities devised to lead a group of people, usually with-out performance backgrounds, through a kinesthetic and aesthetic experi-ence for the purpose of learning (Bolton & Heathcote, 1995; Needlands & Goode, 2000; O'Neill, 1995). The multiple modes of literacy and role-play involved in a process drama provide rich possibilities for learning through students' negotiations within a created imagined world. Engaging students' multiple senses by employing different modalities through drama supports emergent bilingual students to use their funds of knowledge, practice oral language skills and critically negotiate meaning within the metaphoric imagined world.
>
> How a teacher can create a process drama (Schroeter & Wager, 2016):
>
> • Select a topic to explore. Brainstorm drama activities, including strategies that integrate multiple modalities: visual, spatial, audio, linguistic, and gestural (e.g., mapping, voting, tableaux). Create a sequence of 3–5 drama activities that gradually increase the engage-ment required (such as writing-in-role, warm-ups, tableaux, etc.).
> • Make a list of the different "players" within the process, as well as the setting, and think about power structures and languages throughout the process. Plan when you will act in-role and select a prop or costume to distinguish the imagined role from your teacher role. Choose a noisemaker—a chime, drum, or flute—to make transitions between activities.

- Set the scene! Rearrange the classroom and welcome students into the imaginary world by way of props, music, or odors. Improvise in-role and accept new ideas when students make suggestions. Step out-of-role to discuss and problematize things that occur in the imaginary world.
- Leave 15 minutes or more to reflect with students. Debrief about connections between the process drama and students' lives, the decisions they made and conflicts they may have experienced while acting in-role.

Role-play: Much of the work that I have done is specific to using drama in education to create alternative realities for students to play in. For example, in my ESL classroom in Peru, students used drama tools such as role-play to discuss local political and educational issues. While the teachers were on strike in the small village of Chachapoyas in the Andes Mountains, the adolescent students wrote questions in English that they could ask as news reporters. We then worked together to answer the questions in English using sentence strips, specific vocabulary, and expanding on the grammar lesson of the week. Next, they role-played the strike while certain students switched off being the news reporters asking questions in English about why they were on strike and what they hoped could change in the educational system. This role-playing created a space for the young people time to critically think about the reasons for the strike while engaging in new language learning. Students were able to further their acquisition of the English language through the multimodality of drama by writing, asking, and answering questions in their made-up alternative reality of being the teachers, administrators, and news reporters of the school strikes. The use of role-play encompasses various modes of meaning-making, such as gesture, gaze, image, sound, speech, writing, and body posture.

Hot-seating: Hot-seating is an improvised tool where students explore a certain character in a book or story. One student or teacher will sit in a seat, dressed in costume as and role-playing a specific character, while the other students ask the character questions. Answers are based on your interpretation of the character you are hot-seating. This helps build empathy and understanding for characters in stories. Students should prewrite their questions and practice asking each other prior to asking the character in-role.

Reader's Theatre: To engage students in English literacy practices and connect to their backgrounds, I used reader's theatre and role-play throughout my English language arts block in my bilingual Spanish/English classroom. The students were highly engaged in the process and it increased their reading fluency rapidly. Students would take a script home and, on their own accord, memorize it by the next day. You can find many scripts online and it is easy to write scripts from any children's book verbatim. Choose books that connect to your student's backgrounds, cultures, and interests. Reader's Theatre also led to a school-wide "Family Reading Night" where families first watched a performance by a local theatre company and then chose which Reader's Theatre classroom in the school (based on multiple bilingual children's literature books, such as *Chato's Kitchen*) they wanted to participate in with their children.

Tableaux: The use of tableaux, or fixed group images using the body, is extremely supportive for emergent bilingual students' language acquisition process because students express their emotions or their reactions to a text via their body, in a group setting, and then discuss what they see. For instance, after reading a story about a lost dog, a group of kindergartners can create a group tableaux expressing how they think the owner felt.

Creating a Graphic Novel: Expanding on Park and Simpson's graphic novel interrogations, these are preliminary steps for students to create a graphic novel. They need to know what story you want to tell; it could be a story from interviewing a family or community member (similar to the graphic novel *Sugar Falls*), it could further their own autobiographies and dig deeply into the past (similar to the graphic novel *7 Generations*), or it could be a story that they create drawing on current events. Encourage students to share stories from their communities and incorporate their native language when creating "dialogue" for the characters. There are important parts of the story that students need to consider prior to creating the graphic novels, such as plot, setting, characters, the problem, and the solution. Worksheet templates that can easily be found online can assist students prior to creating their graphic novels:

- **Story Organizer Worksheet**: Write the title, problem, solution, characters and the introduction, rising action, climax, falling action, and resolution to the story.
- **Storyboard Worksheet**: Illustrate the major events of the story.
- **Character Maps**: For each character brainstorm actions, feelings, what they say, and appearance.

Once students have filled out the worksheets, they should be ready to create a graphic novel. They could do this by hand or digitally using one of the free comic software programs below:

- **Make Beliefs Comixs** www.makebeliefscomix.com/Comix/
- **Marvel Kids** http://marvelkids.marvel.com/comics
- **Pixton** www.pixton.com/ca/for-fun
- **ToonDoo** www.toondoo.com/
- **Strip Generator** http://stripgenerator.com/strip/create/

Encourage students to read culturally and linguistically diverse graphic novels, such as those mentioned above and *American Born Chinese*, *Soviet Daughter: A Graphic Revolution*, *Persepolis*, and *Baddawi* (to name but a few).

Mentor Artists/Community Members: Mentor artists allow teachers to bring alternative, and often absent, histories and perspectives into the classroom. Maxine Greene (1995) writes that we need to "make poetic use of our imagination to be able to grasp another's world" (p. 4). For students who rarely see themselves or their experiences represented in the curriculum, inviting local artists who are community members (including family members) into the classroom, speaks to their own funds of knowledges, confirming their perspectives.

References

Bolton, G., & Heathcote, D. (1995). *Dorothy Heathcote's mantle of the expert approach to education*. Portsmouth, NH: Heineman.

Greene, M. (1995). *Releasing the imagination: Essays on education, the arts and social change*. San Francisco, CA: Jossey-Bass.

Needlands, J., & Goode, T. (2000). *Structuring drama work*. Cambridge: Cambridge University Press.

O'Neill, C. (1995). *Drama worlds: A framework for process drama*. Portsmouth, NH: Heinemann.

Schroeter, S., & Wager, A. C. (2016). Blurring boundaries: Using drama to examine 17th Century witch-hunts. *Journal of Adolescent and Adult Literacy*, *60*(4), 405–413.

AFTERWORD

Wayne Au

Arts education is so important for engaging all of our children in learning. That's why I am continually disappointed in what I see happening in public schools today: High-stakes testing has been squeezing art, along with other areas of schooling so critical to children's well-being and success like physical education, social studies, science, recess, and even lunchtime, out of the curriculum and out of school budgets since the No Child Left Behind Act of 2001(Au, 2007). Fortunately, arts education hasn't disappeared entirely, and some schools have made purposeful efforts to maintain art as important in the education of children, especially marginalized, working-class, Black, and Brown kids—many of whom are multilingual immigrants. The chapters here in *Art as a Way of Talking for Emergent Bilingual Youth: A Foundation for Literacy in K-12 Schools*, represent some of the best of these efforts.

The importance of arts education in reaching and teaching the diversity of our students has been made personal for me in recent years through my son, Makoto. As of this writing Makoto is a second grader at John Muir Elementary in Seattle, a public school that reflects our Rainier Valley neighborhood. Sixty-eight percent of Muir's students qualify for free and reduced lunch, 33% are state-designated as transition bilingual, almost 50% are African American—with many from recent East African immigrant families, 10% are Latinx, 11% are Asian American, and 11% identify as multiracial (Office of Superintendent of Public Instruction, 2017).

As a family and a school, we at John Muir know we are lucky. Not only do we have a fantastic art program, but our art teacher, Julie Trout, is committed to a politics of racial and social justice through arts education. Ms. Trout knows that one of the best ways to make education meaningful for the students at John Muir Elementary is that it needs to connect to their lives and experiences as immigrants, as bilingual students, as students of color, and as working-class students. She knows that they need to see themselves and their cultures reflected through the beauty and power of art (Alexander, 2017).

One of my favorite pieces of art that my son, Makoto, has brought home was from when he was in kindergarten. It is a picture of a dinosaur DJ spinning records on two turntables—clearly a combination of his then-love of dinosaurs and the fact that we have DJ turntables and records in our living room. Makoto's dinosaur DJ, while cute, wasn't necessarily remarkable in itself. What was remarkable to me was this: On the bottom corner of his art piece was his name signed under a crown. When my spouse and I asked him about his beautiful art piece, he replied, "That's my Basquiat." I was blown away. Mako's art teacher was teaching Basquiat to this incredibly diverse crew of kindergarteners. Since then I've witnessed kids at Muir do reproductions of Jacob Lawrence's "Migration" series, portraits of Frida Kahlo, and Hokusai's waves, among others.

The arts education program at Muir so strongly represents the power of bringing together art, the politics of social justice, and the education of a diverse, multilingual group of students. The chapters here in *Art as a Way of Talking for Emergent Bilingual Youth* reflect this power in so many ways. Drawing deeply on students' funds of knowledge (Moll, Amanti, Neff, & Gonzalez, 1992), these chapters remind us that our kids come to us as multilinguistic geniuses, and that we as educators need to be smart enough to recognize this genius in our curriculum and instruction. Further, this volume reminds all of us how powerful language is: We express familial relations, culture, connections to ancestors, sense of place, our history, love, anger, name our sustenance, express need, and communicate *who we are* through our language. As a collection, *Art as a Way of Talking for Emergent Bilingual Youth* yells this fact for the world to hear and makes the argument that we are harming our kids when we do not incorporate their home languages in our classroom practices.

Art as a Way of Talking for Emergent Bilingual Youth does this work in such wonderful ways because it operates at the intersection of multilingual education, multimodal arts, and teaching for social justice. Here we see students using technology, making picturebooks, getting their hands dirty, doing drama, using hip hop and spoken word, taking photographs, making digital art, and constructing graphic novels, among other forms, all as examples of authentically cultivating student voice in pedagogically rich ways. All this is done as part of cultural recovery, cultural maintenance, and, fundamentally, as a practice of linguistically decolonizing our classrooms. Better still, it is done here in ways that are lovingly grounded in students' communities.

There is so much more speaking through *Art as a Way of Talking for Emergent Bilingual Youth* as well. For instance, bringing together the arts, social justice, and multilingual education is a wonderful expression of healing and humanizing education—core tenets of the burgeoning K-12 Ethnic Studies movement (Acosta, 2015). Similarly, using arts-based multiliteracies (Gee, 2000; New London Group, 1996) to read the world clearly channels the liberatory pedagogy of Paulo Freire

(1974). The contributions to this collection also point to a kind of Vygotskian Zone of Proximal Development (Vygotsky, 1987) where students are clearly using art as a curricular tool in the development of their own critical consciousness (Au, 2011).

As the contributors of *Art as a Way of Talking for Emergent Bilingual Youth* also show us, the power of art education makes particular sense within the context of bilingual, multilingual, and second language acquisition. Art education is an incredible tool for reflection. It moves us to reflect on, process, and make sense of our past experiences and present conditions. Just as importantly it enables us to envision new possibilities and futures. Because of this, arts education for our students who speak multiple languages and/or who are acquiring English becomes a natural vehicle for making our teaching and instruction culturally relevant and for helping students better understand the conditions facing their communities. Similarly, arts education also inspires these same students to envision the possibilities of a different, more socially and culturally just world for themselves and their communities. In this way, merging the arts, politics, and multilingual education is fundamentally an act of teaching for social justice and educational equity (Rethinking Schools, 2003).

Finally, I have to note that *Art as a Way of Talking for Emergent Bilingual Youth* is especially important in our current political context. Right now immigrant youth, Black and Brown youth, and Muslim youth in particular are experiencing increases in incidents of bias, intolerance, racism, and expressions of white supremacy in our schools (Costello, 2016; Rogers, 2017). The anti-immigrant racism of some teachers has been highlighted through social media, while students, parents, and school communities openly worry about moms, dads, uncles, aunts, and grandparents being deported—fears that have sometimes left young children crying in their classrooms (Au, 2017; Kamenetz, 2017). This is our current white nationalist governmental reality, and this context makes the chapters of *Art as a Way of Talking for Emergent Bilingual Youth* even more pressing and important. Arts education in the ways included in this book—ways that honor students' home languages and cultures and ways that empower them to think more critically about their sociopolitical conditions—play the important role of both humanizing our students in the face of dehumanizing white supremacy and preparing students to see themselves as powerful activists and change agents in their own lives and in the world.

References

Acosta, C. (2015). *The impact of humanizing pedagogies and curriculum upon the identities, civic engagement, and political activism of Chican@ youth* [dissertation]. Phoenix: University of Arizona. Retrieved from http://hdl.handle.net/10150/556592.

Alexander, G. (2017, August 30). *Could you be making this common cultural mistake?: Understanding cultural appropriation with art and kids.* Retrieved December 14, 2017, from www.parentmap.com/article/how-avoid-teaching-cultural-appropriation.

Au, W. (2007). High-stakes testing and curricular control: A qualitative metasynthesis. *Educational Researcher, 36*(5), 258–267.

Au, W. (2011). *Critical curriculum studies: Education, consciousness, and the politics of knowing.* New York, NY: Routledge.

Au, W. (2017). When multicultural education is not enough. *Multicultural Perspectives, 19*(3), 1–4. https://doi.org/10.1080/15210960.2017.1331741.

Costello, M. (2016). *The Trump effect: The impact of the presidential campaign on our nation's schools.* Montgomery, Alabama: The Southern Poverty Law Center. Retrieved from www.splcenter.org/sites/default/files/splc_the_trump_effect.pdf.

Freire, P. (1974). *Pedagogy of the oppressed* (M. B. Ramos, Trans.). New York, NY: Seabury Press.

Gee, J. P. (2000). New people in new worlds: Networks, the new capitalism and schools. In B. Cope & M. Kalantzis (Eds.), *Multiliteracies: Literacy learning and the design of social futures* (pp. 43–68). New York, NY: Routledge.

Kamenetz, A. (2017, March 9). *I have children crying in the classroom.* Retrieved March 14, 2017, from www.npr.org/sections/ed/2017/03/09/518996780/i-have-children-crying-in-the-classroom.

Moll, L. C., Amanti, C., Neff, D., & Gonzalez, N. (1992). Funds of knowledge for teaching: Using a qualitative approach to connect homes and classrooms. *Theory Into Practice, 31*(2), 132–141. https://doi.org/10.1080/00405849209543534.

New London Group. (1996). A pedagogy of multiliteracies: Designing social futures. *Harvard Educational Review, 66*(1), 60–92.

Office of Superintendent of Public Instruction. (2017). *John Muir Elementary School.* Retrieved April 19, 2017, from http://reportcard.ospi.k12.wa.us/Summary.aspx?schoolId=1039&reportLevel=School&yrs=14.

Rethinking Schools. (2003). Rethinking our classrooms: Teaching for equity and justice. *Rethinking Schools, 18*(1), 1–5.

Rogers, J. (2017). *Teaching and learning in the age of Trump: Increasing stress and hostility in America's high schools.* Los Angeles: UCLA Institute for Democracy, Education, and Access. Retrieved from https://idea.gseis.ucla.edu/publications/teaching-and-learning-in-age-of-trump

Vygotsky, L. S. (1987). Thinking and speech. In R. W. Rieber & A. Carton (Eds.), N. Minick (Trans.), *The collected works of L. S. Vygotsky: Problems of general psychology including the volume thinking and speech* (Vol. 1, pp. 37–285). New York, NY: Plenum Press.

ABOUT THE CONTRIBUTORS

AgitArte mission is to create projects and practices of cultural solidarity with grassroots struggles against oppression, and propose alternatives that generate possibilities for transformations in our world. We initiate and lead community-based educational and arts programs, along with projects that agitate in the struggles for liberation. In the past 20 years, AgitArte has developed cultural organizing projects alongside community partners in the US and Puerto Rico, including the curation, writing, and design of the book, *When We Fight, We Win!* Over the course of AgitArte's history, we have created over 50 original cultural projects, many with communities that geographically are not our own, but that we have built solidarity and kinship with. Our body of work includes toy theatre, puppetry, Cantastorias, mask-making, large-scale art builds for protests and actions, and art publications.

Cristina Alfaro, Ph.D., is a Professor and Chair in the College of Education at San Diego State University in the Dual Language and English Learner Education Department. Her area of specialization is in preparing critically conscious teachers with a focus on biliteracy processes that explicitly address language ideologies, progressions, demands, and scaffolds that are utilized to bring cultural and linguistic democracy into classroom practice.

Coert Ambrosino is an elementary educator who specializes in language development and culturally responsive pedagogy, and a poet who has performed in various spoken word competitions and shows, published multiple poetry chapbooks, and facilitated writing workshops for elementary, middle, and high school students. He currently teaches fifth grade in Commerce City, Colorado and helps coordinate the SESLA program for emerging bilingual fourth-eighth graders in

Ann Arbor, Michigan. His academic writing has been published in the TESOL Press, the Huffington Post, and ASCD Express. He earned his BA in Latin American Studies and his MA in Elementary Education at the University of Michigan.

Dr. Jeffrey Paul Ansloos is a psychologist, educator, researcher in the areas of youth and social policy, mental health, and Indigenous rights. He holds a PhD in Clinical Psychology from Fuller Graduate School of Psychology, and completed his post-graduate studies at University of Manitoba. Ansloos is Assistant Professor of Indigenous Mental Health and Social Policy in the department of Applied Psychology and Human Development at OISE. His research is focused on sociopolitical dimensions of mental health. He also researches Indigenous youth political mobilization, specifically at the intersections of criminal justice reform, suicide prevention, racial justice, and Indigenous rights. He is the author of *The Medicine of Peace: Indigenous Youth Resisting Violence and Decolonizing Healing* (Fernwood, 2017). Ansloos is Nêhiyaw (Cree) and English, and is a member of Fisher River Cree Nation (Ochekwi-Sipi; Treaty 5). He was born and raised in the heart of Treaty 1 territory in Winnipeg, Manitoba, and currently lives in Toronto.

Wayne Au is a Professor in the School of Educational Studies at the University of Washington Bothell, and he is a longtime editor and author with the social justice teaching magazine, *Rethinking Schools.*

Lilia Bartolomé received her BA from the University of California, San Diego, MEd from the Harvard Graduate School of Education (HGSE) and her PhD from Stanford University. She is currently Professor of Applied Linguistics at the University of Massachusetts at Boston. Bartolomé previously taught at HGSE, San Diego State University and worked as an elementary school bilingual teacher and bilingual reading specialist before entering the academy. As a teacher educator, her research interests include the preparation of effective teachers of linguistic minority students in multilingual contexts as well as working with immigrant parents in order to better assist their children. Bartolomé's publications are extensive and include the following books: *Ideologies in Education: Unmasking the Trap of Teacher Neutrality* and *Dancing with Bigotry: The Poisoning of Cultural Identities* (with Donaldo Macedo).

Berta Rosa Berriz, EdD, concluded her 33 years in Boston Public Schools as a Founding Co-lead teacher of the Boston Teachers' Union School (2008–2013). Including distinctions such as National Board Certification (2006), doctoral studies in culture and learning from Harvard Graduate School of Education (2005), Massachusetts Teacher Scholar (1992), faculty at Lesley University (1990 to present), Berriz was awarded a Lucretia Crocker Fellowship—TEAMSTREAM (1990)—for integrating bilingual students with special needs and gifted students through a collaborative arts approach. Recent publications include *Art as* *voice: Creating access for emergent bilingual families and communities* in the Journal of Pedagogy, Pluralism, and Practice (2017) Amanda Wager & Vivian Maria Poey, co-editors. "Looking Forward Backwards: Teaching Freedom and Democracy in the Classroom" in *Why Teach Now?* Sonia Nieto, Editor (2015); "Multicultural Teaching Story: Boston Teachers Union School: Teacher Leadership and Student Achievement" in (2013) *Affirming Diversity: Sociopolitical Context of Multicultural Education.* bberriz@lesley.edu.

Sally Brown received her PhD in Language and Literacy from the University of South Carolina. She teaches undergraduate and graduate literacy courses at Georgia Southern University. Her research interests focus on supporting diverse young children as they learn to read in English only classrooms by utilizing available technologies. She recently published articles in *The Reading Teacher* and *Journal of Research in Childhood Education.*

Jamall Bufford has been a recording and touring rap artist for over 15 years, both as a solo artist and as a group member. He is currently a member of rap's first performing arts group, The Black Opera. When he's not focusing on his music or leading youth workshops on writing and hip hop culture, Bufford is a Special Needs paraprofessional at Tappan Middle School in Ann Arbor, Michigan. Prior to his work at Tappan Middle School, Bufford was the Music Coordinator at Ann Arbor's famed youth center, The Neutral Zone. Bufford earned his BA from the University of Michigan in General Studies with a concentration in Sociology.

Laura Cranmer is of 'Nαmgis and Haida descent. Dr. Cranmer obtained her BA in English (1997) and her MA in Curriculum Studies (2002) from the University of Victoria, and her PhD in Language & Literacy Education from the University of British Columbia (2016). Laura applied her knowledge as a professor in the First Nations Studies Department at Vancouver Island University and to deepening her understanding of the continuing impact of Canada's colonial history on her community and her family. Recently retired, Laura's research interests include autoethnographic writing, theatre, film studies, arts-based research, and Indigenous language revitalization from within a critical Indigenous Studies framework which interrogates the master narrative. Laura looks forward to resuming her Kwak'wala work full time. Recent publications include: (2013) Nanaimo Indian Hospital, Vancouver: UBC Press and (2010) Exploring Indigenous oratory through image-based theatre as one possibility for cultivating Indigenous knowledge in the academy. E. Sojka & T. Sikora (Eds.).

Katherine Egan Cunningham, PhD, holds a doctoral degree from Teachers College, Columbia University, specifically focused on curriculum and instruction with an emphasis on literacy teaching and learning. She is an Associate Professor at Manhattanville College in the Literacy department. Katie is the author of *Story:*

Still the Heart of Literacy Learning (Stenhouse, 2015) and co-author of *Literacy Leadership in Changing Schools: Ten Keys to Successful Professional Development* (Teachers College Press, 2016), and co-author of the popular blog *The Classroom Bookshelf*. Her research, scholarship, and teaching focuses on children's literature, new technologies, professional development, and intentional teaching towards student and teacher happiness.

Jocelyn Difiore is a fourth-year student majoring in First Nations Studies at Vancouver Island University, located on the west coast of British Columbia. She owns and operates a thriving market garden business and takes great pleasure in nourishing her community.

Rianne Elsadig is a daughter, a student, a leader, a poet, and an activist. She is Sudanese but born and raised in Lynn, Massachusetts. She currently is obtaining her BS in Sociology, Social Change and Non-Profit Business at Lesley University. She has been a leader and an advocate for linguistically and culturally diverse communities. She demonstrates this through her poetry. Her poems have been published three times.

Grace Enriquez, PhD, is an Associate Professor of Language and Literacy at Lesley University, centers her teaching and research on critical literacies and reader response; intersections of literacies, identities, and embodiment; and children's literature for social justice. She is co-author of *The Reading Turn-Around: A Five-Part Framework for Differentiated Instruction* (Teaches College Press, 2010), co-editor of *Literacies, Learning, and the Body: Putting Theory and Research into Pedagogical Practice* (Routledge, 2016), and co-author of the *School Library Journal* blog, *The Classroom Bookshelf*. Grace earned her doctorate from Teachers College, Columbia University.

Shabaash M. Kemeh, PhD, is an Assistant Professor and Director of the Creative Arts Early Childhood and Elementary Program in the Graduate School of Education at Lesley University. He obtained his MA and PhD from Kansas State University; and Postgraduate Certificate in Education from Bretton Hall College of University of Leeds, UK where he honed his educational drama and theatre practices in British schools and colleges. He loves imparting his expertise in disciplines for integrated curriculum pedagogy in areas such as literacy, language arts, social studies, and multicultural education to teachers in Lesley Creative Arts programs nationwide. Facilitated workshops with UNESCO/UNFPA/University of Ghana **theatre for development** in Ghana; including K-State/Ford Foundation workshops on diversity and social issues in K-12 schools. Publications include *"Using Solo Drama to Make the Teaching of Social Studies Engaging for Students"* in Procedia—Social and Behavioral Sciences Journal (February 12, 2015), Vol. 174. mkemeh@lesley.edu.

Debi Khasnabis, PhD, is a Clinical Associate Professor at the University of Michigan School of Education who teaches courses in multicultural and multilingual education and co-coordinates the ESL endorsement program. She has been a leadership team member of the Mitchell Scarlett Teaching and Learning Collaborative, a partnership across the School of Education and Ann Arbor Public Schools, where she has regularly designed professional development opportunities for teachers and family engagement programs that aim to build connections between families and schools. Prior to her work at the University of Michigan, Debi was an elementary bilingual teacher (Spanish and English) in southwest Detroit. She earned her BA in Spanish and MA in Elementary Education at the University of Michigan, her Educational Specialist at Wayne State University in Bilingual Education Curriculum and Instruction, and her PhD in Literacy, Language and Culture in Educational Studies at the University of Michigan.

Dorea Kleker, PhD, is an instructor in Teaching, Learning and Sociocultural Studies at the University of Arizona where she teaches courses in children's literature and language and literacy development. Her research interests lie in the areas of multicultural children's literature, intercultural education, and the power of story to build stronger school-family partnerships. Recent publications include *Engaging Young Children with Global Literature* and *Thinking with Teacher Candidates: The Transformative Power of Story in Teacher Education*.

Whitney J. Lawrence, PhD, received her Doctor of Philosophy in Language and Literacy from the University of North Texas. She is currently an instructional specialist at an elementary school in the Southwest. Her areas of interest are multimodal literacies, art-infused curricula, and critical literacies.

Janelle B. Mathis, PhD, received a Doctor of Philosophy in Language, Reading, and Culture from the University of Arizona. She is currently a Professor of Literacy and Children's Literature in the Department of Teacher Education and Administration at the University of North Texas where her areas of interest are critical literacy, multimodality across the arts, and critical content and visual analysis of children's literature. She recently collaborated as an editor and author of *Critical Content Analysis of Children's and Young Adult Literature: Reframing Perspective* (Routledge, 2016).

Jessica Martell is an elementary school teacher with over 20 years of experience working with diverse student populations in New York City's public schools. She is co-author (with Souto-Manning) of the award-winning book *Reading, Writing, and Talk: Inclusive Teaching Strategies for Diverse Learners, K-2*. In 2017, she received the New York City Department of Education's Big Apple Award, which celebrates and recognizes teachers who inspire students, model great teaching, and enrich their school community.

Mary Beth Meehan Photographer and Educator. Director/Artist in Residence, *Documenting Cultural Communities* project at the International Charter School, RI 2009-Present.

Meehan received her BA in English at Amherst College and her MA in Photojournalism at the University of Missouri. As a photojournalist, her work has been funded by the National Endowment for the Arts, the Massachusetts Foundation for the Humanities, the Rhode Island State Council on the Arts and the Rhode Island Council for the Humanities; and featured in *The New York Times*, *The New Statesman* (United Kingdom), *Le Monde* (France) and *Vision Magazine* (China). Meehan's most recent series, *SeenUnseen*, combines image, text, and public installation, engaging communities around questions regarding visibility, inclusion, and cross-cultural connection. *SeenUnseen* artist's residencies in Providence, RI, through the City of Providence Department of Arts, Culture and Tourism; in Newnan, Georgia, through the Newnan Artist's Residency, and in Silicon Valley, CA., through Stanford University Departments of Communications and Fine Arts.

Beth Murray, PhD, is an Associate Professor of Theatre Education at the University of North Carolina-Charlotte. Years as a public-school theatre teacher, a teaching artist, a program development facilitator, and a playwright/author/director/deviser for young audiences undergird her current research and creative activity centered around multimodal, multilingual literacy and arts-driven community engagement.

Dr. Sonia Nieto, Professor Emerita of Language, Literacy, and Culture, in the College of Education at the University of Massachusetts, Amherst, has devoted her professional life to questions of diversity, equity, and social justice in education. She has taught students from elementary school through doctoral studies. With research focusing on multicultural education, teacher education, and the education of students of culturally and linguistically diverse backgrounds, she has written or edited 11 books and dozens of book chapters and journal articles, as well as a memoir, *Brooklyn Dreams: My Life in Public Education.*

Julie Nora, PhD, is a bilingual educator in K-16 educational settings for the past 25 years. She is passionate about issues of social justice and equity. She received her BA in US Intellectual History (U.C. Berkeley); MA in Teaching English to Speakers of Other Languages (San Francisco State University); and PhD in Education with a Specialization in Language, Literacy and Culture (University of Rhode Island/Rhode Island College). Nora has taught, researched, and advocated for bilingual education in a variety of settings, including international students at Bryant University; middle school in Providence Public Schools; and as a researcher with Education Alliance at Brown University. Nora is Director of the International Charter School in Pawtucket since 2003. Nora embraces the dual language bilingual education which emphasizes the assets students bring to school, including those whose first language is not English, with an intentionally diverse student population.

Jie Park, PhD, is an assistant professor of education at Clark University. She holds a BA and MA from Stanford, and a PhD (2010) in Education (Reading, Writing, and Literacy) from the University of Pennsylvania. Her research focuses on youth literacy and language practices in school and out-of-school settings. Currently she is involved in a variety of research projects around teacher and youth-research, multicultural and multilingual curricula in high school classrooms, and the intersection of youth literacy, language, and identities. Her most recent work has been published in the *Journal of Adolescent and Adult Literacy*, *English Education*, *Journal of Language and Literacy Education*, and the *International Journal of Multicultural Education*.

Mika K. Phinney is an early childhood educator currently teaching in a two-way dual immersion kindergarten classroom at Holbrook Language Academy in Concord, California. With a strong background in arts and literacy, she believes that arts are a fundamental element to providing equity in education. This belief has guided her classroom teaching as well as her work as a K-5 visual arts teacher, arts instructional support provider and literacy coach.

Vivian Maria Poey is Associate Professor in Creative Arts and Learning at Lesley University. Vivian earned an MFA from the Rhode Island School of Design and an MEd from Harvard University. Before joining Lesley, Vivian was a mentor at the Manchester Craftsmen's Guild, an artist in residence in Pittsburgh public schools, and an artist teacher at the Children's Studio School in Washington DC. Vivian has exhibited widely and collaborated with teachers and emergent bilingual students at schools in the Boston area. She is the recipient of the 2017 Massachusetts Art Education Association Higher-Educator of the Year Award and her publications include *Strategies to Integrate the Arts in Science* and *Imaging the Spaces Between: Art an Inclusive Pedagogy* in *Transforming Classroom Culture*. She is also co-editor of *Art as voice: Creating access for emergent bilingual families and communities* in the Journal of Pedagogy, Pluralism, and Practice. vpoey@lesley.edu

Catherine H. Reischl, PhD, is a Clinical Professor at the School of Education, University of Michigan. She earned her MEd at Harvard Graduate School of Education and her PhD at Michigan State University. She is the Coordinator of the Mitchell Scarlett Teaching and Learning Collaborative, a partnership between the School of Education and Ann Arbor Public Schools. Cathy teaches in the areas of elementary literacy instruction in multilingual contexts, English language development, and classroom management. Her research interests focus on the intersection of language, culture, and schooling in teacher education contexts.

Yoselin Rodriguez is an Educator and Fine artist in Massachusetts. She holds a BFA in Fine Arts and an MEd in Art Education, both from Lesley University. As a graduate of the Boston Arts Academy who has continued to contribute to the school, she is deeply aware of the many benefits that art brings to the academic and personal growth of students in the educational system. As an immigrant, Yoselin understands the need for culturally responsive teaching and advocates this through the use of visual art. Currently she teaches visual art at an arts-integrated Boston public school where she works with elementary grades. In addition, she also serves as a museum educator where she works with groups of students of all ages and from various districts at the Museum of Fine Arts.

Robert Shreefter is an artist-educator, curator and gallery director. He recently retired from his position as Professor at Lesley University, in Cambridge, MA, as a faculty member in the Creative Arts and Learning Division in the Graduate School of Education. His primary work was in the Graduate Art Education Program and the Integrated Teaching through the Arts Program. He was the director/curator of the Marran Gallery and Atrium Galleries at Lesley, exhibiting work of students, faculty and community artists.

Shreefter has taught in workplace/adult literacy programs, been an artist-in-residence in schools, community organizations, etc. with diverse populations including pregnant teenagers, homeless people, migrant youth, special education students, and incarcerated youth.

Shreefter is an active studio artist; his prints and handmade books have been shown in university and commercial galleries.

Currently, he is a principal artist and curator of the Off Main Gallery in Wellfleet, MA, a community-oriented gallery created to promote local artists from the Outer-Cape.

Alysha Mae Schlundt-Bodien has been an advocate for Community Media, media literacy, and free speech since 2006. She is currently a Training and Facility Coordinator for Community Television Network of Ann Arbor, where she instructs youth and adults to create video content for local cable channels and online. She is President of the Michigan Chapter Alliance for Community Media (ACM) and Vice Chair for the Central States Region ACM, who promote and preserve the right to media training, civic engagement and education in support of diverse community voices through Public, Educational and Government Access channels. She graduated from Central Michigan University (CMU) with a BA in Integrative Public Relations studying communication, journalism, broadcasting and multimedia.

Lori Simpson is an ESL teacher in the Worcester Public Schools District in Massachusetts. She holds a BS from Southern Nazarene University and a MEd from Clark University. Her research focuses on ways to enhance the academic literacy of students using graphic texts and poetry. Currently she is on her school's instructional leadership team where she represents the interests and advocates on behalf of English language learners in her school. Her work has been published in the *English Journal*.

Mariana Souto-Manning, PhD, is an associate professor at Teachers College, Columbia University, where she serves as Director of the Doctoral Program in Curriculum and Teaching and Director of the Early Childhood Education and Early Childhood Special Education Programs. From a critical perspective, Professor Souto-Manning's research examines in/equities and in/justices in early childhood teaching and teacher education, critically recentering methodologies and pedagogies on the lives and experiences of people of color and other historically minoritized communities.

Amanda Claudia Wager, PhD, is an Assistant Professor at Lesley University where she prepares teachers to integrate the arts within bilingual and literacy education. As an educator, artist, and researcher she explores how multiliteracies, such as drama, visual arts, and media, support language acquisition and culturally responsive education. Amanda's dissertation, *Applied Drama as Engaging Pedagogy: Critical Multimodal Literacies with Street Youth*, was the recipient of the AERA 2017 Arts and Learning Dissertation Award. This community-based research project investigated how a youth activist theatre production created multimodal learning spaces for eight youth-researchers in Vancouver, British Columbia. Along with Vivian Maria Poey and Berta Rosa Berriz, she edited the Journal of Pedagogy, Pluralism, and Practice's Special Issue 2017, *Art as Voice: Creating Access for Emergent Bilingual Families and Communities*. Amanda's passion lies in building democratic spaces in which individuals can creatively and critically co-construct pedagogy. *awager@lesley.edu*

Gustave Weltsek, PhD, is an Assistant Professor of Arts Education/Research at Indiana University. Gustave's Educational/Scholarly/Artistic work emerges within a commitment to social justice and equity. His publications include; *Deconstructing Global Markets Through Critical Performative Experiences*. He was a writer of the US Standards for Theatre Education, received the 2013 AATE research award and is a past editor of The Youth Theatre Journal.

INDEX

Page numbers in *italics* indicate figures and in **bold** indicate tables on the corresponding pages.